EXHAUST THE LIMITS

For Bart —
The best friend
and neighbor anyone
could hope to have.
All the best.

Dan

Advance Praise

"I can't put it down. There's a crafting between big thinking, written influences, and the personal reflection that is so well done that it seems effortless, but I know it's not. I love it!"

Mark Weiss
Education Director
Operation Respect

"When you want to have lots of adventures and are committed to helping others, you end up with a fulfilling and exciting life, as Chic Dambach attests in his wonderful memoir. We are all richer for having Chic's energy, caring, and intelligence working for peace and justice."

Susan Hackley
Managing Director, Program on Negotiation
Harvard Law School

"The book is an engrossing look at a fascinating life and our remarkable times. Dambach is a rare leader of principle, accomplishment and adventure. And he writes his life with terrific interest and skill. Few other people have started so high up and have maintained influence in so many fields. And few people have been so honest with themselves along the way."

Bob Berg
Senior Advisor
World Federation of United Nations Associations

"*Exhaust the Limits* joins *Profiles in Courage* as testimony to what the best in American values in action has achieved."

Christopher Czaja Sager
Concert Pianist
Berlin

"It's a fascinating book about a fascinating life."
Dan Fesperman
Author
Steel Dagger Award and Hammett Prize Winner

"I absolutely love the book. It is difficult to put this down once you start reading. It is truly fascinating."
Outi Flynn
Director, Knowledge Center
BoardSource

"It is a great work—inspiring, impressive. The book is powerful. I enjoyed it all."
Rob Ricigliano
Director, Institute of World Affairs
University of Wisconsin, Milwaukee

"This is a remarkable story of an individual who has done his best in a variety of ways to make our world just a little bit more peaceful. It needs to be told."
Kevin Quigley
President
National Peace Corps Association

"The author shares his life's journey and lessons learned in a most reflective and engaging manner. He inspires the reader to work for social justice and peace at home and around the globe—always, always emphasizing our common human aspirations."
Sherry Lee Mueller, Ph.D.
President
National Council for International Visitors

EXHAUST THE LIMITS

The Life and Times
of a Global Peacebuilder

Charles F. "Chic" Dambach

Apprentice House
Baltimore, Maryland

Library of Congress Cataloging-in-Publication Data

Dambach, Charles F.
Exhaust the limits : the life and times of a global peacebuilder / Charles F. (Chic)
Dambach ; introduction by Congressman John Garamendi ; foreword by Peter
Yarrow.
p. cm.
Includes bibliographical references and index.
ISBN 978-1-934074-57-2 (alk. paper)
1. Peace-building. 2. Humanitarian intervention. 3. Dambach, Charles F. I. Title.
JZ5538.D27 2010
327.1'72092--dc22
[B]
2010022705

Printed in the United States of America
First Edition

Design by Kathleen M. Boehl and Amy M. Scioscia
Cover design by Brooke Hall Creative
Edited by Melissa Henderson
Author photograph by Hilary Schwab

Cover: From the 1968 front page of *Porvenir*, The official Peace Corps Colombia
newspaper, courtesy of the Friends of Colombia Archives, American University
Library, Washington, DC.

Published by Apprentice House
The Future of Publishing…Today!

Apprentice House
Communication Department
Loyola University Maryland
4501 N. Charles Street
Baltimore, MD 21210
410.617.5265
www.ApprenticeHouse.com

To my enablers —
Kay, Alex, Grant and Kai
— with deep gratitude.

And in memory of Dale Stockton.

TABLE OF CONTENTS

"TELLING HIS STORY"

When the border war broke out between Ethiopia and Eritrea, I knew who to call. Chic Dambach would know what needed to be done and how to do it. We assembled a small team; we worked with the leaders of both countries, and we helped them bring peace to their people.

Exhaust the Limits is the inspiring and powerful memoir of one man with high ideals who set out to make a difference—and did it. The story includes a dramatic encounter with cruel racism, student activism, the Peace Corps, the Olympics, and building peace across the globe. His family's courageous struggle to save their child's life while battling with health insurance companies is so compelling, I used it in my first policy speech on the floor of the Congress to help pass health care reform.

Many of us have urged Chic to tell his story to the world. Here it is—to be read and enjoyed.

THE HONORABLE JOHN GARAMENDI
MEMBER OF CONGRESS
UNITED STATES OF AMERICA

FOREWORD
PETER YARROW
(OF PETER, PAUL AND MARY)

In my experience, people write autobiographical books for very much the same reasons that I write songs. The urge among writers, poets, and songsmiths—and here expressed by a person with an amazing story to tell—is more than anything an act of faith.

A person who does not possess an intense faith in the ultimate triumph of goodness of human beings would never write words like those in this book. Chic Dambach's story will uplift and inspire many of us to action and commitment. Just as Woody's guitar bore the words "This guitar kills Fascists," because his songs expressed concern for the common person, Chic's words provide an antidote to apathy, indolence, selfishness, and a loss of hope. They also pose a threat to those who seek to destroy what is good, real, honest, and humane in us and in our world. Chic bravely exposes the greedy "emperor" who has no clothes.

We should read, absorb, and understand what Chic has to say in *Exhaust the Limits*, not to discover some remarkable force that we might harness to do good work, but to know that we can become enriched simply by enriching the lives of others. He redefines the notion of "winning" not as at another's expense, but by virtue of our actions; that is, we win with actions that create more love, equity, and fairness in the world so that others win, too. Also, in this kind of "win" we need not count the blessings we bestow, nor weigh the gifts that we give or assign them a monetary value. We realize, as we read Chic's book, that the more he gave to others, the more his heart and life was enriched. The more powerfully he was devoted to his beloved, remarkable sons and his super-human, courageous wife, the more he was able to apply that same type of passion to his efforts to build peace and bring understanding to the world .

As his ability to affect world events grew in ways that are almost hard to believe in terms of scope and effectiveness, Chic's humility and his love of others grew exponentially. He also grew to appreciate others' gifts and talents and revel in the sheer delight of living with the kind of enthusiasm and optimism that, I suspect, no other way of life could ever have given him. Through Chic's book, we come to realize that the kind of evolution that he enjoyed as a person is something that we, too, might achieve. It is not only available to the very wise, the very talented, or the very lucky. This evolution is immediately before us and available to everyone, if only we live, truly live, in the present wonderment of the life that is before us.

Chic's global perspective provides us with a blueprint for how we might cease to stand on the side, helpless, as we passively watch what is precious in the world be destroyed. Chic, without ever telling us what we have to do, let's us know how he did the "impossible" that became surprisingly possible, as he overcame enormous odds and great oppositional forces.

The book's message: "We can do that, too!"

My mother Vera Yarrow, a teacher, taught me that we learn by imitation. This is how we learn from Chic as we read about and discover his remarkably humble, yet also remarkably larger-than-life, life. He is propelled by an uncommon humility and an unquenchable moral determination to seek to right what is wrong and honor what is beautiful, truthful, and sacred. Also, it is true that Chic, in the despair of loss and overwhelming misfortune, turns such challenges into greater love and appreciation of others. In this way, Chic distinguishes himself from many of us who succumb to self-pity and disenchantment of life. This victory over adversity—often assumed to be so much "tilting at windmills"—becomes Chic's most profound achievement.

In Chic's relentlessly honest telling of his story, he inspires us to feel more confident in the rightness of our pursuit of similar dreams for a better world, less embarrassed to believe in what others label as unrealistic or impossible, and less wearied by the realities of the clock-of-progress that ticks ever so slowly. He extracts from us a patience that we must learn so that we can carry on with full heart as we pursue our own quests and dreams.

INTRODUCTION

"Chic, my friends are killing each other, and we have to do something about it." John Garamendi was terribly concerned about the brutal border war between Eritrea and Ethiopia. John had the audacious notion that we might be able to help stop the death and destruction. "I have no idea what we can do," I replied cautiously, "but let's give it a try."

We formed a team of former Peace Corps Volunteers, and over the next two years we worked regularly with the leaders of both countries. We pressed the case for peace, and we became a primary conduit for communication between the adversaries. When the killing finally stopped, they invited us to the treaty-signing ceremony in Algiers, and Ethiopia's Prime Minister, Meles Zenawe, thanked us, "for creating the momentum and the spirit which made this historic achievement possible."

My life and career have careened from one passion and cause to another, but my commitment to peace has been constant and consistent. I can't stand the notion that some human beings believe their nations, tribes, gangs, or congregations have a right or obligation to kill and destroy others in order to advance their cause, ideology, faith, or economic interests. I know mankind has always done it, but that doesn't make it right, reasonable, honorable or acceptable.

We don't allow our children to settle their disputes with knives, guns and grenades. Neighbors don't plant landmines to mark property lines. We would never tolerate people in our cities and states who destroy life and property to fulfill their desires. We arrest them, put them on trial, and, if convicted, we incarcerate them. Why, then, do we accept, even canonize those who fight, kill, and destroy on the national or international scale under the pretext of patriotism and national interest? It makes no sense. So, I've spent most of my adult life tilting at the pervasive war mentality with my tiny lance made only of goodwill and firm determination.

Early experiences and influences at home, school, sports and summer jobs provided a solid foundation for a life of meaning and adventure in the pursuit of important social causes. Like so many of my generation, I was moved by President John F. Kennedy's challenge to "ask not what your country can do for you, ask what you can do for your country." The momentous music of the great folk singers like Pete Seeger, Bob Dylan and Joan Baez as well as Peter, Paul and Mary inspired me to care about the human condition. Close encounters with blatant racial brutality compelled me to act, and several writers caught my attention and shaped my beliefs and values. The murder of my best friend and mentor made my own life all the more intense.

In *Essays on the Myth of Sisyphus*, Albert Camus quoted the Greek poet and philosopher Pindar, "O my soul, do not aspire to immortal life, but exhaust the limits of the possible." Sisyphus, according to Homer, was condemned to forever push a rock up a mountain only to watch it roll back to the bottom where he must start again. An eternity of futility was the ultimate punishment imposed by the gods for Sisyphus' impertinence. Camus, however, saw in Sisyphus the existential human condition—striving for survival and meaning only to fail, die, and disappear into the void. But Camus found something far deeper, more powerful and profound. He saw existential meaning, value and virtue in the very act of putting one's shoulder to the rock and pushing with all of one's might—rebelling against the inevitable, rejecting futility. Camus ends this compelling essay:

"I leave Sisyphus at the foot of the mountain! One always finds one's burden again. But Sisyphus teaches the higher fidelity that negates the gods and raises rocks. He too concludes that all is well. This universe henceforth without a master seems to him neither sterile nor futile. Each atom of that stone, each mineral flake of that night-filled mountain, in itself forms a world. The struggle itself toward the heights is enough to fill a man's heart. One must imagine Sisyphus happy."

Sisyphus is the perfect metaphor for the peacebuilders of the world. We are often maligned as delusional idealistic fools, pursuing an impossible dream. Yet, we push back against the cynics with the same joy Sisyphus must have known. We are building a more peaceful world, and the frequency and severity of violent conflicts has actually declined. Like pushing the rock, building peace is hard work, but it makes life safe and secure for innocent people. We are neither delusional nor foolish for trying to make it happen. We don't always succeed, but we achieve something magnificent on the way to the top. When the rock falls back, we pick ourselves up, dust off and always try again.

Inspired by Camus, I was determined to find a meaningful rock and exhaust the limits of my possibilities—to see as much as I could see, do as much as I could do, know as many people as I could know, and fill every day with value and the joy of life. It meant staying on the move physically, intellectually, and spiritually—always exploring, always searching, always open, and always asking questions and looking for answers. Since college, I have held fifteen different jobs, lived in thirteen cities, and traveled to fifty-seven countries.

I have been incredibly fortunate to connect on a deep level with some of the world's most intelligent, dedicated and talented people. They have made my life a joy and they are responsible for anything I may have achieved. This is my tribute to them, and it is their story as much as my own.

President John F. Kennedy often said, "One person can make a difference, and every person should try." I have tried, and perhaps, I have made a difference. Not by plan but rather by happenstance, I found myself immersed in peace activism, and that evolved into Peace Corps service and then peacemaking initiatives in Africa. From there a peacebuilding career emerged. This is the story of the early experiences that shaped my values and ambitions, and the adventures, challenges, opportunities, triumphs, tragedies, failures and successes that made it all worthwhile.

VALUES

The values that drive and guide my pursuit of peace and justice were formed very early. My family and teachers and the powerful social and political movements of the times inspired me to be independent and determined to make a difference.

When I was eighteen months old, our family moved from the city—Columbus, Ohio—to a classic large old house on four acres of fertile land. We were a mile and a half from the tiny village of Linworth (and its elementary school), three miles from Worthington (and its middle and high schools) and about ten miles from Columbus and The Ohio State University—where Dad taught natural resources management and from which all of us were expected to graduate. We raised chickens and a pig or two, and we cultivated a highly productive vegetable garden. Our small orchard provided an abundance of succulent apples, peaches, and cherries.

Dad was abandoned by his parents; spent his early years in an orphanage, moved in with an abusive aunt, escaped as a teenager and sustained himself in the woods by rummaging through garbage and roasting captured animals. He survived through sheer grit and hard work, and he was eventually taken in by the Kibler family to work on their farm. He excelled in school, and he went to college at Ohio State where he ran track on the Buckeye team with the great Jesse Owens. He earned a Ph.D., and became one of the most important figures in research and support of the conservation of natural resources in Ohio history. A nature preserve near his childhood home in Geauga County bears his name, and a bronze likeness of Dad greets students and faculty in Kottman Hall and the School of Environment and Natural Resources on the Ohio State campus.

Our mother was a classic farmer's daughter in every way. Ernie and Bertha Kibler owned a modest but successful dairy farm just outside Burton in Northeastern Ohio. It provided a comfortable home, and a self-sufficient existence as they grew virtually all of their own food, and made money with their top quality dairy and maple syrup. They took my dad in, put him to work, and helped him through school. They gave him a home and his first experience of a loving family. Mom was the older of two daughters, and closer to Dad's age. They fell in love, married, raised a family and shared a remarkable life. Mom was a good student and modest and responsible in everything she did. She was liked and trusted by everyone who ever knew her. She gave absolute support and devotion to our father—the proverbial strong woman behind the successful man. For us, she was supermom.

Mom had her own career as a dedicated and beloved home economics teacher, but her career always took second place to home and family. She took time off to raise us when we were young, and even when she returned to the classroom, she was always there for us. Our parents adhered to a basic mission in life to leave the world better than they found it. They did, and nothing less was expected of their three children.

Since we lived in the country, there were only a few neighbors within walking distance. My older brother George, sister Charlou and I played kick-the-can with the McLaughlin kids until it was too dark to see the can. Weekly radio shows like *The Shadow*, *Jack Benny*, and *Gun Smoke* provided the only mass media entertainment until we bought our first TV when I was in my teens.

For the most part, I had to find my own pleasure, and I found it in the woods and streams. Our house was between the Stillson and Antrim farms and both of them had ponds and creeks. I spent every possible hour fishing in their ponds and wading in their streams catching turtles, tadpoles and salamanders and turning over rocks to discover whatever might be living in that dark, damp environment. I have enjoyed solitude in the wilderness ever since.

George was the classic scholar-athlete who excelled at everything. Later in life he would lead the development of a new medical school at Florida International University in Miami. Charlou was the oldest, and she stayed close to home and followed our mother's model—beloved teacher, caring wife and mother. Whenever I need to re-connect with America's heartland, I call Charlou.

≈

I loved all sports, but football was *my* sport. I started playing organized ball in junior high school, and I was a starting linebacker on defense and pulling guard on offense with the varsity team in my freshman year—a rare achievement at any school. I wasn't as big or fast as the others, but I worked hard to overcome any inherent deficiencies. To grow stronger, I actually dug a pond with a shovel and wheelbarrow in our backyard during the summer between my freshman and sophomore years. It was the real thing—twice the size of a hockey rink and over six-feet deep. Over the next few years I did 500 push-ups and sit-ups every day to continue to build strength.

As a star high school athlete, I was invited to at least a dozen campuses, where coaches tried to persuade me to join their programs. Instead of Ohio State, I chose Oklahoma State University in Stillwater (the better OSU, I like to say) where head coach Cliff Speegle was a basic good guy who seemed to respect the appropriate place of the game in our lives. His Cowboy teams were less than powerful, but always respectable. They played by the rules (mostly), and tried to build character as well as athletic prowess. It was big-time football, which appealed to my ego, but it was modest enough for me to feel comfortable.

The day after high school graduation in 1962, I flew to Stillwater to meet with the coaches, and they took me in a single engine plane across the Oklahoma plains and into New Mexico, directly to the TO Ranch. The coaching staff had arranged a physically challenging, but fascinating, summer job for me as a real cowboy on the cattle ranch near Raton. The owner, Jack Renfro, had been a wrestler at OSU, and he liked to hire athletes for the summer work load. The TO had 153,000 acres and 4,000 Hereford Whiteface cattle, including a Grand National Champion bull named Real Silver Domino 283. It was perfect for an adventure-seeking kid to spread his wings.

While working on the ranch and listening to the radio in a pickup truck, a whole new sound with powerful lyrics came on my favorite "top 40" station. I stopped the truck and absorbed every word of Peter, Paul and Mary singing "If I Had a Hammer." This wasn't just music. This was philosophy. It was sociology. It was politics. It was heart and soul. It was inspiration. It was a movement, and I wanted to be part of it.

That fall, I moved into Bennett Hall, the OSU athletic dorm, with a bit of arrogance, mistakenly thinking standards in Ohio must be higher than those on the lonesome prairie. However, my parochial Buckeye pride was badly misplaced. Many of my new classmates at this modest Land Grant school were absolutely brilliant. I wasn't close to their intellectual level, and most of the faculty gave no grace. I actually had to study for the first time in my life. I still only did the minimum to get by, but I really did study.

There was one exception to the rigorous academic demands: a special class had been arranged for athletes who were slow of mind and needed to pass math to remain eligible to play. In "Jock Math" or "Fun with Numbers" as the class was known among students, we learned basic addition and subtraction, and I believe we even progressed to three digit multiplication and division. The instructor was barely over five feet tall; he weighed no more than 110 pounds, and he had a squeaky, whiney voice. He looked scared every time he entered the room, and a bit relieved when class ended—probably with good reason. He was surrounded by the largest and most aggressive men on campus. Yes, the class was all men, and all of us passed.

We had several notable characters on our freshman team, including Walt Garrison—the ultimate cowboy. When not riding broncos in rodeos Garrison scored touchdowns for us. He eventually became a famous running back for the Dallas Cowboys, and he is even better known as the iconic television spokesman for Skoal chewing tobacco, encouraging macho men to "Put a *peench* (of Skoal) between your cheek and gum."

Today, everyone living in southern Arizona or Orange County California knows the name Jim Click, a ubiquitous car dealer. Jim was far too small to be an interior lineman in the Big-8, but he had a spirit and drive that just couldn't be denied. He had unbelievable energy, optimism, and enthusiasm, and he beat players who outweighed him by thirty or more pounds for the starting center position. No one anywhere lives larger than Jim Click. He always beams a broad smile, and he knows how to have a good time—no, a great time! His family resources (his dad was a very successful car dealer in Altus, Oklahoma) meant he had virtually no constraints. Jim lived without limits then, and he still does today.

Slingin' Sammy Baugh was our freshman team coach. Sammy Baugh was a football legend, one of the greatest quarterbacks ever to play the game, and one of football's most colorful characters as well. His recent death was headline news on national television and on the front page of virtually every newspaper in America. As an all-around athlete, Baugh may well have been the very best ever. Known primarily for his passing, he was also the best punter in the history of the game, and some of his records still stand. We were in awe of this great man, and he didn't disappoint. Even in his fifties, Baugh could pass and kick better than anyone in the game. If a forward pass could be captured, framed, and displayed, Sammy Baugh's would belong in the Louvre. He could punt a spiral almost as tight and accurate as his passes. It was a privilege to be in his presence.

My football career, however, almost ended my freshman year with my fourth shoulder separation. I was holding my own among some bigger and faster players, but my left shoulder had been weakened by a childhood injury and two more separations playing high school ball. This one caused serious nerve damage, and my left shoulder and arm went numb. I lost use of the deltoid muscle, and I could barely use my left arm at all. The feeling began to come back just before planned surgery, and it recovered enough for me to try again in the spring.

Starting that year, I had a brief but intense flirtation with evangelical Christianity. I was "saved" and joined Campus Crusade for Christ; read the entire *Bible*; witnessed for the Lord, and attended Billy Graham rallies. However, it didn't take long to realize that while the *Bible* offers profound guidance, it is also seriously flawed. The books of Leviticus and Deuteronomy, for example, are downright dreadful. Furthermore, the concept of salvation and bliss for born again true believers, but eternal painful damnation for everyone else is revolting. Thomas Jefferson edited the *Bible* by taking out the miracles and salvation parts, while leaving the moral teaching in place. I appreciate his version of the *Bible*, and I can relate to his vision of faith and theology. I simply try to live a spiritually aware, moral, and ethical life—as best I can. I respect and enjoy enduring friendships with people of deep religious faith. All I ask is respect for my views in return.

Dorm life was intoxicating. We discovered new people with different ideas, and we engaged in stimulating discussions and debates on politics, religion, and girls well into the night. The music of the time was particularly significant. Perhaps more than at any other time in history, the words of popular music carried a powerful message. Peter, Paul and Mary came out with new albums with compelling lyrics. We played them over and over enjoying the sound, but also analyzed the meaning of every phrase. I couldn't get enough of Pete Seeger and his fervent songs of peace and justice. His rendition of "Turn, Turn, Turn" turned over in my mind for hours at a time. At the time, I didn't know his historical significance as a social and political activist, but there was something uniquely authentic in his voice, his music, and in his message.

In the fall of 1962, the U.S. and the Soviet Union marched to the brink of mutual annihilation over missiles in Cuba. Both sides demonstrated the will and the capacity to destroy all life as we know it with a nuclear holocaust. I was clueless about international relations and foreign policy nuances, but I knew we were the good guys and the Soviets were bad guys. Castro was a commie, and he was our enemy. That was all any of us needed to know. I didn't like the idea of nuclear war, but we had to protect America against Godless communist dictators at any and all costs.

We gathered in small groups in our dorm rooms to listen to the latest news on the radio, and we speculated about what might happen, and what we should do. Classes and practices lost their meaning for a very tense week. Most of us, me included, were ready to leave school and join the Marines to fight. We felt brave, strong, and patriotic. Nevertheless, we were tremendously relieved and grateful when the Soviets backed down and removed their missiles from Cuba. My children read the Cuban Missile Crisis story as distant history. For me and my generation, it is very personal, powerful and terrifying reality.

In the off season, our head Coach Cliff Speegle was fired, and replaced by a completely different staff led by Phil Cutchin. Cutchin had been an assistant to the great Bear Bryant at Alabama, and the campus and alumni were excited at the prospect of championship football coming to OSU. Cutchin took great pride in being the toughest coach in America, and we became known as Cutchin's Cowboys, a moniker we embrace to this day. Under Cutchin, we defeated Oklahoma twice, but that was because they were bad, not because we were good. Otherwise, the experience was dreadful for most of us, and our record was pitiful.

During Cutchin's first spring training, nearly two-thirds of the team quit. Dozens of young men who needed athletic scholarships to afford college expenses and earn a degree walked away because it wasn't worth the humiliation and pain. I'm not sure how I survived that spring, but somehow I did. As I recall, the coaches went a bit light on me due to my injured shoulder.

Practices were brutal for everyone, but they were twice as hard on the black players. They were called every derogatory and condescending epithet available in the English language. Cutchin and his staff were über racists at a time when racism was rampant, even displayed with smug satisfaction in much of the South. After a while, we white players noticed the black players were absorbing the abuse and coming back for more. Most of them desperately needed their scholarships to get an education, but I suspect their collective honor was a major factor. They refused to let the racist coaching staff get the better of them. They would not allow anyone to accuse black men of quitting. It was an impressive demonstration of pride, courage and discipline.

I returned to Stillwater in August for two-a-day workouts and high hopes of playing for the Cowboys in real games. This was 1963, and the racial tension was palpable throughout the nation. We read news reports about civil rights advocates risking their lives, and some had been killed. Were they heroes or fools? It wasn't yet clear to young people still learning the ways of the world. Our mixed-race team functioned with awkward collegiality. We were teammates on the field, but separate in every other way. Whites and blacks were never assigned to the same room in the dorm; we rarely sat together in the cafeteria, and no one expected anything else.

Meanwhile, something strange and disquieting was happening in far off Washington, D.C., that would change America and much of the world forever. Over 250,000 people had gathered in front of the Lincoln Memorial to demand civil rights for Negroes. I had known a little about the movement growing up in Worthington. A local Methodist pastor was involved, and a few of us held discussions about it. The pastor received little support from our comfortable almost all white suburban community, but it seemed to me he was on the right side of the issue. After all, my best friend Paul Jones was a Negro. He was about the finest kid in our school, and his entire family embodied the very best qualities. His father was like a second father to me. How could Paul, anyone in the Jones family or anyone like them be denied the right to eat wherever they wanted to or have the same job as anyone else? My heart and mind were in the right place, but I didn't do anything about it at the time.

Exhausted after another brutal morning practice, we gathered in a large room in the basement of Bennett Hall, with a formally integrated but socially segregated team, and a racist coaching staff, dreading the afternoon practice, and watched cultural history unfold. My favorite folk musicians, Peter, Paul and Mary, sang "Blowin' in the Wind" and "If I Had a Hammer," and I finally grasped the full meaning and power of those great songs and the lyrics. Then, Martin Luther King, Jr. spoke. I couldn't hear very well, as the TV was small and the room large, but I was moved to the core of my being. His dream became my mission. I would speak out for justice and equality in solidarity with anyone any-where who was the object of oppression. I didn't muster the courage to become a street marching activist right away, but I was starting on that path.

My dad came to Stillwater to watch our practices, and after a few sessions he took me to dinner and asked me to leave the team. He could see that my left arm and shoulder were weak, and he feared permanent damage. I knew he was right, but I couldn't quit. The young-macho-athlete-pride thing prevailed in my immature value system. I told him I couldn't quit, but if he asked me to, I would. He asked, and I did. We re-turned to Worthington and I spent my sophomore year at nearby Ohio Wesleyan University.

Wesleyan is a superb liberal arts college with high standards, and I hadn't yet developed the motivation or discipline to study hard. I passed, but barely. Ohio Wesleyan wasn't the place for me, however, and I still felt disappointed with myself for leaving the Oklahoma State team. I had lost my scholarship when I left, but, reluctantly, my parents agreed to cover the tuition costs, so I returned to Stillwater the next fall. I told Coach Cutchin I wanted to try again. He gave me a chance, but I had to earn my scholarship back with a strong performance on the field. Practices were still brutal, and I nursed splitting headaches every day from the fierce head-to-head collisions. I stayed with it, however, and I remember with pride the day Coach Cutchin pulled me aside and said he liked what he saw, and my scholarship was reinstated.

The season opened against Arkansas in Little Rock where 50,000 screaming fans enjoyed watching the defending national champions whip us. I rode the bench anxious for my first taste of game action in big time college football, but Cutchin's Cowboys were no match for Frank Broyles' Razorbacks, and there was no hope for substitutes to see action.

A few weeks later, my teammate and friend Earl "Bud" Jones injured his knee, and it would probably end his playing career. I admired Bud as an extra special nice guy and excellent student as well as a tenacious lineman. Like me, he was too small to excel in Big-8 football, but he was very good. We had taken a Biology class together as freshmen. When the professor posted the grades on his door, Bud and I walked across campus together to see how we did. I got a C, and he had earned an A. I knew then he was exceptionally bright and capable with his mind as well as his body.

Under NCAA rules, injured athletes kept their scholarships until their graduation date, but you lost your scholarship if you quit. White athletes had no problem, but the coaches did everything imaginable to force the black players to quit and forfeit their scholarships. Bud was black.

His injury came the week before we were to play Tulsa, a team we should be able to beat easily but for their All-American quarterback Jerry Rhome and superstar receiver Howard Twilley. Since Bud couldn't practice on his bad knee, the coaches told him to play the role of Rhome and stand in the "pocket" where the quarterback would—behind the offensive line, ready to make a pass. Jones would provide a target for the defensive line to practice their pass rush. Our second string offensive linemen were to block as the first and second string defensive lines took turns charging the quarterback. Everything seemed normal until defensive line coach Jim Stanley gave more specific instructions to the defensive linemen. "Your job is to attack Jones, and the play will not stop until everyone hits him as hard as possible—*with your helmet on his knee.*"

His demand was deplorable, so no one took him seriously. The first play began with a whistle, and we blocked as best we could to protect the "quarterback", but eventually everyone broke through and hit Jones. But they didn't hit him hard or on his knee, and Coach Stanley was furious. In a rage, he stormed up to each defensive lineman, grabbed their face mask, yanked their helmet off, hit them with their own helmet and screamed, "I said hit him hard and hit him in the knee!!!"

It took a few rounds for the defensive linemen to comply, but they finally did, out of self preservation. Play after play we blockers did our best to provide protection, but our task was impossible. Action never stopped until all five defensive linemen had hit Bud hard on his knee. After the first string did their damage; the second string followed, and then the rested first string lined up, charged, and hit him again.

After each round, Coach Stanley roared at Jones, "Are you quitting, Nigger?!? When you gonna quit, Nigger?!?" Bud was knocked to the ground each time, but he picked himself up and defiantly stood his ground. My admiration for him grew with each hit, and my anger at the coaching staff mounted as well. After a while, Jones couldn't muster the strength to stand, so he stayed on his knees facing the relentless taunting from Coach Stanley and the onslaught of big, powerful defensive linemen.

Finally, Jones could no longer even rise to his knees. He lay on the ground but the attacks and the unrelenting taunts continued. Finally, after at least thirty minutes of this torment and torture had passed, head coach Cutchin descended from the lofty tower he used to monitor the whole practice field. He came straight to our area walking fast and his face was taut in fury. He looked down at the proud but fallen Earl Bud Jones and simply said, "Get out of here, Nigger."

The rest of us moved on to continue the practice session in another part of the field, while Jones slowly crawled off and into the locker room. I let my friend down that day, and I never recovered from the guilt. If any of the white players had one percent of the courage, integrity and character of Earl Bud Jones, we would have walked off the field in solidarity with him. Instead, in collective shame, we went on with our practice, and Earl disappeared.

More than forty years later, Jones found me through the "Cutchin's Cowboys" email service that keeps us informed about our team-mates—usually news of a serious illness or death. I had responded to the passing of Rex Russell, one of the upper classmen who had been an inspiration to those of us who were freshmen during his senior year. By now, Jones had dropped the nickname Bud, and went by Earl. He sent me this note:

"Chic: I had seen your email address on several of the emails from some of the old Cutchin Cowboys and finally decided that was really you and sent you a direct email. I do remember the tough Worthington Ohio kid with the toughness of a bull-dozer and when Frank Shidler stopped by just before Xmas to visit me, your name came up often. I promised him I would get in touch, but took forever to do that. After finishing my ROTC commitment in 1969, I had a 30 year career with AT&T Bell Labs as a computer scientist, and then retired here in Florida in 1998. Like most of us in our 60s life is mostly good. Be well old friend, and I look forward to chatting with you. Earl"

I was busy at work in the office when this message appeared in my email inbox, but I broke down in tears. I had thought of him often over the years, and I had recounted the story of his torment several times with teammates to remember it and to verify the fact that it actually happened. I had also used it as an example for the few people I know who doubt the significance of racial discrimination. I had just written the above description a few weeks before Earl's message arrived, so it seemed mystical that he would contact me.

I had thought I would never see or hear from Earl again, but he reached out to me, of all people. I called him immediately, and we talked long about our experiences then and since. He told me he still suffered nightmares; he had been through therapy, and his knee had to be replaced. Yet, he has enjoyed a good life and very successful professional career as a computer engineer with Bell Labs.

Earl and I began talking and exchanging email messages regularly after reconnecting, and I sent him a copy of the story I had written. I shared it somewhat reluctantly, however, fearing it may awaken dark memories he would rather have kept hidden. When I expressed my concern, he responded with this amazing message:

"Chic,

I have been sleeping like a baby the last few days, so not to worry. Your note did something for my memories that I have not been able to do for myself. What I have decided to do was to take the 1965 preseason media booklet (the only documentation I kept from OSU) and go through each player and coach in it and try to write down as much as I can recall about each. In most cases, it will be minimal, but it might provoke me into some more recall.

My shrink tried to get me to do something similar years ago, but I thought it a tad silly. Today as a senior citizen, it should be easier and more rewarding. I say all of that to say thank you for jump starting my memory and my exodus from the dark side.

As for you and I, we are connected in ways most people will never be, and I suspect one way or the other we will stay that way.

Be well my friend and stay that way.

I will keep in touch.

E"

No one on earth deserves a good life more. I will go to my grave happy to know Earl Bud Jones is well.

After we lost the 1965 season opener in Arkansas, Missouri came to Stillwater for a conference game. J. B. Christian, the starter ahead of me suffered a mild injury in the third quarter, and I finally had my chance. The first play was a punt, and I took my position next to center Jim Click and stared across the line into the mean eyes of the biggest man I had ever seen. Click snapped the ball, and before I could set my feet to block, I had been knocked most of the way back into our own punter. I was dazed but regained consciousness in time to make sure all of my teeth were in place and look down field to see All-American running back Johnny Roland racing straight at me with knees pumping high and touchdown on his mind. I should have been 40 yards down field with the other linemen to stop him there, but I was way back where a safety would be. Nevertheless, I was the only body between this lightning fast, super agile, very large national sports hero and a Missouri touchdown.

I got him. I don't know how, but I did. The home town crowd cheered wildly, and I was a college football hero for a fleeting moment. That was the beginning and the end of my college sports success. May it live forever.

I played about a quarter of the game before Christian returned. In that brief time, I turned in the single worst performance by an Oklahoma State athlete in any sport in the entire history of the school. It may have been a national record, but the NCAA doesn't maintain those statistics. On one play—*Fake 6 Utah*, as I recall—I completely missed my block; Walt Garrison was stopped behind the line of scrimmage, and Russell Washington, an enormous Missouri player, hit me so hard I went airborne and landed on the other side of the pile of bodies. The coaches played and replayed the film of my aerobatics in the post-game review to a mixture of laughter and disdain.

Fortunately for the team, I managed to re-separate my shoulder — *for the fifth time*—a few weeks later, and that was the end. There would be no more football ever. But it was a blessing in two ways I could not anticipate or appreciate at the time. First, it enabled me to get out of a miserable football program gracefully and remain in school on scholarship. (Since I was white, the coaches were content to let me stay on scholarship without pressure or torture. Coach Bentley even pulled me aside and acknowledged it was a good thing for me. I had a sense even he was growing weary of the Cutchin brutality.) Second, it rendered me ineligible for military service. The war in Vietnam was growing, the military draft was gearing up, and that injury may have saved my life.

Coach Cutchin and his staff were supposed to help build character and guide young athletes in moral as well as athletic standards. Instead, they displayed deplorable values and demonstrated dreadful qualities. When Cutchin was finally fired three years later, he had ruined the college athletic experience for hundreds of young men, and he had produced a miserable win—loss record to show for it. Coach Speegle had achieved a modest 36-42-3 win-loss-tie record. After inflicting torturous practices and humiliation on his athletes, Cutchin went 19-38-2. In spite of it all, several teammates went on to stellar professional careers in business, engineering, and education, and we enjoy the enduring camaraderie among Cutchin' Cowboys.

Furthermore, the experience had a powerful impact on my sensitivity to racial issues and it helped shape my social and political values. It was my new awakening to the challenges others face and to the social and political struggles ahead. Earl told me the torment he survived on the practice field made him stronger. Seeing his courage and resilience in the face of the assault by the Cutchin staff gave me inspiration and courage.

BEYOND THE CLASSROOM

With my football career over and much of my own theological center formed, I began to search for other sources of interest, information, and philosophy. I read at least two books every week beyond the required course work because I was eager to make up for years of lost learning opportunities. The first non-required book I read was William Golding's *Lord of the Flies*. The narrative was compelling, and the profound insight into the potential for human depravity was alarming. It was just the beginning of a lifetime of reading and learning.

I read and absorbed every book and quality magazine I could find and afford. *Saturday Review* (now defunct) became a favorite weekly, but I also read *The Nation* and *The New Republic*, and for another point of view I subscribed to and read *Commentary* and *National Review*. *Ramparts* and some other radical magazines were available, and I read them from time to time, but I focused on more solid and mainstream journals including *Time, U.S. News and World Report* and *Newsweek*. I formed a group of very bright students to share what we could learn from these publications. Gene and Kathy Reid, Doug and Sherry Caves, and others each took responsibility for a few publications, and everyone prepared reports on the most important information and ideas. We met weekly to review the reports together and discuss the pertinent issues. We filled notebooks with quotations and data; we became exceptionally well informed, and it helped shape our political views and career aspirations.

In addition, I read everything by Albert Camus and Herman Hesse, and I found the works of Bertrand Russell to be fascinating. The great World War II era theologians like Dietrich Bonhoeffer and Paul Tillich had a profound impact on my values. Bonhoeffer's book on *Ethics*, with the essay, "What Is Meant by Telling the Truth?" written in the early 1940s during his active opposition to Nazi Germany, was most influential. Bonhoeffer was a major inspiration for my determination to take action wherever and whenever possible and to overcome injustice and violence. For me, the task has been easy. For Bonhoeffer, it meant a one way trip to a concentration camp and execution. As a Christian rather than a Jew, he had nothing to fear from Hitler; but as a man of integrity, he chose resistance. He lived and died by the ethics he taught.

Humanists like Julian Huxley and Aldus Huxley were also influential, and I identify with the community of "secular humanists" to this day, in spite of the vilification of the term by religious and political zealots. The liberal utilitarian philosophy of John Stuart Mill seemed about right. Early American philosophers like Ralph Waldo Emerson and Henry David Thoreau were heroes, and I read and re-read their works. I studied the popular existentialists, but Albert Camus made the most sense. The logical case for nihilistic existentialism was persuasive but not satisfying. Camus turned nihilism on its head. From a cosmic perspective, our lives may be irrelevant, but we make our own relevance and meaning through rebellion against inevitable oblivion by embracing the purpose we find for ourselves and interaction with those around us.

I had also embraced the enriching life of the performing and visual arts. I had developed a taste for great music, thanks to a wonderful music appreciation class at Ohio Wesleyan. It had been recommended to help my dreadful GPA, but understanding and appreciating classical music didn't come easily. At mid-semester, I had no interest in the music; I had barely earned a D, and I risked flunking out of school. But the music of the romantic period clicked. The Max Bruch "Violin Concerto

#1" did it. I listened to it over and over, and let the rich harmonics and the passion penetrate into my heart, mind, and soul. Soon other classics began to make sense, and I was hooked—destined to be a great music devotee forever. Along with music came an interest in literature, and along with literature came an interest in studying just about everything. It was a whole new world, and I couldn't get enough. An integrated framework of philosophy and aesthetics began to shape my values and propel me toward a lifetime devoted to building harmony among people and cultures.

The summer between discovering music at Ohio Wesleyan and the return to football at OSU, I made a special trip to Aspen, Colorado to see Laura Jane Clayton, a piano student at Ohio State. My cousin Cheryl Beales had introduced us, and I was smitten. She was an amazing musical talent and drop-dead beautiful. At Aspen, she was studying under the master teacher Madame Rosina Lhevinne. Laura Jane dumped me (gracefully but definitively), but I fell in love with Aspen—unique and pre-glitz Aspen—and its mountains and music. Laura Jane also introduced me to Christopher Czaja Sager, another of Madame Lhevinne's prize students.

The following summer, Christopher and I shared a small cabin on Ute Ave. on the edge of tiny Aspen. I worked hard labor clearing the trails that would become the Snowmass at Aspen Ski Resort. When I returned physically exhausted at the end of each day, I would lie on my bed and listen to Christopher practice on his Baldwin baby grand. He had just won the prestigious National Piano Auditions, and he was on his way to a brilliant career as a concert pianist, but for those glorious days, I was his audience of one.

Christopher persuaded Madame Lhevinne to ask the Festival management to provide me with comp tickets for the music festival concerts. The minimum wages I earned went for food, rent and gasoline. I could never have afforded the tickets. Madame Lhevinne told the Festival staff I was her driver for the summer, and all I asked in return was a season ticket. She never intended to sit in my little Volkswagen beetle, but she liked me, and she did the favor. She was impressed that a football player enjoyed good music, but she particularly liked my plan to go into the Peace Corps. That was the real reason she helped. I got to spend a summer listening to great music in a magnificent setting, and more often than not, I sat with one of the greatest piano teachers of all time.

Madame Lhevinne was always surrounded at the concerts by admiring (or terrified) students. The great Beveridge Webster had just finished a solo, and as the applause was dying down, the eager students began their critiques. "His timing was a bit off in this passage... He missed three notes... It was too soft... It was too fast..." Madame Lhevinne raised her hand to quiet them, and said in her thick Russian accent, "Please, please. Practice is for criticism. Performance is to be enjoyed. I came here to enjoy." I've always cherished that wonderful wisdom. It's easy to find fault. If anyone in the world was qualified to criticize Webster it was the great Madame Lhevinne. But she was there to enjoy the concert. The rest of us could, too.

I developed an interest in students from other countries and Iran was particularly intriguing. I became friends with Mehrdad Johanne (John), an engineering student from Tehran. OSU attracted many students from Iran and the Arabian countries because of its focus on petroleum engineering. John and I spent countless hours listening to music and discussing current events and politics. He also spent a few weeks with me in Aspen during the summer months. I was fascinated by his culture and his views. Iran was ruled by the Shah at the time, and he was our ally, and all seemed well—or so I thought. John dropped occasional hints that all was not well, but I didn't catch them until the dramatic changes and some deep reflection many years later.

That same summer, I took a solo excursion into the mountains above Independence Pass. I couldn't afford a backpack, so I used clothesline for shoulder straps to rig a facsimile of a pack for my sleeping bag, food, fly fishing gear, and extra clothes. I went without a tent because even the cheapest were far beyond my price range. The rope dug into my shoulders, but it got me through. It was my very first overnight totally alone, and there was not another person within miles. I went through a full range of emotions from fear to a profound sense of freedom and elation. I talked to myself out loud. I sang, and even danced. I didn't catch any fish, but I had packed enough food, including some canned beans and peas.

I was well above the timberline, so it took a while to gather enough leaves, twigs, and branches from the brush for a fire, but I built a nice little pile of sage and other dry plants. I struck a match to light the fire, but it went out in the thin air and slight breeze. I lit another, and it went out. I held two matches together, but the flame vanished. Three together did no better. Faster and faster, I lit matches until there were only two left, and I was shivering while looking at cold cans of beans and peas for dinner. I gathered my wits, and carefully re-built the pile with the very thin twigs and dry leaves positioned perfectly for protection from the breeze and where they might catch the flame. Slightly larger fuel was right next to the smallest kindling, and larger material was piled next to that. I took a deep breath and tore the last two matches from the book. I cupped my hands around the matches, and held the strike pad right against the target. I struck the matches towards the fuel to minimize the time between the strike and ignition of the kindling. It worked. I carefully coaxed a tiny flame until I could add the larger fuel and then more until I had a real camp fire. It cooked the best hot meal of my life—beans and peas out of the can by a lovely, lonely mountain lake. I curled up right next to the fire to sleep as I was badly under-equipped for the mountain cold. The fire didn't last long, but it helped me get to sleep. I awoke shivering, but I had survived my first solo night in the wilderness.

It is dangerous and perhaps foolish to trek through the mountains alone, but that experience whetted my appetite. I've done several solo mountain excursions since, and these days I cherish the solitude of a day alone on the river with my fly rod. Someone once said, "You are what you are when there is no one else around." I have found and become reacquainted with myself again and again by making time to be alone.

≈

I became a speech major simply because I earned my first college "A" in an introduction to public speaking course. I had finally discovered something in the academic world that I could do well. Like most students, the prospect of facing an audience, not to mention the professor, was terrifying. To my amazement, however, I actually enjoyed the experience. I had no idea if there would be career opportunities associated with such an obscure major, but speaking came easily, so that was it. It proved to be a fortuitous choice as the ability to communicate effectively has carried me throughout my multi-faceted career.

Dale Stockton, the debate and oratory coach at Oklahoma State, was one of the great men in the field of speech and communications. His own speeches (and his sermons whenever he substituted for local preachers) were memorable, but his ability to teach and inspire others was beyond compare. His "Introduction to Public Speaking" became the most popular course on the entire campus, and his debate teams became national powers. Only in his early 30s, Dale was emerging as a major figure in the field of social ethics as well as communications.

Dale took special interest in a few of us, and we spent countless late night hours in his living room. He was our Socrates, asking penetrating questions and exploring every angle before we could reach any conclusions. He taught us to respect and listen to others and other points of view, and he presented us with profound moral and ethical conundrums and challenged every response we could devise. It was exhilarating and exhausting.

Socrates said, "The unexamined life is not worth living." Most of us cruise through life in the safe lane with a career, family, pets, and hobbies towards the ultimate end without a second thought as to the rationale for our religious faith, values, government, or much of anything else. We evade fundamental existential questions and settle for simplistic answers. Physical comfort, financial security, and a good time with family and friends suffice. Socrates had challenged his pupils to seek more and to question and re-examine often. Dale challenged us. It makes life a bit more difficult, but it is ever so much richer and fuller.

The local Kentucky Fried Chicken let us buy their cooked but unsold pieces for a dime each after they closed at 11. We filled a bucket with chicken parts and ate while we debated until midnight, 1 am, 2 am, or later several nights each week. It's a wonder his wife Judy didn't divorce him on the spot, but she seemed to tolerate his drive for knowledge and his engagement in national and world affairs. She even made sure we were comfortable and felt welcomed. We did more homework to prepare for the sessions with Dale than we did for our formal classes.

Dale insisted that I read Viktor Frankl's classic *Man's Search for Meaning*. I still have the copy I purchased in 1967, and it is filled with fading highlighter yellow—a reflection of the intensity of my interest in nearly every word. Frankl had studied survivors of the Holocaust and he found a remarkable common characteristic: for the most part, those who survived did so for the sake of others. Victims whose motivation to survive was purely for their own sake were more likely to perish. Those with an external cause—family members, their work, or a life mission—were more apt to survive. Life purpose or meaning, he concluded, is essential for human survival, and meaning is found outside oneself. Frankl said, "Life ultimately means taking the responsibility to find the right answer to its problems and to fulfill the tasks which it constantly sets for each individual." He also quoted Nietzsche, "He who has a *why* to live for can bear with almost any *how*."

I joined the OSU debate team, and it changed my life in unforeseen ways. The debate topic for that season was, "Be it resolved, the United States should significantly reduce its foreign policy commitments." We attended the national debate conference in Missouri before the start of the season to meet and greet other debaters and to learn more about the topic. The keynote speaker at the event was a former national debate champion and obscure U.S. Senator named George McGovern. I happened to sit next to him during a lunch break, and we struck up a conversation. He had expressed concern about the war in Vietnam in his address, but few people responded with any interest in the topic. America was in Vietnam to defeat Godless communism. Case closed. I shared that view, and I told McGovern I didn't agree with him. He didn't argue or reject my views. Instead he listened patiently and respectfully, but he also suggested I do a little research before dismissing the case against the war.

Oklahoma State was, and is, a very conservative campus. We knew we would face criticism if the OSU debate team chose to argue for U.S. withdrawal from Vietnam. Upon returning from the conference, however, we pored through the literature. The deeper we looked into the history and the data, the worse the war looked.

McGovern encouraged me to read the works of the great French journalist Bernard Fall and the I. F. Stone newsletter. Fall was an expert on the folly of the French occupation of Vietnam, and he knew the Vietnamese were fighting for national pride and independence. They were not part of a global communist movement to conquer the world. The leaders had embraced communism because they believed (rightly or wrongly) it provided an economic model to overcome gripping poverty. Fall also knew it would be impossible for an occupying force to prevail, regardless of its military superiority. The human spirit of independence and cultural identity are more powerful than any army.

Stone had poor hearing, so he avoided press conferences where journalists were told by government officials what to report. He went to original source documents from the Pentagon, State Department and Congress, and he discovered a very different reality in the written record. From Stone, I learned the shocking truth that the attack in the Gulf of Tonkin was a fabricated fiction. Yet, it was used to justify the Congressional resolution authorizing the military escalation—the transition from an advisory role to combat. Stone was vilified by the establishment for his work, but he, along with Daniel Ellsworth and a few other courageous dissidents, were the true patriots of the era.

The war started with a lie. Stories of the Vietnam communist threat and falling dominoes were nonsense; and our own government officials knew it. Decades later, even Defense Secretary Robert McNamara admitted as much. Nevertheless, they convinced a loyal and patriotic public to believe it. Reports of light at the end of the tunnel were pipe dreams that ran counter to everything that was actually happening on the ground. The rationale for war and the prospects for success in Vietnam were false. The government of the United States of America, which I had grown up respecting and admiring with every cell in my body, had betrayed us. I have never been able to trust media reports or public relations hype from the government or corporate America since then. I always look deeper. I look for the truth beneath the hype.

McGovern was right. The war was wrong. It was a quagmire from which withdrawal would be embarrassing and ugly, but inevitable. Dale had been an opponent of the war all along, and he was thrilled to have his debate team discover the truth and take on the lie. From our perspective, the only question was how long the U.S. would prolong the killing, the damage, and the destruction before facing facts and leaving. We argued that leaving immediately would be far better than a prolonged disaster. We won many tournaments with our case. It was rock solid. We lost a few times however, when judges marked their ballots with notes indicating we were anti-American and odious communist sympathizers.

Making the case against the war to win a debate tournament, however, was more than an intellectual exercise. I had become convinced the war really was wrong, and I could not limit my engagement to the sterile debate environment. We had to take it to the people. One of my colleagues, Bill Dawson, and I persuaded several residence halls to let us present forums in their common spaces. We gained a bit of a reputation, and we attracted substantial crowds. Many of the students refused to believe that we, as students, could possibly know better than our national leaders, and some accused us of treason, but we made remarkable headway. We helped ignite an anti-war movement that eventually permeated the entire campus, and my own path was becoming clear.

'60s ACTIVIST & PROUD OF IT

It only took me five years to complete a four year degree, and the 1966-67 school year was my fifth and best. I only had to complete a few courses to graduate, so I added some graduate level classes, but still kept a light load. Dale Stockton invited me to move into his garage so we could spend more time thinking and working together. Dale was establishing a communications consulting firm, and he had political ambitions. He wanted me to be his partner in both endeavors. His wife Judy never seemed pleased with the arrangement, but she was always gracious, and I was thrilled.

By this time, my athletic scholarship had expired, but I was invited to teach the beginning speech class as a graduate assistant. That meant a modest income, and I was invited to the College of Arts and Sciences faculty convocation before classes started. Dr. James Ralph Scales had become Dean the year before, and he had gained widespread respect among the faculty. He was an established intellectual figure, and a great advocate for the arts. But I was skeptical. Scales had been president of Oklahoma Baptist University before coming to OSU, and that was not a good sign. OBU was as conservative as a campus could be, and I wanted to see OSU become more open to diversity of opinion and part of the 1960s social and political movement. In the midst of his speech, Scales noted the turmoil sweeping campuses all across the country. "I don't want the boat rocked," he pleaded, "because I'm in it."

That was all I needed to hear. As far as I was concerned, Scales was on the wrong side. I could expect and accept that attitude from the deans of Agriculture, Engineering, or Business, but Arts and Sciences should be in the vanguard of change. Scales was the wrong man in the wrong place at the wrong time. Bill Dawson and I shared a cubicle office in Morrill Hall as graduate teaching assistants, and we stayed up most of that night crafting a letter to the editor of the *Daily O'Collegian*, the student paper, to express our outrage.

The letter dripped with sarcasm and it reeked of disdain for anyone who would dare tread on academic freedom. Scales was our immediate target, but we were speaking to the entire campus and the authoritarian administration. "But, really, Dean Scales, we cannot agree with you. We feel that enlightenment is the object of true education. Emanuel Kant once said that to be enlightened one must have the courage and ambition to use his own intelligence. But since our exposure to controversy has been nullified, our ambition for intellectual pursuit is being stifled. Our courage has no testing ground." We concluded, "We hope we have misinterpreted you, Dean Scales, but campus atmosphere and conditions indicate otherwise. Nevertheless, if we have, we hope you will set us straight with a reply."

Dr. Fred Tewell, head of the speech department, knew what we were doing, and he was not pleased. He answered to Scales in the university's chain of command, but we didn't care. We were right; Scales was wrong, and we had to speak out. As we arrived at work the morning the letter appeared in the *O'Colley*, the office phone Bill and I shared began to ring, and we knew what was coming. The Dean wanted to see us immediately. Others in the department feared we might be expelled, or at least lose our teaching positions. They wished us well as we left to see Scales, but Bill and I marched straight to his office with foolish youthful confidence and only a touch of anxiety. There, we found a remarkably warm and gentle gentleman. Scales was tall, dark tanned, and very distinguished, with a bit of a Will Rogers look in his chiseled face.

"I have read your letter," he began slowly and then paused for effect. "It's very well written." Another pause. "But you have the wrong man," he concluded. Scales explained he was speaking with irony, even sarcasm, when he said he didn't want to be in a rocking boat. He agreed OSU needed to change, and he promised to work with us to make it happen. Bill was skeptical, but I was ready to give him a chance. The next day, a hand written note was delivered to my desk. "Now that we have met, please don't neglect me." It was signed James Ralph Scales.

Dr. Scales was true to his word. For the next nine months, the rest of the school year, he served as a mentor, advisor, and friend. I became engaged in every activist initiative on campus—anti-war, free speech, civil rights, the environment, and publication of an underground newspaper—and Scales helped me push the envelope as far as possible without tearing it apart.

Late in the spring of 1967, I was about to graduate and go off to serve in the Peace Corps when Dr. Scales called and asked if I would do him a favor. He was a candidate for the presidency of Wake Forest University, and he wanted me to be a reference for him. We both laughed about how far we had come from our first encounter when I had blasted him with my "well written" letter to the editor.

Four Wake Forest trustees crowded into my tiny cubicle to ask about Dr. Scales, but I was afraid to tell them the truth. Wake was known to be a very conservative Southern Baptist school in North Carolina. How could I tell them about his support for our activist anti-establishment initiatives without ruining his chances? Tom Davis, chair of the trustees and chairman of Piedmont Airlines, started the conversation by saying, "Wake Forest needs to change. It has to become a progressive university. Now, please tell us about Dr. Scales. Can he make that happen?" With that introduction, I was free to tell the whole story, and I did. Dr. Scales became president of Wake Forest, and he turned it from a mediocre conformist college into a progressive school ranked among the top academic institutions in America. We corresponded while I was in the Peace Corps, and I had the privilege of earning a second degree from him ten years later. The arts center at Wake is named in his honor.

≈

I had become a member of the OSU Student Forum Committee, the group that presented the campus speaker series. The chairman, John Hancock, was perceived by the rest of the committee as being too timid and accommodating to the administration's restrictions on the topics and speakers. He was establishment, and we were anti-establishment. He was cautious, and we were aggressive. In a secret meeting, the group agreed John had to go, and I should take over. They also asked me to break the news to John. He and I weren't close, but I liked him and hated to cast him out, but the issues were too important. The right of students to listen to controversial people and to be exposed to new ideas was at stake. John would not challenge the established order, but the rest of us would, so I prepared a detailed and rock-solid case against him.

When the next committee meeting started, I asked to be recognized, I laid out our case, and John took it remarkably well. He was not totally surprised, as he knew discontent had been brewing. He offered his resignation on the spot; we accepted, and I became committee chairman.

We had executed a successful coup, and we were ready to take on the campus tradition and authority. We had a small budget from student fees to pay speakers, and we developed a careful plan to present a balanced, but provocative series. We brought Barry Goldwater to speak from the conservative, pro-war perspective. Scales arranged for us to pick up Goldwater in Columbia, Missouri in a private twin-engine plane owned by a Stillwater banker and ardent Goldwater backer. David Block, the most radical member of our committee, and I had the privilege of a lengthy airborne dialogue with the voice and conscience of conservative America. Goldwater was terrific, and I thoroughly enjoyed spending the day with him. He asked us more questions than we asked him. He wanted to understand why we were so vigorously opposed to the war in Vietnam. We didn't change his mind, but he listened, and we respected him for it.

He also shared a delightful story about his recent trip to Spain to meet with General Franco. "El Caudillo" had mentioned to Goldwater that an American named Billy James Hargis would be visiting with him the next day. Hargis was a famous televangelist crook from Tulsa. "What should I tell this American," Franco wanted to know. Goldwater replied, "Bolt everything down, and tell him no!" We knew then Goldwater was not the humorless right wing ideologue of his reputation. Libertarian, yes. Right wing, no. Humorless, absolutely not. Goldwater filled the arena with 8,000 students and faculty, and I was very proud to introduce him and to have been part of it.

We attracted Vice President Hubert Humphrey, and he also filled the arena and defended the war policies. The Humphrey program even made national network news. Some friends from Worthington sent letters saying they had seen me on national television introducing and questioning the Vice President of the United States. I admired Humphrey, but I had come to despise his policies on Vietnam. It made for an interesting though mutually respectful confrontation. We grilled him thoroughly that day.

The rest of the speakers were lower profile, and very different in their perspectives. Julian Bond, a controversial leader of the civil rights and anti-war movements from Georgia, made the administration nervous, but they could not ban him. He was an elected member of the Georgia legislature. The eminent historian Henry Steele Commager came to address the war issue. The administration hated it, but there was little they could do. He was a revered academic, and the U.S. Senate Foreign Relations committee had invited him to testify. If he was acceptable to the U.S. Senate, why couldn't OSU students hear him?

These speakers threatened campus tranquility, but the university had no legal or policy basis for blocking them. The university's odious gag rule was very specific. No communists, and no atheists—period.

None of us on the Forum Committee were communists, and while some of us had become agnostic, none of us were out to convert anyone or destroy their religious faith. We simply believed that, on a college campus in the land of the free, we should be able to hear views we didn't understand or agree with. That, we argued, was fundamental to a well rounded education.

The book *God is Dead* by Anglican Bishop A. J. Robinson had just been published, and the whole concept of religion and faith was a hot topic. We wanted someone who could represent a skeptical point of view, since fundamentalist Christianity was preached in dozens of local churches and reinforced at several university-sanctioned faith-based clubs and centers. Evangelical Christian doctrine was ubiquitous and rarely challenged in Stillwater, Oklahoma, not even on the state university campus. Robinson was high on our list, and he wasn't even an atheist, but university president Robert Kamm absolutely prohibited it.

Our other target speaker to challenge the rule was the prominent Marxist historian and political activist Herbert Aptheker. Aptheker was speaking on campuses all across America, and we wanted him in Oklahoma. Why should OSU students be denied access to this a famous and influential man and his views? Try as we might, the administration refused to allow student fees or campus facilities to be used for a communist.

That ruling prompted a well organized campus protest that attracted a large crowd in front of the library, and it generated a lively debate. The theme was "No Thought Control," and a stream of passionate student and faculty leaders spoke out. Dean Scales dared not attend, but he followed the event with great interest, and he commended us for doing it right. There was no violence, and everyone was respectful. We even kept our hair cut short, and we wore sport coats and ties to make it hard for anyone to accuse us of being un-American, hippies or radicals.

David Block had learned that Dr. Han Suyin, a prominent novelist was touring campuses with a message we might find interesting.

Dr. Suyin had written the very popular romance novel, *A Many Splendored Thing*. It had become a movie and hit song as well, so she was safe from the censors. I told Dr. Kamm we planned to bring this novelist to campus, and he was most pleased. Not very innocently, however, I neglected to mention Dr. Suyin was also an ally, friend, and advisor to Chinese Communist Party Chairman Mao Zedong. We promoted the speech with posters and newspaper ads identifying Dr. Suyin as a famous romance novelist, but we also spread the word among friends and friendly faculty this was not to be missed. We held the event in a small but comfortable 300-seat theater in the student union, and the crowd was standing room only.

The only reference to *A Many Splendored Thing* was in my introduction. Dr. Suyin spoke eloquently and persuasively about China and its Cultural Revolution. We gained an extremely valuable insight into the challenges China faced and the rationale for the Revolution. Of course, all of us have learned since how dreadful the Cultural Revolution was. Millions of innocent Chinese peasants and intellectuals were murdered by Chairman Mao and his troops. His may have been the most monstrous regime in all of history. But I am proud we brought his spokesperson to our campus. We lived our freedom, and we learned a tremendous amount.

In fact, Dr. Suyin taught me one of the most powerful lessons of my life. It has enabled me to be effective as a mediator and negotiator in several serious conflict environments. I can't recall the exact words, but the essence of her message is burned into my memory:

Imagine that you live in Beijing, and you are responsible for the safety and security of a billion Chinese people. You look out at the world around you, and what do you see? There are 400,000 American soldiers fighting a war of aggression in Vietnam, right on your border. Vietnam is a small country with no political or economic consequence to America, so why are you there? It is obvious. You are in Vietnam to establish a stronghold from which to invade China. There are another 50,000 troops in Thailand. Why are they there? Obviously, for the same reason.

You Americans are concerned that China is taking steps to fortify itself. We are threatened, and this is our self defense. When, on the other hand, you felt vulnerable because of a few missiles being shipped to Cuba, ninety miles off your coast, you were prepared and willing to launch a nuclear attack that could have destroyed every living thing on this planet. You think the world has reason to fear us. You are the ones to be feared.

I heard these stinging words sitting behind Dr. Suyin on the stage, and I watched the audience. Everyone was spellbound. We had never heard such a thing. We had never seen the world from the other side. That night we did, and we are all better for it.

I was not then, and I certainly am not now a communist sympathizer. Almost everything about the practice of communism runs diametrically opposite my own social, political and economic philosophy. Mao, even more than Stalin, was a monster who delighted in brutal and totalitarian control. I would have the world community establish legitimate mechanisms to topple such men, put them on trial, and imprison them for life at hard labor. Nevertheless, it was tremendously important for us to hear and understand his perspective. To my knowledge, no one that night became a Mao sympathizer. But we left knowing and understanding much, much more about him and the complex challenges beyond our borders.

To no one's surprise, I was invited to see President Kamm the next day. My lifelong friend and Forum Committee colleague Gene Reid accompanied me for moral support. Dr Kamm let me know, in no uncertain terms, he was not pleased, and that I had deceived him. I had said nothing untrue when informing him we were inviting Dr. Suyin, but I hadn't told him the whole truth, and I admitted as much. But, I said, "Dr. Kamm, three-hundred OSU students heard a message they had never heard before from a perspective they may never hear again. They have gained new knowledge and insight. That is what a university education is for." I went on to say, "The sun rose this morning just as it did yesterday before Dr. Suyin spoke. It will set again tonight as it does every night. The only thing that has changed is that we have some better informed students who will be better citizens for it. I seriously doubt any of them will join the communist party because of what they heard, but they may try to understand global issues from a broader perspective. How can you object to that?" Kamm was still unhappy, but he had to admit I was right.

The next year, while I was in Colombia in the Peace Corps, my successors on the Forum Committee successfully brought Herbert Aptheker to Stillwater. He was denied access to university facilities, but the Methodist Student Center allowed him to speak there. OSU's own little Berlin Wall of repression was crumbling. The gag rule was a farce, and it was eventually rescinded. The American birthright of freedom of expression and the right to listen and learn had been delivered to future generations of students, even in Stillwater, Oklahoma.

Today, free speech is often challenged by the left as well as the right. Racists like David Duke are barred from speaking for fear they may offend minorities. He offends me, too, but he should be allowed to speak if someone wants to invite him. We can stay home if we don't want to hear him. Better yet, we can listen and challenge him in a serious dialogue. Louis Farrakhan is often barred because he offends the Jewish community and others. He offends me, too, but let him speak, and let an informed public judge his words and respond.

Throughout the OSU campus, like-minded, high spirited, independent, and active students found each other through informal networks, and we formed a group we called the Friday Afternoon Tea and Glee Society, the FATAGS. Many years before, some enterprising students had created a social network by that name, and they had left it registered as an official campus club. The club had been abandoned, so we adopted its name. After all, we weren't making trouble. We were just meeting on Friday afternoons to drink tea and enjoy fellowship. There were no dues, formal registration, or mailing lists. We just knew each other and spread information and news by word of mouth.

Over time the group grew to dozens of members, including most of the sociology department faculty and students. Nearly all, but not 100 percent, of the eager students Dale Stockton had assembled aligned themselves with the FATAGS. The brain power was high, and the enthusiasm was higher. These were some of the brightest students on campus, and we were determined to change OSU now and the world later.

Bob Swaffar was the only other scholarship athlete in the FATAGS. Like me, Bob was no longer active in sports due to an injury, but his story made medical history. Bob was a 6' 9" basketball player and architecture student whose arm was ripped off just below the shoulder in the athletic department's centrifugal dryer in a freak accident. Fast action by teammate Gary Hassman and the team physician, Dr. Donald Cooper, preserved the severed limb. Bob and his long arm were rushed to the University of Oklahoma Medical Center nearly two hours away where a surgical team had studied and practiced for major limb re-attachment. Bob's arm was stitched back in place, and after months of therapy it actually became functional. It was only the second successful major limb re-implantation in medical history. He never played competitive basketball again, but he has enjoyed a normal life, including two years as a Peace Corps Volunteer in Ethiopia and a successful career with the architecture department at the University of Texas. His long, tall, and prominent presence at our FATAGS sponsored events gave us extra recognition.

FATAGS members had various interests and priorities, but the group provided a point of contact for anyone interested in promoting changes. We worked for civil rights, against the war, for free speech, and for the environment. When the Oklahoma legislature tried to cut funding for higher education, we protested that as well. Our signature became an unofficial, underground newspaper we called *The Drummer*. We borrowed the name from Henry David Thoreau, "If a man does not keep pace with his companions, perhaps it is because he hears a different drummer. Let him step to the music which he hears, however measured or far away." At OSU, we were different, and proud of it. *The Drummer* gave a public voice to several very bright, well informed and articulate students who preferred to eschew the controlled official publications and sanctioned outlets.

Just for fun and to taunt university officials, we often met for picnics on the large manicured lawn in front of the Student Union. We called them Frodo picnics in honor of the hero in J. R. R. Tolkein's popular *Lord of the Rings*. On occasion, men in dark suits with dark glasses and large black bellow-lens cameras appeared and took our pictures. We knew they were with the FBI, and we resented the government intrusion, but we made the best of it. In a strange way, it was actually amusing, and we enjoyed mocking the agents. We provided them with comic poses, and wished them well. Years later, I would learn my FBI file, picnic pictures and all, had followed me through my first few jobs and relocations.

A few years ago, Jerry Gill, an old Cowboy football teammate and subsequent president of the OSU Alumni Association, gave me a tour of the marvelous new Alumni Center on the campus. The Center's Legacy Hall features photos of significant events in the history of the university, and the very last picture in the series shows a crowd of students assembled in front of the library holding a protest banner: "No Thought Control." Jerry looked closely at the people in the photo and asked, "Where are you, Chic?"

"Jerry, I was one of the speakers," I answered.

"I should have known," he replied with a big smile. After all these years the school that tried its best to shut us up and put us down has honored us in their proud hall of history.

≈

My antipathy toward the war in Vietnam grew by the day. Friends and friends of friends were killed or permanently maimed. Innocent Vietnamese were killed by the thousands, even tens of thousands, each week by my friends and neighbors using chemical weapons financed with our tax dollars. Because of my study of the issue on the debate team, I knew the facts inside and out. I was also heavily influenced by Senate Foreign Relations Committee Chairman J. William Fulbright. His committee hearings focused a bright light on the flaws in the policy. Fulbright's book *The Arrogance of Power* captured the essence of America's mistake in Vietnam, and I believe it remains one of the most important books on foreign policy ever written. (Sadly, the lesson on arrogance has been lost on the recent national leadership, and we have paid the same devastating price once again.)

Opposing the war in Vietnam was easy at Wisconsin, Berkeley, and Columbia. On those campuses, protest was the norm to which everyone was expected to conform. OSU was a very different matter. It took courage to speak against the war when surrounded by ROTC cadets and flag waving super-patriots wearing cowboy hats and boots. When they couldn't respond to our facts and logical analysis of the fallacy and the moral depravity of that war, they would revert to the comfortable God and country argument punctuated with, "My country right or wrong," and, "Love it or leave it." Since we loved America, we wanted to improve it—help mend its ways. The few of us willing to speak out were often accused of treason by other students, but we stood our ground.

We organized rallies and created opportunities to confront anyone anywhere to make our point. We did so respectfully, and peacefully. We respected the soldiers who had been pressed into service, but we vigorously opposed the policies that forced them to kill and be killed. I also opposed radical activists on the left who resorted to violence. I wanted an open, honest and peaceful dialogue, and I believed that an informed public would eventually recognize and embrace the truth and value of our message.

In December, 2008, a fellow OSU student whom I barely knew at the time found me on Facebook and sent this message:

Hi Chic, You probably don't know me but I watched you sitting in a booth in the student union arguing decisively against the Vietnam war with uninformed students. Your facts and presentation made an impression on me—so much so that I began my own fact-finding mission about the war.

You and my Elements of Persuasion and Debate instructor were instrumental in changing my world view. It's interesting that I can remember your name and not my professor...

In any case, at 63 years old, I'm still that old fiery check out the facts person that you inspired me to be so many years ago.

Hope you're doing and well and since you're in Washington, D.C., can you say hello to the incoming president? I'm not na-ive enough to think our new leader will be able to turn this place around quickly. I just hope that he has enough support to start repairing the damage from the last eight years.

Many blessings to you,

Sharon Gafford Furstenwerth

I was tremendously moved by her message, and we have continued to correspond ever since. The instructor she remembered was, of course, Dale Stockton, my friend and mentor.

By the time I graduated, we had made a mark on campus. When classes started in the fall of 1966, there was barely a whisper of controversy. Classes, fraternities, parties, and the new football season dominated social conversations. When the school year finished nine months later, OSU's isolation from the great movements of the time was gone, and tranquility had been shattered. We even gained national press attention when all but one member of the sociology department resigned in protest over administration repression. Free speech and anti-war demonstrations stirred both patriotic and revolutionary emotions, while students and faculty eagerly anticipated the arrival of each weekly edition of *The Drummer*.

Even the race for student government offices were waged on serious issues like intellectual freedom. It was a different place, and we, the FATAGS, made it happen. *The Daily O'Collegian*, the official student newspaper which had published our letter blasting Dean Scales, gave me the *O'Colley Salute*—their choice for the outstanding student of the spring semester of 1967. I was even named the "Outstanding Graduate Teaching Assistant" of the year by the Alumni Association and the Blue Key honor fraternity. That was more a tribute to Dale and to my activism than to my teaching ability, but I was proud of the recognition.

My parents came for graduation, grateful that their son, who barely survived high school, had actually completed college. Dale showed them the story in the *O'Colley* honoring their son, and I think their sense of relief that I actually graduated turned into some small measure of pride.

The 1960s began in tranquility, but they ended in turmoil. The serenity masked a nation that practiced apartheid, restricted basic freedoms, ignored a rapidly deteriorating ecosystem, and blindly followed national leaders regardless of their merit. America began the decade with a low-grade but expanding intrusion into the internal affairs of a small Southeast Asian nation ten thousand miles away. The decade ended with unspeakable death and destruction, and the nation's innocence in shreds. The turbulence we generated helped expose the sins, and it forced changes in policies and behavior. We were on the right side of every issue, and all of the changes were needed. I did my small part to expose the flaws and press for a new America. I'm proud of what we did. Our country and the world are better for it.

THE PEACE CORPS ADVENTURE

I was accepted into the Peace Corps program in Colombia, and like most newly appointed Volunteers, I ran to the library to learn where it was and what it would be like. Right after graduation and the day before leaving campus, one of the more innocent and provincial Oklahoma State students approached me in the student union with a worried look on her face. She had just learned I was going into the Peace Corps. "You wouldn't, would you?" she asked plaintively.

"Wouldn't what?" I asked.

"Marry one of *them*," she blurted out. I laughed and assured her I was going off to work, not to seek a wife, but I also told her I could make no promises. She walked away perplexed and quite concerned.

Between graduation and the start of Peace Corps training, I took an adventuresome and low budget trip to Washington and New York, just to connect with those magnificent cities before leaving the country. Connie Kantzer, one of my best friends on the Forum Committee and the FATAGS, accompanied me on the trip. Connie and I had never really dated, but we were quite fond of each other. This trip wasn't exactly a date either, but we laughed, talked, and hugged as only very dear friends could.

My aunt and uncle, Charlotte and Wendell Beales, lived in Westfield, New Jersey near New York, and I had arranged to stay a few nights with them to save money during the New York part of the trip. I told them a friend was coming with me, but I said nothing about my companion's gender. I pulled my green Volkswagen beetle into their drive-way; they saw a girl in the car with me, and a look of terror struck their faces. As quickly and discreetly as possible, they rearranged the rooms so Connie and I wouldn't be sleeping together! After a night with the Beales family, Connie and I spent the rest of the New York portion of our trip in the Manhattan apartment of my pianist friend Christopher Sager. Christopher had no such moral qualms. He expected us to sleep together. Indeed, we shared a small bed in his apartment, but we re-ally did sleep, nothing more. That wasn't my plan, but Connie and her Oklahoma values prevailed.

After our scandalous trip, Connie returned to Oklahoma, and I moved into a dorm at George Washington University in Washington, D.C., to begin training to become a Peace Corps Volunteer. The forty-five trainees began as strangers, but we bonded quickly. We all faced the same rigorous training regimen and the prospect of living and working in a strange land, speaking a new language, eating different food, and surviving on $100 per month. It was exciting, invigorating, and terrify-ing all at once.

I had much more trouble than most of the others learning Spanish. My mind froze as I tried and tried to memorize new words and mas-ter the grammar. The classes, from the very first minute, were taught entirely in Spanish, and I just didn't catch on. I deeply feared failing and "de-selection" from the program. De-selection was the Sword of Damocles over every trainee. Our status as Peace Corps trainees could be terminated at any time by the staff, and the prospect of a humiliating return home was more than any of us could bear.

Early in the program, Gretchen Handwerger came to monitor our program for the headquarters office, and rumors spread among the trainees that she was there to start the dreaded de-selection process. When she observed my struggle in Spanish class, I feared the worst. She pulled me aside, and I knew it was all over. I braced myself for the sword to drop and pierce my dreams. Instead, she said she had noticed my anxiety, and she gently gave me the guidance and confidence I needed to survive. She told me I was trying too hard. I simply needed to relax and allow the new language to flow into my mind and become part of my experiences. I couldn't force it. I had to open up and let it happen. I did, and it worked.

I saw Handwerger again many years later at Peace Corps events. She had become acting director of the Peace Corps and then she became the World Bank's liaison to the UN and special representative to the Organization for Economic Cooperation and Development. She didn't remember my traumatic encounter with her during that training program, but I was very pleased to have an opportunity to thank her. Without that brief meeting with a wise and caring mentor, I would have failed in the Peace Corps, and I doubt I would have ever recovered.

The second half of our three month training regimen took place in Bogota. On our last night in Washington, several trainees took a city bus to the historic Carter Baron Amphitheater in Rock Creek Park for a Peter, Paul and Mary concert. With their themes of peace and understanding, we felt the music was just for us. It would be our last direct contact with American musical culture for two years, so we inhaled and absorbed every word and note.

Bogota was a large and crowded city of two million high in the mountains where buses were jammed with passengers on the inside and half a dozen fearless others hanging onto the outside. There were a few prosperous neighborhoods and elegant hotels like the famous Techendama, surrounded by sprawling unspeakable poverty. We were there to deal with the poverty. During training, we lived with host families in modest but not impoverished neighborhoods. It was part of a gentle transition to the real thing. My family was middleclass by Colombian standards, and I appreciated them very much. I regret deeply that I have forgotten their last name and that I failed to maintain contact with them, but I didn't have a chance to get to know them well. The husband was named Alfonso, and they had relatives in Hackensack, New Jersey.

They spoke no English, and at that time my Spanish was miserable. We communicated primarily with hand signals.

The room was comfortable with a hard bed and plenty of blankets to keep warm during the cold, damp Bogota nights. Bogota is near the equator, but it is also nestled at 9,000-foot elevation. The temperature hovers between forty-five and sixty-five degrees nearly every day. The locals are used to it, so they have no heat in their homes, but it was a shock to my system. The house had a shower, but the water was heated by a small electrical element attached to the shower head. It scared me to death, and the water was always either scalding hot or freezing cold. I never found the trick to getting it right.

I took a public bus from the barrio to CEUCA, an education center affiliated with a group of liberal arts colleges in the Great Lakes region of the U.S. CEUCA's director John Martin was unpleasant, condescending and authoritarian from the very beginning. The rest of the trainers, however, were superb. Sam Farr, and Dave and Nora Fretz had been with us at George Washington, and a new set of Colombians and a dashing Argentine gentleman (who knew Che Guevara) added an exciting dimension to the program. We had already bonded with the trainers who had been with us at GWU, and the new ones in Colombia were delightful. Some fulfilled our fantasy vision of handsome and suave Latin *caballeros*, and beautiful, elegant *damas*.

We took field trips to some of the poorest barrios in Bogota, and the first experience was very disturbing. Thousands upon thousands of people lived in shanties made of scrap wood and metal sheets on steep hillsides with no running water or power. They were barefoot and dressed in rags in spite of the constant cold. On my first trip, a chilling rain filled gullies with yellow-brown clay saturated water, and it carried trash and sewage alike downstream to an unknown destination. There were no schools for the children; no one could read or write; and unemployment exceeded seventy percent. They survived by begging and stealing, and I came to view both professions as noble. When your family is starving, you do what you must to survive. To me it was Hugo's *Les Miserables* come to life. For the first time in my sheltered and protected life, I came face-to-face with reality for the billion people who miss meals regularly because they have no food. I felt troubled and inept, and I've never been fully comfortable since that experience. Why was I born into affluence when so many are born into so little? Where is the justice?

Peace Corps training went well, in spite of occasional unpleasant encounters with Martin, and we settled into a routine. Even the fear of de-selection seemed to subside, until a few weeks before training was to be completed. A troubling rumor spread like fire, and it was quickly confirmed. Comandante Martin had determined that our friends and colleagues Joe and Sarah Walsh were to be de-selected, and our favorite trainers like Sam Farr, Dave and Nora Fretz and some of the Colombians had been fired for refusing to accept his dictum.

Joe and Sarah were the only trainees in the program without college degrees. Joe was a trained and experienced carpenter, and Sarah was a nurse. They actually had something to offer the Colombians. The rest of us were liberal arts college graduates with nothing but our spirit and goodwill. We had no skills whatsoever to teach anyone. Furthermore, we loved Joe and Sarah and found them to be among the best in our group. Yet, Martin wanted them out.

We trainees gathered immediately and debated our response options. We could accept the decisions of those in authority, continue our training and become good, compliant Volunteers; or we could rebel. The momentum moved firmly toward a revolt. If there was to be a revolution, however, unanimous consent among the trainees was imperative. Any softness, any yielding to authority, would doom the rest of the group to expulsion. It was all or nothing. Some in the group were reluctant to risk their opportunity to become Peace Corps Volunteers, but peer pressure prevailed, and we achieved unity.

An effective revolution needs leadership, and I was elected to take the lead. I guess all of those free speech and anti-war rallies at Oklahoma State gave me some experience and credibility as a revolutionary. Fortunately for all of us, Howard and Shirley Marcus became part of the leadership team. Howard was a lawyer with a cool head, and he and Shirley kept us from doing anything too radical or stupid. I'm not sure that could have been said of me.

We developed a strategy and defiantly declared *"huelga"*—a strike. We would refuse to take training classes under Martin's program unless the Walshes were reinstated and the trainers rehired. Obviously the Peace Corps could have sent all of us home in disgrace, but we knew if we stayed together the disgrace would be on the hands of the Peace Corps, not us. This was, after all, 1967—the age of protest and revolution. Rightly or wrongly, we were absolutely confident we held the higher ground.

The trainers were tremendously appreciative of our courage and effort, and they gave us their full support. Martin had been isolated. The trainers even set up an alternative informal training program for us. They weren't paid, and our training didn't count, but we did it anyway.

Our small leadership team met with Martin whose voice quivered when he spoke. I was never sure if it was out of rage that his authority had been challenged or out of fear that his leadership and reputation were being destroyed. Perhaps it was both. Regardless, he refused to yield, and so did we. Bill Dyal, the Peace Corps country director became personally involved, and he sent subtle signals that he was on our side, even though he could not say so in his official capacity.

The stand-off had lasted about two weeks, when Peace Corps Director Jack Hood Vaughn flew down from Washington to investigate and resolve the matter. He met with Martin, with the trainers, and with our rebellious junta. After hearing everyone out, he reached his verdict. He called us all together, and said, with a mischievous smile, "You guys are pretty impressive. You already have what it takes to be effective as Volunteers, and you don't need any more training." We were two weeks shy of the required three months of training, but he swore us in as Volunteers, including Joe and Sarah, and he sent us on to our sites to begin serving.

I have asked friends in high places at Peace Corps headquarters to look into the records, and as best we can tell, this is the only trainee strike, or strike of any kind, in Peace Corps history. We're proud of it. Sam Farr was elected to the U.S. Congress in 1993 to fill the term of Leon Panetta who had been named Chief of Staff for President Clinton. At the time I was president of the National Peace Corps Association, so Sam and I were able to reconnect in Washington with our special bond. Time and time again, we have been together to speak at Peace Corps functions and we take great pleasure in retelling our story.

≈

I was assigned to the barrio Ceballos on the Caribbean coast, near Cartagena. Ceballos was a shantytown—an "invasion" barrio—a parcel of useless land upon which peasants from the *"campo"* (the country) had migrated and settled in search of a job and paycheck in the city. My new friends and neighbors were "squatters" with no financial assets whatsoever. Very few actually found work, and conditions were bleak. Most of them lived in one-room dirt-floor shanties, many had one change of worn out clothes, and the wealthy ones had shoes.

At the same time, Cartagena itself is a lovely city with a colorful and proud history. The old city is surrounded by a 17th century stone wall, and the grand fortress San Felipe overlooks the city and the bay. The wealthy barrio Boca Grande had large lovely homes, tourist hotels, and a long beach. Cartagena was beautiful then, and it is even more so today. The social and economic chasm between the wealth of the old city and Boca Grande and abject poverty of Ceballos and dozens of other communities, however, was enormous. About ten percent of the population lived in luxury in a tropical paradise. The rest survived in paradise on one or two bowls of rice plus whatever fruit they could find and whatever fish they could catch. Their homes were made of bamboo poles tied together with hemp and plastered with cow dung. The floor was dirt, the roof was palm thatch, and there was no electricity or running water. The more prosperous barrios had cinder block houses with tile or tin roofs, a communal water supply and some even had electricity a few hours each day. Ceballos, however, was at the lowest end of the scale.

At first, I occupied a room in a two-room home and paid monthly rent of fifty pesos—about $3.50. The other room held the family of five, with another child on the way. My rent payments enabled the family to eat more than they would otherwise, but there were times when they skipped meals. Sadly, the man of the house was abusive, frequently beating his wife and children. I objected, but I was not able to persuade him to change. It was his paternal duty, he explained.

Eventually, I moved to the neighboring barrio of Albornos. My excuse for moving was that there was an opportunity to create a fishing cooperative in Albornos because it was right on the water. The real reason I wanted to move was to get away from the violent household where I was powerless to make a difference. I have always been bothered that as a Peace Corps Volunteer—I couldn't bring peace to that one home.

Before leaving, however, I had helped bring the *Junta de Accion Communal*, the local community action council, together to agree to build a school. My hero was the president of the junta, who went by the name Ciriaco. Ciriaco had migrated to Ceballos from the Chocó region of Colombia, the rain forest area near Panama where annual rainfall exceeds 400 inches. Ciriaco was highly respected by the whole community, and he inspired volunteer initiative to improve living conditions for everyone. The population was 100 percent illiterate, and there was no school to enable the next generation to do any better. Now that these former *campesinos* lived on the edge of the city, they knew education was the key to progress, but they had no clue as to how to make it happen. My job was to help them figure out how to do it.

Community action programs in Cartagena's barrios were supported by a small government agency run by the unforgettable Tito Bechara. Tito was small in physical stature, but very large in life. A Piel Roja cigarette made with strong black tobacco and no filter hung from his lips and bounced up and down as he talked. And Tito never stopped talking or smoking. Tito only needed one match to start the day, as each new cigarette was lit by the one he was finishing. His arms waved constantly, and he never sat down. He had too much energy to sit. Tito cared deeply about the people in the impoverished barrios, and he inspired the Peace Corps Volunteers as much as he entertained us with his antics. We adored that man.

With Tito's support, I went to the department of education office in Cartagena and learned the government would provide teachers if the community built a school facility. I reported the news to the junta in Ceballos, and they agreed to do it. I could have written to my family for the money to build the school, but that was not the Peace Corps way. We wanted the community to make it happen themselves with their own resources, and they did.

We found four molds for cinder blocks, and there was plenty of sand all around us. Cement, however, would cost real money, or so I thought. However, a few Ceballos residents had construction jobs, and whenever we needed another bag of cement one would appear. I never asked where it came from or who paid for it. I was just glad it was there. Each day we plastered four blocks in place, and poured the sand and cement mix into the molds to produce four more. The project continued for months after I had moved on to Albornos, and the local volunteers built the school—four blocks at a time.

Ceballos was a mere twenty minute walk from Albornos, and I visited regularly to maintain friendships and to monitor the school progress. I also joined the celebration when the school was completed. I accompanied the Junta leaders to report the news to the department of education, and true to their word, the government provided four teachers, one for each of four rooms in the school. Crude wooden benches served for chairs and desks, and paper and pencils were scarce, but the teachers were wonderful, and the children learned to read and write. I didn't do it. They did. It was theirs. I just provided a modest stimulus and I gave them some respect and confidence that they could improve their own lives.

≈

In Albornos, I enjoyed the luxury of a one room cinder block home all to myself. It even had a concrete floor and a spliced wire for electricity. Rent was double the rate in Ceballos, but with my $100 per month stipend, I could afford it. I hung a hammock between the walls and draped a mosquito net from the ceiling. The windows had no glass, which was preferable as air circulation was essential. Unfortunately, however, privacy was not possible. The town's crazy lady, known affectionately to everyone as *"La Loca"*, took a special liking to me. She was tall and pencil thin, with a gaunt face and penetrating eyes. She stood outside the window, pushed the cheap, unprotected curtain aside, and watched my every move. She left only to sleep at night or when I left, but she was back within five minutes whenever I returned. The neighbors tried to get her to leave me alone, but she would not be denied. I just learned to live with it. She was harmless.

I never fully adjusted to the constant sound of babies crying, pigs squealing and chickens crowing throughout the night. That is a lifelong constant for the people of the barrio. For me, it was a mere two-year inconvenience. Several animal guests moved into my abode during my eighteen months in Albornos, including a friendly boa constrictor who settled in for a few weeks. Then he moved on without even leaving a note. He wasn't large enough to hurt me, and since boas aren't poisonous, I didn't mind. Then a vine snake appeared. That caused more concern as the vine snake is highly venomous. But he was gorgeous and elegant—a rich, brilliant green color on a long pencil thin body and narrow elongated head. I just kept my distance and admired his graceful movements. He wouldn't attack me unless I threatened him, and I wasn't about to do that. Sadly, one day the kids in the neighborhood came to visit; they saw my long green friend, and screaming, "Culebra, culebra!" they killed him. I know they were proud for "saving" my life, but I felt bad for the snake. There were always lizards, including a few iguanas, scurrying about, and crabs came and went as though they owned the place. A bat also took up residence in the ceiling, and he was still there when I left.

With a small electric wire in my home, I went upscale with a lamp and hot plate. Unfortunately, however, they rarely worked. The electricity was stolen from a power line that ran past the barrio. Someone had been brave (or foolish) enough to tap into it, and the single line ran through much of the community. However, it was spliced in dozens of places, and it broke in the slightest wind or disturbance. Someone had to tie the hot wires back together to restore power, and that could take days. To access the power for my place, I used a pocket knife to strip the insulation and expose the bare wire and make a hot connection with the community line. I took a few hard jolts in the process. At best, we had power five to ten hours per week, so I was never convinced it had been worth the risk of serious electrocution.

Water was available through a single spigot from a pipe in the middle of the barrio. Every day, all day, a long line of friends and neighbors waited their turn to fill their containers. It often took an hour or more. I was on my own schedule, but as an impatient Gringo I hated wasting so much time in line. Every day when the sun rose, my young friend Miguel Angel pounded on my door with the same joyous declaration, "Carlos, Carlos… agua, agua." Miguel Angel was about 9 years old, and I paid him a few pesos, a nickel or a dime, to wait in line and fill my ten gallon water tank. When he returned with the full tank, we lifted it to the roof where it would warm in the sun. By late morning, the water was tepid, and I could take a very pleasant solar heated shower using a plastic tube to siphon the water and let it run over my hot sweating body.

Sometimes I had to leave the barrio before the water was warm, so I took cold showers, but that wasn't so bad in the steaming tropical heat.

The water was not suitable for drinking, so I tried to boil it or treat it with chlorine tablets before cooking with it or drinking it. Despite the care, however, I contracted amoebic dysentery just like all of the other Peace Corps Volunteers. I spent a few days every month with wrenching stomach cramps and severe diarrhea. It was just part of the experience.

Organizing a fishing cooperative in a place like Albornos wasn't exactly a nine-to-five job. There were days when nothing could be done. Other times, I worked long hard days and weeks without a break. I went out on the bay in dugout canoes with the fishermen where I was able to build a trust relationship and explain business concepts and describe the value of an incorporated cooperative. Of course, before going to Colombia, I had known nothing about business or cooperatives, but I could read the books and figure it out. I studied regularly and stayed a step ahead of my friends and colleagues in their canoes.

Changing the fishing habits was imperative. The locals had taken to using dynamite stolen from construction sites to improve the daily catch. They would paddle the canoes out into the bay and search for a school of tarpon or snook. A designated fisherman would light a stick with a short homemade fuse and throw it into the middle of the fish. The concussion would shock or kill most if not all of the fish in the area, and everyone would jump in and gather them up.

It was very effective, but it was also dangerous and destructive. The fish population was in steep decline as the small fry as well as larger fish were all killed at once. Furthermore, the makeshift fuses were unreliable and sometimes the dynamite exploded in the hand of the fisherman. Albornos was heavily populated with "mochos"—one armed fishermen. I was terribly troubled every time I saw a mocho paddle his canoe with one arm, find a school of fish, and light another stick of dynamite with the match held in his teeth. It can only be understood and explained in the context of abject poverty. When the choice is between risk and hunger, one takes risks.

My objective was to provide a viable alternative to dynamite fishing. With a formally incorporated cooperative, the fishermen would be eligible for loans from the *Caja Agraria*, the agricultural bank. With some working capital, they could purchase motors for their boats to get to more fertile waters quickly, and they could purchase nets to fish effectively and safely and without killing everything in range. We created the coop; got the loan; purchased a few small and inexpensive but reliable British Seagull motors and some nets. We even expanded the reach of the enterprise to other fishing villages in the area, including Baru.

The tiny village of Baru is located at the point of a long narrow peninsula with the same name. I had been told it was accessible by land after crossing the Canal del Dique, but I had no vehicle, and the best way to reach the village was by boat. The Peace Corps procured a small second, third, or fourth hand fiberglass boat and a very used Johnson 33 horsepower motor for me, and I used it to reach Baru and other fishing villages along the coast.

Baru and the nearby Islas del Rosario are the picture of a tropical paradise with pure white beaches, magnificent coral reefs, coconut palms, abundant fruit trees, tropical sun and a steady sea breeze. The residents were entirely Afro-Colombian descendents of slaves who had built a comfortable and tranquil life for themselves. They ate fresh, ripe mango, papaya, and other luscious tropical fruits picked from trees just outside their homes. They had enough fish to provide protein, and they grew rice and yucca to fill out their diet. I fell in love with Baru, its people and their way of life. I was tempted to settle down for life.

My only concern in Baru was the dynamite. Just as in Albornos, the fishermen had succumbed to the temptation of quick catches from the explosion, and they were ruining their own piece of heaven and losing hands and arms in the process. Sadly, some of the magnificent coral had already been shattered by the explosions, and it could all be ruined in a few decades. I hoped to be able to change it through the coop.

The village leader was affectionately known as *El Viejo*, the old man. I wish I could remember his real name, but that's what everyone called him, and I did as well. It was a term of endearment and respect. *El Viejo* became my friend and mentor, and I've never known a finer gentleman. He was in his 70s, and he had built a very attractive and comfortable thatched roof home with a spectacular view of the sea and the Rosario Islands. He had a delightful, friendly, and gracious wife and many, many children, grandchildren, and great grandchildren. They spent a few hours each day catching fish and tending to their gardens. The rest of the time they enjoyed friendly and lighthearted social interactions playing dominos and sharing gossip.

The people in Baru were as wealthy as any community I have ever known. They had no cash, but instead they had abundant fresh food, comfortable homes, fantastic views, family and friends, and no stress. This was paradise. They had no electricity, and they didn't need it. They had a central well for fresh, clean water, and they had plenty of time to fetch it. Gathering water was a pleasant social event. A few villagers had battery-powered radios, and they could receive faint signals from Cartagena, so they heard the news, but their primary interest was the daily novellas—radio soap operas—not the hard news of political strife, war, and famine in far off places.

I was in this remote Colombian fishing village with no electricity or running water on July 20, 1969, when Apollo 11 landed on the moon, and my countrymen began to walk on and explore the earth's only natural satellite 238,857 miles away. Everyone in the village gathered around the few radios in town to listen to the live broadcasts with great interest. However, virtually everyone in Baru believed this was actually the climax to a dramatic *novella*—a sci-fi soap opera like Buck Rogers. It could not possibly be true, but it was a great story with superb actors. I tried to explain it was real, only to be ridiculed with knee-slapping laughter. How could anyone be so naïve? *El Viejo*, however, knew it was real.

With the greatest respect, he looked at me moments after Armstrong took his small step for a man and one giant leap for mankind, and said, *"Felicitaciones. Tu pais ha hecho algo magnifico."* Congratulations, your country has achieved something magnificent.

In order to encourage a switch from dynamite to net fishing, I wanted to show my friends in Baru a Spanish-language film about a successful coop that had been created among fishermen in Puerto Rico. It might help them understand the concept and its value. I borrowed the film, a projector, and a generator from the U.S. Information Center in Cartagena. Unfortunately, the load was more than my small boat could safely handle, so I also borrowed a van and set out to drive.

A Colombian colleague from a local development agency joined me, and we departed for paradise together. We crossed the canal on a wood raft that barely floated with the weight of our vehicle. On the peninsula side, a dirt path with faint tire tracks marked the way. The further we went, the less visible the path, but on the narrowing peninsula there was only one way to the point so we continued. However, about half way to the end, we encountered steep rocky hills on one side and the soft white sandy beach and crystal clear sea on the other. The beach was the only way forward, so we proceeded until we became hopelessly embedded in the sand with wheels spinning.

So we were trapped on a beautiful beach at least 15 kilometers from the village with a heavy load to transport. Dejected, we left the van and its contents to walk the rest of the way to let the villagers know we had tried but failed to make it, and to seek help to extricate the van from its sand trap. The sun was directly overhead, there was not a cloud in the sky, and the cooling afternoon sea breeze would not start for hours. Most of the trip was in the soft sand making walking slow and laborious. We became seriously dehydrated, but as we came close to the village of Baru, we found a large healthy mango tree filled with rich, ripe fruit hanging just above eye level. We picked them gleefully, bit off the end of the firm skin and sucked out the delicious juice, one after another. We savored the moment and smiled and laughed with the succulent relief.

When we arrived in the village and told our story, the entire group of fishermen mobilized to save the day. They walked to the truck, and they carried all of the equipment, including a heavy generator, by hand, back to the village. I don't think it was because they were so anxious to learn about coops. They, and their families, wanted to see a movie—any movie.

As the sun went down, we set up the projector, cranked up the generator, and presented the film. The entire village came for the show. Most left after the movie but the fishermen stayed and we engaged in a healthy discussion about the glories of cooperative enterprises. While this was happening, however, my tongue and throat begin to swell and my face began to itch with hives. By the time we finished, my eyes were swelling shut, and I could barely breathe. I was on the edge of panic. It grew worse by the minute, and I anticipated a painful death by asphyxiation, and there was nothing anyone in this remote village could do. Fortunately the swelling in my mouth and throat stopped expanding with a tiny passage still open to gasp for air. I didn't sleep all night, and it was barely better in the morning, but I had to return to Cartagena for medical attention as quickly as possible. El Viejo and the other fishermen carted the equipment back to the van, and they helped me make it on foot as well. They also put their shoulders to the task and freed the van from the sand. My colleague drove us back as fast as possible along the bumpy path to the raft-ferry and across the canal and from there on to the city.

We went straight to the Peace Corps office where we called the doctor in Bogota. He asked me to describe what had happened, and as soon as I got to the mango tree, he knew the cause. Some people are deathly allergic to mango, and obviously I was one of them. I had enjoyed mango often, but always in modest proportions. Furthermore the toxins are in the skin, not the fruit. By biting off the ends, I had ingested a very high quantity of poison, and my dehydrated body absorbed it thoroughly, making matters even worse. The doctor prescribed a strong antihistamine and admonished me to avoid mango for as long as I live. I love the taste of mango, but every time I see it in the store, on a menu, or in a salad, I remember Baru and I stay far away.

After that experience, the good people in Baru realized vehicle traffic between their village and Cartagena might bring more economic opportunities and modern conveniences, so they went to work on the path. All on their own and entirely by hand, they brought rocks and stones up from the sea bottom and down from the hillside to cover the soft sand where I had been trapped. They broke large stones into pebbles, and they made the roadway passable. Indeed, more people from Cartagena discovered Baru, and economic growth arrived. I was told on a visit back to the village a decade later that it all began with my excruciating trip.

Sadly, it may be the worst thing that ever happened to Baru. This remote, heavenly haven has since been discovered by hotel chains that have driven the native population out to make room for their buildings and tourists. The entire tranquil way of life has been destroyed. There are paying jobs for some, but most villagers have been left out of the prosperity. Furthermore, these people never needed a paycheck. They had lived happily and comfortably off the land and sea for centuries.

Google recently led me to this sad story from Reuters dated February 21, 2007.

ISLA BARU, Colombia (Reuters)—To visitors, it is a paradise of white beaches and brilliant blue waters, but Colombia's Isla Baru has been scarred by a long fight for control between Afro-Colombian residents and hotel developers.

Armed security guards, paid by the government and private business groups, this month fired around the feet of locals trying to plant fields on contested property worth millions of dollars near the booming Caribbean coast tourist city of Cartagena.

No one was wounded but residents are scared. "Now we know they have orders to shoot at us, we're afraid for our lives," said Carlos Rincon, a farmer. "This is getting worse."

What local media have dubbed "The Battle for Baru" started in the 1970s when the government says it bought 300 hectares from business groups that say they still hold 200 hectares.

Together they have drawn up plans for a luxury resort and want to start building.

But the Afro-Colombian descendants of slaves who say they hold land titles dating back to the 1590s insist the purchase documents were falsified and that they never sold to anyone.

This news is particularly personal and troubling since I played a small role in the story. It almost certainly would have happened with or without out my ill-fated trip, but it did happen, and I feel badly about it.

≈

Cartagena was and it remains well known throughout South America as a delightful resort, and most Peace Corps Volunteers serving in other regions made at least one pilgrimage to our coastal heaven during their two year service. As a result, I had frequent house guests. Albornos was anything but a resort, but the beautiful beaches were accessible by a long bus ride, and the room was free—about all any Peace Corps Volunteer could afford.

Walter Davis, one of the fellow strikers from our training group, came for a visit with his girlfriend from Kentucky. I needed to visit some sites several miles up the Canal del Dique to provide a report for Tito Bechara on their recovery from flooding, so I took Walter and his friend along. The Johnson motor for my little boat worked most of the time, but it was never reliable, so I always took a few basic tools in case of an emergency, even though I had no clue how to fix an engine.

New houses had been built in the flooded village, and we wanted to know how the villagers were doing in their new, improved homes. We expected effusive gratitude for the U.S. foreign aid gift of solid houses made of cinder blocks with concrete floors and tile roofs. They looked terrific to this North American. But the villagers had already built their own structures made of bamboo, dried cow dung, and palm thatch roofs—their traditional building materials—nestled between the hard block houses, and no one was living in the lovely new modern structures. Chickens, pigs and goats occupied the block houses. I asked why, and the answer was simple. The concrete homes had poor circulation, and they were five to ten degrees hotter in the tropical climate than the traditional structures. I discovered the concept of appropriate technology that day.

Shortly after we boarded the boat to return home, the erratic motor stopped. I yanked on the rope over and over, and Walter took his turns as well, but nothing happened. We drifted down the canal towards the bay and the Caribbean as we tried everything we could think of to get the Johnson to start. I sprayed an entire can of ether starter fluid into the carburetor to no avail. Helplessly and under a burning sun, we drifted out of the canal, into the bay, and with an outbound breeze, we found ourselves slowly sailing out toward the open sea and out of control.

Walter's friend was very fair skinned, and she was wearing a sun dress with her shoulders and arms exposed. She was cooking in the sun, and she was in agony. I didn't let on I was scared, but I was. I had always been able to start the motor before, but I was running out of options this time.

I had no training as a mechanic, and family and friends can attest that I am useless under the hood of a car. But we were desperate. I removed the motor cover, examined every inch of the mechanism, and made a wild guess that the carburetor was seriously fouled. As I removed it, and disassembled it to clean the parts, I very carefully memorized the sequence and what parts connect to what other parts for reassembly. I cleaned everything very carefully and reassembled it as the coast slipped further and further away.

The first few pulls on the rope gave no sign of hope, but as fuel worked its way through the tube and into the engine, there was a small sputter. Then with more pulls, there were more pops and finally ignition. I carefully adjusted the choke to make sure it wouldn't stall, and we steered straight back to Cartagena. As the dock in Boca Grande came into view, the motor stopped again. This time, however, we were out of gas, having used much more than anticipated due to the trip out to sea. A coastal police boat had just passed us, and I had become friends with the officer on board due to my work with fishermen. He had arrested some of my friends for using dynamite, and I had pleaded their case promising they would change their behavior. Just as our boat settled into a powerless drift, he looked back to wave again. His smile changed to a look of concern, and he turned back; threw us a rope, and towed us to safety.

Walter and I met up recently for the first time since we bid farewell in Bogota at the end of our service. He was a conscientious objector to the war in Vietnam, and he went to Canada to avoid the draft. After President Carter issued a pardon to draft resisters, he returned and built a career as a community organizer and activist based in Tennessee. Now, he is Executive Director of the National Organizers Alliance, and I have joined up. He's another of the really good people in my life for whom I have undying appreciation and admiration.

≈

I spent most of my time as a Volunteer in Albornos, Ceballos, Tierra Bomba, Baru and other fishing villages, but I also met with some of the corporate leaders while seeking their advice and support for some of our projects. The large Standard Oil refinery was managed by Martin

King, a smart and sophisticated Harvard MBA graduate. We became friends, and he invited me to his home for occasional dinners and a real shower. His driver would pick me up in Albornos and take me to his large, elegant home on Boca Grande. King co-owned a sixty-five-foot schooner with the famous Colombian artist Fernando Botero, and I got to share in this floating luxury several times. Martin shared my concern about poverty, and he believed in making an investment to make a difference. Like me, he opposed the war in Vietnam, and even though he was a Republican, he was skeptical of President Nixon, so we found substantial common ground. He had known and even played his guitar and sang with Pete Seeger as an undergrad student at Harvard. That alone made him fine with me.

King introduced me to his deputy manager, a Canadian petroleum engineer whose son Randy was about my age, and Randy was dating a stunning Colombiana named Cecilia. Cecilia's best friend was Marta Inez Hernandez, and Cecilia and Randy set us up on a blind date. Marta turned out to be even more beautiful than Cecilia. She was also lively and engaging, and I fell for her on the spot.

Colombian women are well known for their looks and for their affinity for beauty pageants. There are national queens for every industry, and Marta had been Colombia's national queen of cotton. The number one song on the radio and Colombian hit charts at the time was *"Se llama Marta Inez, la Reina del Algodon"* ("Her name is Marta Inez, the Queen of Cotton"). The song described a vision of loveliness, and that exquisite fantasy was my new girlfriend Marta.

Getting to her home in Boca Grande from Albornos required a two-kilometer walk, long wait for a bus, a forty-five-minute bumpy ride, a transfer to another bus, and finally, two hours after setting out, I was there. Unlike Marta's wealthy suitors, I had no money for movies and dinner, but she seemed to like me anyway, and we dated whenever I could make it. Instead of spending money on meals and movies, we spent most of our time walking the romantic narrow streets of Cartagena and on the beach at Boca Grande. The courtship was further complicated because I had no means of telecommunication. There were no phones in or near Albornos. We had to make arrangements for the next date at the end of each one, and if something came up to prevent it, there was no easy way to re-schedule. Somehow, however, we surmounted the obstacles, and eventually we were married in the Naval Club in Cartagena on May 3, 1969, four months before the end of my Peace Corps service. We lived at her parent's home during that period as she wasn't about to live in a place like Albornos.

By that time I had been elected by my peers as the Regional Peace Corps Volunteer Leader, and my tasks had changed from field work to administrative duties and coordination of and support for all of the Volunteers in the region. Therefore, I worked out of an office in downtown Cartagena, and the new living arrangement made sense. I maintained contact with the fishing villages, but they were ready to manage their coop on their own.

I had developed a friendship with Senator Fred Harris of Oklahoma during my student activist years, and we corresponded several times while I was in Colombia. He asked me to write an account of my experiences and I produced a fifty-page document for him. As a Member of Congress, he wanted a personal connection with the Peace Corps, and I was it. He sent a very kind letter of appreciation after reading the report, but I was a bit skeptical. The letter could have been written by his chief of staff Leslie Kreps who had been one of my professors at Oklahoma State. However, I met with the Senator after returning to the States, and he referred to several specific items in my document. He actually read it, and remembered it in some detail.

≈

The experience in Colombia from the summer of 1967 to the fall of 1969 was transforming, but it took me out of the United States during a tremendously dramatic period for politics and social change. Race riots burned inner city neighborhoods and challenged all pretense of domestic tranquility. Demonstrations against the Vietnam War escalated in size and intensity. Martin Luther King, Jr. was assassinated, and then Robert Kennedy met the same fate. The 1968 Democratic Party convention in Chicago became a battleground in Grant Park and within the McCormick Center. The party didn't recover in the eyes of the voting public until President Nixon made Republicans look even worse.

I followed all of these events closely on Voice of America radio, and we received complimentary copies of *Newsweek* magazine whenever we could get to the Peace Corps office, but we were far removed from the political action. On the other hand, I had a special opportunity to observe it all from afar and to see our troubles through the eyes of others. When King and Kennedy were killed, I was surrounded by Colombian friends who mourned as deeply as I. At the same time, they were bewildered by the political chaos and the race riots. I felt the angst, and I corresponded as frequently as possible with my brother and other activist friends to stay connected, but it wasn't the same as being there. I even missed Woodstock, but I was where I belonged.

≈

I am convinced the primary difference between prosperous countries and those mired in poverty is cultural and attitudinal. We in the U.S. progress, at least economically, because we wake up believing we can make this day better than yesterday and tomorrow better than today. In most underdeveloped societies, the vast majority believe their lot in life has been ordained. They accept underclass status as the fulfillment of God's will, *"Si Dios quiere."* Too many believe there is nothing they can do or even should do to change it.

Successful Peace Corps Volunteers change attitudes, and we instill pride and confidence among people who have been told they are lesser and unworthy creatures. I saw it in the people I lived and worked with. The more we worked together, the more confident they became. The more confident they became, the more they were able to do for themselves. By the time I left, they looked me in the eye with pride, and they believed in themselves and their future.

At the same time, my friends and neighbors on the coast of Colombia taught me far more than I could possibly have offered them. Even though many missed a few meals now and then, their lives were meaningful and enjoyable. If they could smile with nothing but the warmth of the sun, why couldn't I be happy with so much? Some people with trust funds and isolated in gated communities are obsessed with wealth and stressed with fear of losing it. I went into the Peace Corps to teach poor people how to become prosperous. My new friends and neighbors taught me a new definition of prosperity.

I came away with a whole new set of values, and a global perspective. John Stuart Mill said, "Human nature is rich and complex. The good life can be lived in several different ways, and each profits from dialogue with the rest." I've lived a rich life, because of a never-ending dialogue with the rest of humanity, and none have meant more than my friends and neighbors in the barrios of Cartagena.

They also shared one of my favorite formulas for living in peace. The coast is known for its relative calm compared with other regions of Colombia that tend to be more violent. When I asked them why they were so peaceful, they shared this wonderful philosophy: *"Cuando queren hablar, hablamos. Cuando queren cantar, cantamos. Cuando queren bailar, bailamos. Cuando queren luchar, corremos!"* Translated it means, if they want to talk, we'll talk. If they want to sing, we'll sing. If they want to dance, we'll dance. If they want to fight, we run!

The last few months in Colombia were filled with dramatically mixed emotions. I felt the glow of my marriage, but I missed the daily contact with my campesino friends. Far worse, however, my father had been diagnosed with liver cancer, and the prognosis was grim. I hated being so far away and unable to help him or my mother. The Peace Corps was kind enough to arrange a special trip home to see them, as there was concern that Dad may not last until the end of my service in late August. The visit home was awkward and depressing. I had no idea what to say to my dying father, and my departure to return to Colombia, knowing he was near the end was excruciating. The Peace Corps was prepared to grant me an early termination, but there is special pride among Volunteers who serve all the way to the end, and I was determined to make it.

Dad was weak but still living and working when I completed my service and we returned to Ohio, so Marta and I spent some quality time with the whole family together. It was very hard on a new bride to start a new life in a new country under such stress, but she handled it quite well.

≈

I had communicated regularly by very slow mail service with Dale Stockton throughout the Peace Corps years. He had insisted I return to Oklahoma State to pursue a graduate degree and help him develop a communications consulting company as his partner. It was an extraordinary opportunity, given Dale's unique intellectual and leadership qualities. We shared political ambitions as well, and our plan was to establish the company, generate the resources and connections we would need, and then Dale would run for Congress. I would be his chief of staff or his legislative assistant, whichever I preferred.

The speech department offered me a generous teaching assistant position, and we moved to Stillwater. Dad was disappointed as he wanted me to stay home with my mother during this difficult period, but he understood my need to build my own life, and we left with his blessing. Just a few weeks later we were back in Worthington for his funeral.

Marta and I settled into a small duplex on Duncan Street a few blocks from campus, while Dale and I slipped right back into our symbiotic partnership studying, teaching classes, and developing our new company, Creative Communications Consultants. I supplemented the teaching stipend with a modest salary from the Peace Corps as the campus recruiter, but that made for an overextended schedule. I was also invited to speak to campus organizations, local civic clubs, and even a few school assemblies around the state to describe the Peace Corps experience. Sometimes they paid as much as $25 plus mileage. Everything was on track, and my entire future was clear and positive in every way.

I also reconnected with the activist community. The FATAGS had become well organized, and they welcomed me home. The free speech movement had won major victories, and the antiwar movement had taken hold, even at OSU. New leaders had emerged by then, so my role was less public, and I had limited time to devote to the cause. Nevertheless, I did all I could with pleasure and enthusiasm.

The National Moratorium against the War in Vietnam drew 500,000 protesters to Washington on October 15, 1969. Many analysts point to that day as the tipping point—the day the tide of public opinion turned irrevocably against perpetuating the insanity of the war. Our FATAG group produced a day-long class boycott and rally for the students who would not be able to travel to Washington for the big national event.

Oklahoma's junior U.S. Senator Fred Harris, for whom I had written the report on the Peace Corps, finally agreed to oppose the war, and he was the keynote speaker at our large and vocal rally. I had commented on the mistaken policy on Vietnam in several letters to Harris when I was in Colombia, and I would like to think I helped change his mind.

Harris committed political suicide in Oklahoma politics that day, but he knew he had done the right thing. Coming from such a conservative state made his position all the more persuasive nationwide. Knowing he had no hope of re-election to the Senate in Oklahoma, Harris launched a campaign for the Democratic Presidential nomination in 1972. Our former Peace Corps Director Jack Vaughn was his campaign manager, and I conferred with both of them several times as they planned the campaign. I was about to quit a secure job and join the campaign staff when it ran out of funds and Harris withdrew from the race. I learned then and there to be wary of a professional political career.

≈

While in the Peace Corps, I enjoyed a deferment from the military draft, but the day my service ended, I was once again eligible to be compelled to fight. I was adamantly opposed to the war, and I was prepared to do whatever was necessary to avoid the risk of killing and being killed for a terrible mistake. I hoped my old football injury would provide a medical exemption, and my Peace Corps physician in Colombia had written a compelling letter on my behalf. Nevertheless, convincing a draft board in Oklahoma that a former OSU football player was not physically fit for military service seemed unlikely. I seriously considered moving to Canada or enlisting in the National Guard as viable alternatives. Conscientious objector status was not an option as I would fail the religious test. Furthermore, I couldn't honestly claim to oppose participation in any and all wars. I would fight in real national self defense, but Vietnam did not qualify. The Guard had the most appeal since members of the Guard seemed immune to actually fighting in Vietnam. But it was a refuge for people with connections and influence. I had a few connections, but I would never ask them to pull strings to get me into the Guard. I loved Canada, but Marta thought it too cold. She also opposed the war, and she didn't want me in the military, so the frigid North seemed to be the only plausible option. I did extensive research on living and working in Toronto.

Indeed, the orders to report for a physical exam arrived, and I boarded the dreaded bus to a military facility in Oklahoma City. The anti-war movie and song *Alice's Restaurant* had just come out, and virtually everyone on the bus sang the words with gusto—to the consternation of the driver, I am sure. My seat-mate on the bus was morose all the way to Oklahoma City. He was sure he owned a one-way ticket to Vietnam. Over and over, he complained that there was absolutely nothing wrong with him. I showed him the letter from my Peace Corps physician, and he was happy for me, but it didn't make him feel any better about his own good health.

The experience was right out of the *Alice's Restaurant* movie. A hundred young men lined up like cattle for a cursory examination of our body parts. The simple word "next" echoed throughout the barren hall as each probable draftee dressed only in briefs or boxers passed from station to station. When the appropriate time came, I presented my letter. The officer in charge read it over, looked at me with moderate disgust and pronounced, "Okay, you'll be 1-Y." 1-Y wasn't quite as good as 4-F, but it would do. 4-F meant you would never be called to serve. I-Y status meant you would only be called if the military ran out of others eligible for service. I hid my joy from view, but the sense of relief was beyond words.

Meanwhile, my bus companion passed from station-to-station without a hitch. He approached the last station, the famous hernia check, in hopeless despair. A medic stuck a finger into his crotch to feel for any intestinal protrusion. The medic stood up and shouted out, "Got a hernia here!"

"I do?!?, I do?!?" my friend cried out in glee. "I've got a hernia, I've got a hernia!!!" He couldn't control himself as he danced in front of a hundred not-so-lucky colleagues. All the way back to Stillwater, the grin creased his glowing face, and he just kept announcing to everyone in earshot, "I have a hernia, I have a hernia!" We shared his joy at the wonderful discovery that he had a medical condition most people would wish to avoid. Nearly everyone on the bus came to our seat to congratulate both of us, and to express personal regret that they were not so fortunate. We could only convey our condolences and best wishes in return. Those were strange times.

TRAGEDY AND A NEW PATH

By the spring of 1970, Dale Stockton, Fred Tewell and I had formed Creative Communications Consultants, Inc., and we secured a contract with Americans for Indian Opportunity (AIO) and the Bureau of Indian Affairs to conduct some workshops on a reservation in Arizona. LaDonna Harris, wife of Senator Fred Harris, was the founder and president of AIO, and we had worked with her on several projects. Dale was to give a speech and cover a debate tournament with his team in Dallas on the weekend while I flew directly to Phoenix to meet with our hosts and make preparations. After meeting with the local organizers, I returned to the airport to pick up Dale. I arrived early and ran into former Vice President Hubert Humphrey, of all people. He was by himself and waiting for a flight, and I introduced myself and reminded him of the day we spent together in Stillwater a few years before.

I chatted with Humphrey for about 30 minutes about the Peace Corps, politics, and the plight of Native Americans before he had to catch his plane. He was the author of the original Peace Corps legislation in the Senate, so he took particular pride in hearing my stories. I chose to avoid discussion of Vietnam where we would have clashed.

Just as he left, I was paged over the public address system to an information desk, and my life took another dramatic turn. Dale Stockton, my friend, my mentor, and my business and political partner would not be arriving in Phoenix. He had been murdered in his hotel room in Dallas.

My shock and disbelief quickly turned to deep grief. It was a profound personal tragedy. I had grown closer to Dale than my own family, and I felt the loss as deeply as if it had been my brother. It was far worse, of course, for his wife Judy and his extended family. The loss was also devastating for the speech department at OSU. The entire department had flourished around his charisma, intellect, and leadership. We were gaining a national reputation, but it was all based on Dale.

I informed our colleagues at AIO, and the whole project in Arizona was cancelled. I returned to Stillwater that night and met immediately with the faculty and staff on campus. We helped Judy plan the funeral, and I served as a pallbearer. The large Methodist Church was filled and overflowing with mourners. The day was cold and overcast with snow on the ground, and it was hard to keep our balance on the ice at the cemetery. Nothing could have been colder than my spirits that day.

We did all we could to help the police conduct an investigation, but the crime was never conclusively solved. Dr. Tewell, the department head, asked me to teach Dale's classes, and I did the best I could, but I was a complete failure. I was not up to the task emotionally, and I was no Dale Stockton. My first lecture was a tribute to Dale, and I simply stumbled through the rest of them until the merciful end of the semester. Ever since, in my own feeble way, I have tried to help fulfill the life Dale might have lived.

The following fall, registration for the speech classes fell dramatically. Over the years, the Speech Department lost support, and it no longer exists as a distinct department. OSU offers a few basic speech courses, but it is a ghost of the shining light Dale had created.

Without Dale, OSU lost its meaning for me. I tried my best to continue my studies for a Masters degree in speech-communications, but the motivation was long gone. Furthermore, Marta had become pregnant while we were in Stillwater, and I had to think seriously about generating enough income to support my new family. OSU had been good to me, and I loved it, but it was time to move on.

≈

Thirty-five years later, I was invited back to OSU to receive the College of Arts and Sciences Distinguished Alumnus of the Year award. In an address to the graduating honors seniors and their faculty and parents, I described the causes we fought for when we were students—civil rights, free speech, opposition to the war, and for the environment. The established university leadership opposed us on all of those issues, but history proved us right on every one. I encouraged a new generation of young people to assert themselves and challenge the order my generation had established. I also encouraged them to explore the world beyond the local, parochial, and the comfortable and embrace friendship as life's greatest treasure… "make friends—make lots of them, nurture them, and cherish every one of them. And, serve your community and your world. Become part of the powerful force of civilization. Lives filled with friendship and service become lives of purpose and joy."

I had feared an ultra-conservative audience at OSU might reject my message, but I received a standing ovation. Jim Huey, who had been recruited to OSU by Stockton, was still teaching speech, and he invited me to address his class. When I finished, Jim came to me and said simply, "Dale lives." It was one of the most moving and gratifying moments of my life. The world lost a great man when Dale Stockton was killed. I am grateful for any opportunity I may have to keep his spirit and values alive.

≈

Instead of returning in the fall to finish my degree and continue teaching Dale's classes, I landed a job in El Dorado, Kansas as executive director of the Mid-Kansas Community Action Program, known as Mid-CAP. The previous executive had been relieved of his duties after causing too much political turmoil. *Time* magazine published a story about the generational, cultural and political divide in America. Their case study to illustrate the clash was Mid-CAP and their executive director, Dave Fretz—the same Dave Fretz who, along with his wife Lori, had been among my Peace Corps trainers. He represented cultural and social change, and the town leadership wanted none of it. Dave had been fired for doing the right thing a few years earlier in Bogota. Now, he had been fired again for taking a stand. I had led a strike in his behalf back then, and I would try to restore his agency and help rebuild his organization, if not his reputation, in Kansas.

I believed firmly in the issues and values embodied in Mid-CAP and advanced by Dave, but my style was much more collegial than combative, and that seemed to be needed at the time. Wounds had to be healed between the organization, the elected officials and town elders. There were also serious problems between the agency and the Department of Labor over procedures and accounting for the Neighborhood Youth Corps program. When I sat at my desk on my first day, the finance manager informed me that we had two months to correct dozens of violations and flaws in the program or it would be closed. We might even be forced to return funds that had already been spent. It would have killed the agency.

We had a small but dedicated staff with several wonderful VISTA volunteers to take our work directly to the people. Together, we went to work on all of the internal challenges and the public relations disaster, while doing our best to fulfill our mission and serve our constituents— the low income people of Butler, Harvey, and Greenwood counties.

At the time, we operated a small Head Start program, the Neighborhood Youth Corps Program and a few other federally and locally supported initiatives. The vast majority of our funds came from the federal Office of Economic Opportunity—the War on Poverty equivalent to the Pentagon. Tense relations with local officials made it extremely difficult to persuade the county governments to provide the required matching funds. Fortunately, the federal officials allowed us to count in-kind donations and volunteer support as part of the matching funds. Without it, we would not have qualified for the federal grants.

Somehow, we met all of the requirements from the Department

of Labor within the allotted time, and the local governments gave us a chance to prove we could meet our objectives without offending the people and institutions the public had elected as their representatives and leaders. We survived.

I wanted to see social and economic changes, and I was determined to do all I could to help people climb out of poverty. I also believed in self-reliance, so I wanted to be sure everyone had opportunities to achieve their potential, but I was not willing to promote ever more hand-outs and welfare. Conservatives have a right to complain about the creation of a culture of dependence. It is real, and it is insidious. My concept of community action was grounded in the community and in action—hard work by everyone to be more productive to make life better, while meeting the needs of those with genuine needs.

I was particularly proud of our efforts to help people create their own opportunities. For example, we worked extensively with an older African-American gentleman to get a loan to acquire a truck and begin his own trash collection business. We taught him how to keep his books, market his services, manage his employees, and repay his loan. He was remarkably successful, and he became a role model.

Our board chair Barbara Gaines gave me full support and wise advice. As a community leader and wife of Kansas legislator Frank Gaines, Barbara had the respect of the establishment, and she had the courage to stand for the rights and needs of the low income and disadvantaged population. I admired her and appreciated her immensely. Together, we rebuilt the agency, and since I left it has grown to serve eleven counties, and it is still helping low income people find opportunities for dignity and prosperity today.

Our son Alex was born November 14, 1970, in El Dorado. In those days, fathers were not allowed in the delivery room, at least not in El Dorado, Kansas. Ohio State played Michigan that day so I had an appealing diversion. I also went to the Mid-CAP office for a while when it was clear the delivery would not come soon. While there, a young lady who did some volunteer work for us came in. She worked at the police station, and she shared some confidential information—there was an FBI file on me at the police station. It included pictures from our "Frodo" picnics at OSU as well as shots taken at anti-war and free speech demonstrations. I was outraged. The day was among the most important in my life because my first child was about to enter the world, but I was furious about the world he was entering. I pushed it out of my mind as best I could, as Marta and I celebrated the arrival of Alex.

≈

Starting as a CEO right out of school was not a smart career building strategy. I needed experience as a subordinate in a larger organization to learn how the mature, seasoned experts do it. Cleveland, Ohio was near the bottom of my preferred places to live, but it had a great symphony, a fabulous art museum, and a job opportunity. It was also closer to my family. The Metropolitan Health Planning Corporation needed a junior planner, and they gave me an opportunity. I wasn't well suited for the job, as it called for technical skills I lacked, but I did an adequate job. I learned a tremendous amount from my highly skilled supervisors, Harry Fisher and Lee Podolin. Harry was a fastidious analyst with a social work background. Everything was to be done by the rules, and I learned to be careful to draw between the lines, at least when I had to. Lee set high standards, far beyond anything I had encountered before. He introduced me to the concept of intellectual "rigor". Every word in every document had to be carefully selected, every sentence had to be properly constructed, and every paragraph had to be important, appropriate, and accurate.

Lee marked my draft documents with a red pencil, and it infuriated me. I thought I was a good writer, but he never failed to mark nearly every line in red with some comment demanding better. Draft after draft went from my desk to Harry's and after improvements to Lee's. They always came back with more red pencil than black type. Four to five iterations were normal before they could leave the office. This was before the age of word processing, so my secretary had to re-type every page with each new draft.

After this process had irritated me for several months, I was determined to provide a first draft beyond the possibility of correction or improvement. Harry was in on the plan, and he thought my carefully crafted draft was perfect. But it came back from Lee marked in red. I made the recommended changes, and it came back with plenty of red yet again. After the fourth round, I re-submitted the original. It came back with a note, "This is what I've been looking for." I went back to Lee's office and placed the marked up original on his desk and the approved final next to it. He read for a few moments, looked up and said with a sheepish grin, "Got me, didn't you." Fortunately, he took it well. I told him how much I appreciated what I had learned from him about quality. All I asked in return was respect for my improved work. We worked well together from then on.

While in Cleveland, Marta, Alex and I visited parks whenever possible to escape the crowded and polluted city. Punderson Lake was a favorite, and we took our family's Old Town wood and canvas canoe to enjoy the lake and wooded scenery. The park was near my grandparents' farm, and my dad had been instrumental in the development of the state park, so it was a special place for us. I had been there with my dad during the restoration of the old mansion as a young child. One Sunday afternoon, we were out on the water when a beautiful, long, narrow wooden boat shot past us.

The muscled athlete propelling the sleek craft was the picture of elegance, grace and power. I couldn't believe how beautiful a boat, water and man in perfect harmony could be. On shore, we saw the man and his boat again, and I asked him what it was. "A racing kayak," he said with a modest foreign accent. "Do you want to give it a try?" Of course I did, but I was not prepared for the experience. With his help, I slipped into the small seat and took the double-bladed paddle in hand. Before I moved an inch from the dock, I had flipped and was swimming. Our new friend, Leslie Nagy, broke out in laughter. He knew what would happen to any beginner.

He explained the boats were exceptionally long and narrow for maximum speed, and they were much harder to learn and balance than a bicycle. (Recreational kayaks are quite stable. Only the racing boats are narrow and tippy.) It could take weeks, even months of trying just to paddle a few hundred yards without swimming. He asked if I wanted to learn; I said yes, and he offered to teach me. Day after day, I failed to get away from the dock, but I was determined, and after months of regular practice, I finally mastered the balance part of the sport. Having done all of that, I felt compelled to go the next step, to become a competitor. Leslie and his friends—virtually all Hungarians who had migrated to Cleveland in the 1950s to escape communism—became our friends, and we traveled to local races together. They won medals, and I learned more with each experience.

The health planning job was not a good fit, and Cleveland was a miserable place to live, in spite of the symphony and our kayaking friends. The city launched a public relations campaign - "The Greatest Location in the Nation" - to improve its image, but everyone knew Cleveland to be "The Mistake on the Lake". It was badly polluted, miserably cold and windy in winter, and crime was rampant. The economy was in decline with little hope for improvement. Aside from Punderson Lake and kayaking, my only fond memory of Cleveland is a fabulous performance of *Jaques Brel Is Alive and Well and Living in Paris*, staged with a local cast in the lobby of a downtown theater that was undergoing renovation. Eventually Playhouse Square emerged from that nascent cultural venue, and it helped stimulate a rebirth of the city. Cleveland has recovered, and it is a reasonably pleasant place today, but I was long gone before its renaissance.

We wanted to move to a warmer climate, and North Carolina was the logical place to go. I was still in touch with Dr. Scales at Wake Forest University, and I still aspired to enroll in the graduate school where he would be my mentor once again. I found a job with the Piedmont Triad Health Planning Council in Greensboro, and we left Cleveland in March, 1974. Blizzard conditions made loading the rental truck difficult, but it confirmed the wisdom of the move. On the other hand, we were in the midst of the gasoline crisis, and our truck got about eight miles to the gallon. Gas stations were only open a few hours per day, and most of them limited the amount of fuel they would sell per vehicle. We had to plan very carefully where and when to refuel for fear of running dry on the remote and often narrow West Virginia Turnpike. Running out of gas on a tight mountain turn could cause a fatal accident.

We made it all the way to the North Carolina border, and as we reached the top of the last mountain before coasting down to the North Carolina Piedmont, the sun came out, the air warmed, and we looked out over the land in front of as with a warm glow and high hopes. Near Mt. Airy, however, we found ourselves down to the last few cups of fuel and the only gas station in sight was closed. We decided to pull in and park under the Shell sign just to be there whenever it opened. We had a travel-weary four year old Alex and two frightened cats, so staying long would not be pleasant. We knew we may have to sleep in the truck overnight, but there were no other options.

The station owner came over to us to say he was closed, but he seemed to grasp our situation, and he asked us to pull up to a pump that was out of sight from the highway. He pumped enough to get us to Greensboro, and I offered an extra $20 for his kindness. He refused the money, and he asked us not to tell anyone what he had done. He had violated the rules to rescue us. I have only passed his station a few times since then, but whenever I do, I stop to fill up whether I need fuel or not.

Greensboro didn't have the Cleveland Symphony or a great museum, but it was a very livable city with decent cultural attractions. Quality restaurants didn't exist, but we couldn't afford them when we were in Cleveland anyway. The climate was delightful, Greensboro had a few solid educational institutions, and making friends came quickly and easily. Lake Jeanette, just north of the city, was a perfect place to kayak. Greensboro was just a very comfortable place, and we were happy to be there.

The job was nothing special. Regional health planning agencies had been created to bring some control to inefficiencies in the rapidly growing U.S. health care system. The proliferation of new facilities and technologies was driving prices higher and higher. Regional planning agencies like MHPC in Cleveland and the Piedmont Triad Health Planning Council in North Carolina were designed to bring costs under control. That meant telling some communities whether or not they would be permitted to build new facilities or acquire the latest technologies. We were Big Brother, with the potential to impact access to and the quality of care for thousands. It made me uncomfortable, but I also knew it needed to be done. It just wasn't my style, so I began looking for something more appropriate soon after starting. I did a decent job for the agency, and we designed a respectable regional system for emergency medical services. Nevertheless, my work would never qualify as a model for best practices.

We enjoyed the Greensboro Symphony and Eastern Music Festival, the museums and community theater, and we made friends with many of the young people who managed the organizations and attended the events. One day a story appeared in the *Greensboro News* announcing the resignation of the executive director of the United Arts Council. That was the job I wanted. I had no reason to believe they would hire me, as I had no arts management or significant fundraising experience. But they did, and a new chapter opened. The main task of the Arts Council was to conduct a campaign to raise funds for all of the approved arts organizations in town. Fortunately the systems and support structure for the drive was in place and I simply sustained it and gave it new energy.

We also managed to contort the rules for a federal employment program to hire Michael and Brenda Lilly and Mary "Cricket" Faran and form a small theater troupe we called The ACT Company. Cricket's husband Tom Huey worked for the Arts Council doing public relations, but his real talent was creative writing, and we enjoyed producing his plays. We presented some cutting edge shows in unusual places like a rundown greasy spoon in downtown Greensboro.

We wanted to add something special to the local arts community, and we found it in the Carolina Theater. The Carolina was a grand old Vaudeville theater that had been built in 1927 as the premier showplace between Washington, D.C., and Atlanta. When we first walked into the smelly, filthy structure in 1975, it was hard to imagine its potential, but our board chair Betty Cone, board member Sam Hummel, and I saw beneath the grime and dreamed of a glistening palace filled with great music and theater.

The community response to our vision of a flourishing arts scene, anchored by the Carolina Theater, in a revitalized downtown Greensboro was tepid at best. The center of the city had been abandoned for the suburbs and shopping malls. The few professionals who still worked downtown left at five every evening with no desire to return until the sun was bright the next morning. Darkness in downtown was for derelicts and the police. No one, we were told would attend anything in the dying heart of Greensboro ever again.

Undaunted, we raised barely enough cash to make the purchase with faith that we would eventually generate the resources to make it shine. The Carolina had become a low-grade movie house, and the carpet held years of un-cleaned Coke and popcorn. If your shoes weren't tied tight, they would stick to the floor and come off when you walked. None of the gold leaf gilt on the large columns could be seen. The lights were kept low with yellow bulbs to mask the filth. The last movie before we took ownership was *Texas Chainsaw Massacre*, a fitting end to a sad period for a grand old entertainment palace.

We recruited volunteer labor to clean the theater up enough to show it to potential donors. Staff members volunteered extra hours to share the burden and demonstrate our commitment. Gail Perry joined us as a summer intern and helped shape our strategies. (Gail went on to become a nationally known writer, consultant and speaker as well as lifelong friend and trusted advisor.) Betty, Sam and other leaders of the effort were from the upper crust of Greensboro society, but they rolled up their sleeves, dug into the dirt and grime, and together we transformed a tawdry den into an elegant facility for the performing arts.

My own volunteer task, carried out on evenings and weekends, was to clean the enormous chandelier. I worked from the balcony where we could swing the unit within reach. It held thousands of glass crystals to refract the light, but every piece had become black with filth. Even with the dimmer at full power, it barely shed any light. That was probably best, because no one would want to see what they were walking on or sitting on. Many of the steel lines holding the crystals in place were old and worn, and they broke at the touch. I had to replace them after crawling on the grimy floor to find and retrieve all of the crystal pieces that fell. It took months to complete the task, but I take special pleasure even today whenever I return to Greensboro and look up at that bright, glorious chandelier.

We had become desperate for cash to keep the project alive, and reluctantly we went to our ace in the hole, Benjamin Cone, Sr. Mr. Cone was the patriarch of Greensboro as Cone Mills, America's prime denim producer, had long been the economic driver of the region. He was also Betty's father-in-law, and it was not easy to admit to him that we were struggling. Betty, Sam and I finally mustered our courage, and we told him we needed some advice. He looked at us as though we were children, knowing full well why we were there. "You don't need my advice," he said with paternal authority. "You need money. How much?"

Twenty-five thousand dollars would enable us to save the project and get us through the next few months, we said. Mr. Cone pushed the buzzer on his desk to summon his secretary. He asked her to bring his check book, and he hand wrote a check for $25,000. He saved the project, and we've always been grateful. The Carolina has become a Greensboro landmark and source of enormous civic pride. Downtown Greensboro may not be Georgetown or SoHo, but it is alive with quality restaurants and a real nightlife, and the Carolina Theater is a magnet. It has been fully restored, and it shines with bright light from the chandelier, and the gold leaf glistens.

We also acquired the old newspaper company building in a special deal with the city government to create a visual arts center to complement the theater for the performing arts. These facilities and the activities they made possible drew people from the suburbs back into the city, gave it new life, and helped rebuild Greensboro into a very attractive and lively city. I worked 60 and 70 hour weeks to make these things happen. After the first year of the project, Betty and I recalled twenty times we had worked all night with no sleep to get everything done.

≈

In addition to the Arts Council responsibilities, I also enrolled in the MBA Executive Program at Wake Forest. This was a full-time, two year program for currently employed and experienced business executives. We attended classes all day on Fridays and Saturdays and studied all week. Between the work load and school, on average, I slept fewer than three hours per night for two years.

Business is far from my area of interest or expertise, but I felt an MBA curriculum would help me become a more effective nonprofit executive. I was not disappointed, but there were many clashes between my values and perspective and those of the faculty and my classmates. On the very first day in our first class finance Professor Jack Ferner walked into the room, looked at us and with no other greeting asked, "What is the purpose of business?" There were forty-five students; forty-four of them worked in the business sector, and they knew the answer. As though they had rehearsed, all forty-four shouted, "profit!" The forty-fifth student, the old Peace Corps guy who was running an arts council scratched his head and wondered how Socrates might answer that question. Surely Dale Stockton would make us examine the query from a dozen angles and plumb the depths of its meaning. By the time I refocused on the class we had moved on to learn how to manage money to maximize profit.

My time at the Babcock School was enlivened and enlightened by my commuting partner Rogelio Tornero. Rogelio is a Cuban immigrant with every ounce of anti-Castro vitriol found in any Miami expatriate. I was never sure whether he placed a higher value on killing Castro or becoming a billionaire. He was passionate about both ambitions. His wife Marta and mine (also Marta) had been childhood friends in Colombia, so we had connected in Greensboro in spite of very different views and values.

Rogelio was always determined to beat the system. For example, during orientation, I took my place in line to register my car and pay for a parking pass. Rogelio and I had planned to take turns driving, so we both needed to register, or so I thought. He walked over to me with a look of disgust. "Dumb Gringo," he said, "get out of that line."

"We need our passes," I protested.

"Get out," he insisted.

"No," I refused to leave, and I registered, paid the fee, and received a permit.

On the way home he explained, "If you register your car, they'll know who you are. No registration, no ticket. Even if you get a ticket, they won't know you're a student and they'll never find you." Sure enough, for the next two years, we drove past the student lot and parked right next to the business school building. While our classmates walked a half mile through the rain and snow, we walked ten steps to the door. We rarely had a ticket, and they never tracked us down. Needless to say, we used Rogelio's car every time.

Just before graduation, Frank Schilagi appeared in our organizational behavior class. He was the Babcock School Dean, and we had heard he was a superb teacher, but we had not enjoyed that experience. We were about to. Schilagi was a short, thin, intense, wiry guy with glasses. He said not a word, but walked to the board and wrote 40,000. He looked at it for a moment and looked up at us. Without a word, he returned to the board and wrote 100,000. He looked back at us and asked, "How much is enough?" (This was 1977 when $40,000 was an impressive salary for a young executive, and $100,000 was a dream. I was earning about $12,000 at the time.)

Then Schilagi gave us a quiz. First question: "How old are you?" Question two, "How old do you expect to be when you die?" Question three, "What one thing, more than anything else, do you want to do before you die?" We turned in our written answers and he read some of them out loud. None of the answers had anything to do with making a large profit. Some wanted to take special trips to exotic places. Others wanted to improve their golf scores to a professional level. A few wanted to do something of real value to humanity. "If that's what you want to do more than anything else, why don't you do it?" he asked with a bit of pique, and he proceeded to lecture on the Socratic maxim that, "The unexamined life is not worth living."

In triumph, I remembered that first day in Jack Ferner's finance class. All of my classmates were so sure of themselves. The purpose of business was, without question, profit. But not according to business school Dean Frank Schilagi. I was right. The Peace Corps guy was right. We should challenge ourselves, ask questions, and look beneath the surface and beyond the obvious. There is more to life, and there is more to business than profit. There is no universal answer to that or other value laden questions, but I was vindicated, and I graduated with a deep sense of satisfaction.

In May, 1977, I was honored to receive my second degree signed by my hero and mentor Dr. James Ralph Scales. We didn't have much time to talk after the graduation ceremony, but we took a moment to reflect on the tense day we had met, our conspiracy to change the political and intellectual climate at Oklahoma State, and my modest role as a reference for him to become President of this great institution. Dr. Scales made a difference in my life, and he made all the difference in a great academic institution. I am honored to have known him, and to have played a small part in his life and career.

≈

With no more classes to attend and relieved of homework assignments, I had at least thirty to forty new hours available every week. Some of it would be devoted to sleep, but some time could be used for other pursuits. Unfortunately, the marriage to Marta disintegrated under the strain of work and school. Alex lived with Marta, but spent considerable time with me as well. While the divorce gave me some freedom, I was emotionally fragile, broke, and burdened with a deep sense of personal failure.

I needed something to rebuild my spirit and self esteem. My racing kayak had been damaged and I couldn't afford another one, so I turned to running (shoes and shorts are cheap). I joined the local YMCA, and connected with a group of runners who met at noon every day. Charles Saunders, a banker; Vance Baron, an attorney and former Peace Corps Volunteer; Bob Foxworth, a salesman; and McGee Porter, a corporate executive, and I met almost every day at noon for a run through the parks and on the tree-lined streets of Greensboro.

Marathon running was just beginning to gain popularity, but that distance was far from my mind. Just a mile was a challenge after two years of school and no time for any rest or exercise. As I ran more and more, however, I added miles and miles to the daily routine. One day McGee came into the Y with entry forms for the New York City Marathon, and he suggested we all enter.

The race was only a few months away, and I had never gone over five miles. But, the old competitive spirit was still alive, and I accepted the challenge. I read *Runner's World*, developed a rigorous training schedule, and dedicated myself to the task. The third Sunday in October, McGee and I found ourselves on Staten Island starting a 26.2 mile endurance test through all five boroughs with some 3,000 other running fools.

The crowd of spectators along the city streets was enormous and very vocal throughout the race. Just after the mid-point, we came off the 58th Street Bridge and turned up First Avenue. A powerful PA system blared the theme from *Rocky*, and the crowd pushed in so close we could slap their hands on both sides at once. It was absolutely intoxicating. Lifted by the crowd, I picked up the pace but kept it under control. Some others sped up too much and paid for it later.

When I finally reached Central Park, with about five miles to go, everything was gone. My training base simply was not sufficient for a marathon, and I faced failure. Yet I kept running, refusing to walk even a single step. The pain ripped through every muscle, and I just tried to make it to the next mile marker, then the next one. With two miles to go, I had reached my limit, and I was within a few yards of collapse, when a spectator handed me a slice of orange. I almost rejected it for fear it would upset my stomach, but I took it and sucked the juice. I could feel my body absorb the liquid and nutrients like a sponge, and I felt renewed. I actually picked up the pace, but it only lasted a mile. When I was about to crash again, I saw another spectator with orange slices. I would have mugged him if he hadn't offered them to me. I inhaled the orange slice, it filled my body with new energy, and I went on. It took one more orange hit to get me to the finish line, but I made it, running every step of the way.

People who have never run a marathon cannot understand the metaphysical experience. It is both Zen and athletics. It is competition, and it is meditation. It is community, and it is solitary. It is endurance; it is survival, and it is triumph. To accept the challenge and to finish is a metaphor for everything else we do in life. If you can finish a marathon, you can survive whatever life throws your way.

I ran seven more marathons over the next two years, including Boston twice and New York again. My times dropped from three hours and twenty-five minutes in New York to consistently under three hours—less than seven minutes per mile. My last New York Marathon was among the slowest, but it was the most fun. I wasn't in good enough shape to try for a personal best, so I started at the back of the pack. By this time the number of entries had reached 5,000. I passed over 4,000 runners on the way to Tavern on the Green in Central Park, and slowed to talk briefly with several fellow runners along the way. It was a 26.2 mile party with no pain.

≈

I was elected chairman of the governing board of the Guilford Wildlife Club, an affiliate of the National Wildlife Federation that leased the right to exclusive use of Lake Jeanette from Cone Mills. It is primarily a bass fishing club, but I used it for kayak training. The board was a collegial group with few challenging issues, but I noted growing tension prior to one meeting as a crusty codger who worked at P. Lorillard Tobacco Company distributed copies of a magazine article about carp to selected board members. He didn't give me a copy, but someone else shared his with me. The article warned pond owners about the risk of carp invading the water because they would multiply and drive preferred species like bass and brim out. I asked innocently if there was a problem with carp in Lake Jeanette, and I was advised I would find out soon enough.

When the name of one of the candidates to be approved for club membership was read, someone uttered the one word "carp" with dripping disdain. The signal had been sent, and the designated board members knew they were to vote no without discussion. I may have been slow and naïve, but I wasn't clueless. Obviously the candidate was black, and the cabal was determined to keep the club purely white.

As a kayaker who had little interaction with other members, the question of race and club membership never even occurred to me, but it hit me square in the face that night. The segregationists on the board didn't want any discussion of the issue because they knew if it was debated they would have to admit their prejudice, and they might lose. As board chairman, I demanded discussion; the blatant racism was exposed, and after a lengthy and testy debate, the membership application in question was approved. Had the vote gone the other way, I would have been forced by conscience to resign from the club and find another place for my boat.

The Woolworth's store in Greensboro had once been the scene of a pivotal confrontation in the early stages of the civil rights movement, but the city had become remarkably integrated and collegial since those ugly days. Nevertheless, vestiges of the old segregationist South remained beneath the radar, and it surfaced that night. This time, however, the dark side lost. The Guilford Wildlife Club is still there, it is integrated, and everyone seems to be content.

≈

The Greensboro Arts Council was a member of the American Council for the Arts and its committee for community arts councils. I was not particularly active at the national level, but I was aware of tension between the committee and the parent ACA. Committee chairman John Blaine and other community arts council leaders were itching to break away and create our own organization, unencumbered by the stodgy arts establishment that dominated the ACA. I feared we weren't prepared for such a bold move, but when the members voted to separate the resolution passed by 97 to 1. I was the one dissenting vote. I am told that after the referendum, Blaine asked of the other leaders, "Who was the smart one?" He knew the group had taken a very risky step to become independent with no defined sources of support. John and I didn't know each other at the time, but we were about to become friends and colleagues.

A few weeks later the newly created and independent National Assembly of Community Arts Agencies began to search for its first executive director, and several colleagues suggested I apply, so I did.

When the selection committee learned I had cast the lone dissenting vote, their interest in my candidacy increased. They liked the idea of someone who was willing to resist the overwhelming flow and think for himself. I was invited to Washington for an interview, and I stayed in the Hotel Intrigue just a few blocks from the interview site in Foggy Bottom. Even though I was within walking distance, I took a cab so I wouldn't have to worry about getting lost. I allowed an extra half hour just to be sure I wouldn't be late, but the driver became confused, and went in the wrong direction—toward Northeast rather than Northwest Washington. When I told him I thought he was going the wrong way, he insisted indignantly that he knew what he was doing. A half hour later, we were completely lost, and a parade was blocking our way. Time for the interview to start was upon me, and I saw my opportunity evaporate. Cell phones had yet to be invented, and the only way to let the committee know was to find a pay phone. I found one; called the hotel; reached the committee; they were forgiving; I was hired, and a new life in Washington was about to begin.

INSIDE THE BELTWAY

Ever since my experiences with Dale Stockton and Peace Corps training at George Washington University, I had dreamed of living in Washington and becoming part of the D.C. milieu. This was my chance, and I was determined to make the most of it.

I moved to Washington in the fall of 1978, and settled into a first floor tiny apartment in a row house duplex on Corcoran Street between 14th and 15th Streets. At the time, the neighborhood was in transition, the epicenter of Washington gentrification. On the 14th Street side, drug traffic and prostitution ruled. Fifteenth Street was already safe and prosperous. Dupont Circle, the cultural and intellectual heart of the city, beckoned just beyond at 18th Street. Most of my neighbors were young professionals striving to make their mark in the nation's capital. I fit right in.

I was far too inexperienced for the responsibility of leading the National Assembly of Community Arts Agencies, but the whole field was young, and underfunded, and I may have been the best they could afford. We had a tiny staff of three and no secure funding base, but we survived. Our signal achievement was the first ever national convention devoted solely to leaders of local arts agencies. Attendance was strong and spirits were high at Denver's classy Metropolitan Hotel in the summer of 1979. After decades as the lesser creatures at conferences of the American Council for Arts, we were on our own, we had grown up, and we reveled in our new status.

New board president Lee Howard arranged for Harry Chapin, the great singer and songwriter best known for "Cat's in the Cradle," to be our keynote speaker. Chapin was also very active in social causes, and he was a remarkably knowledgeable and articulate spokesman for the local arts agency movement. We sought to connect the best in the arts with anyone willing to participate as a celebration of community and as a tool to stimulate integration and interaction among all social classes and racial groups. We promoted arts in education and participation in arts activities for everyone in small town USA as well as the major metropolises. Chapin was one of us, and his speech is still revered three decades later among community arts advocates. He admonished us not to allow the arts to be the band on the Titanic diverting attention away from inevitable tragedy, but rather to climb into the crow's nest to see the icebergs on the horizon and to shout out warnings and directions to help guide the public. We should make the call to social and political action where and when action is needed.

Three very talented colleagues formed an impromptu trio with Jonathan Katz playing the washtub bass, Jack Le Sueur playing guitar and vocals, and Bob Lynch playing mandolin. It was an odd collection of instruments, and the visual impact was striking. Jonathan was probably the tallest and thinnest person in the whole arts community, and Bob the shortest. Somehow, it was perfect. Word spread that they were going to play in one of the guest rooms, and a crowd gathered. Every inch of chair, bed and floor space was filled, as Jack, Bob and Jonathan sang popular songs from the folk, blues, and rock traditions. I sat on the floor with my back to the wall and my arm around my dear friend Molly LaBerge of St. Paul, Minnesota. Everyone sang along way into the night and early morning hours. Jack's performance of "American Pie" was better than Don McLean could have imagined, and it became the theme song for the event. A great tradition in the local arts agency community began in Denver, and I am told it continued for decades with the same trio intact.

My job was to help create a sense of community among the rapidly growing arts councils throughout the country and to build respect and support for the movement among the arts establishment. The first task was fairly easy. The Katz, Lynch and Le Sueur trio unified the community in song, and our policies and programs added the cement. With remarkable and inspired colleagues like Ralph Burgard, Lee Howard and Molly LaBerge providing leadership and inspiration, the community created itself. The second task—gaining respect from the establishment—was another matter.

I arrived in Washington entirely unprepared for the intellectual and cultural confrontation between the "community" arts and the "elite" arts. We were welcomed by the whole arts community as a potential ally to lobby Congress for more support for the National Endowment for the Arts (NEA). Our constituency reached into every congressional district in America, so we could broaden the base of support. However, any effort to promote broader allocation of NEA resources into "community" rather than "elite" institutions met with serious resistance from our colleagues with the American Symphony Orchestra League, American Association of Museums, Opera America, etc. All federal funding for the arts, they contended, should go to institutions judged (by them) to be the very best in the nation.

I never argued against quality as a criterion for grant making. I simply maintained that local arts agencies in places like Kearney, Nebraska; Sitka, Alaska; and Winston-Salem, North Carolina could be the best in the country at developing local and participatory arts experiences, and they too are part of the nation's arts and cultural fabric and worthy of federal support. Hank Putsch was our only advocate among the top executives within the Endowment, but he was a tremendous asset. After lengthy sessions with Senator Claiborne Pell of Rhode Island (known as "Mr. Arts" in the Senate), Congressman Sidney Yates of Illinois (known as "Mr. Arts" in the House) and NEA Chairman Livingston Biddle, we were given a chance to make our case to the National Council on the Arts.

This presidentially appointed body consisted of very wealthy political donors and famous artists such as Van Cliburn and Theodore Bikel. The word elite—in all of its manifestations, both positive and negative—defined this group. Convincing them to embrace the concept of including the lowly "community arts" within their realm was an enormous challenge. They wanted us to persuade Members of Congress from the heartland to vote for appropriations for major cultural institutions in large urban centers, but not a penny should be wasted building understanding of, appreciation for and participation in the arts at the local level. To my surprise, the folk singer and actor Bikel was particularly hostile to our cause. He feared dilution of quality in America's cultural fabric if our constituents were allowed inside the tent. Cliburn, the great pianist, was relatively ambivalent. After all, he was from Kilgore, Texas, so he was pulled both ways.

Ralph Burgard, Lee Howard, and I worked far into the night honing our presentation, and the next day we nailed it. Biddle told us afterwards it was the best presentation he had ever seen before the Council, and we prevailed. The Council (reluctantly) embraced formation of a special program of support for local arts agencies, and Congress granted larger appropriations for the NEA, including funds for a new local arts agency program.

≈

Early the next year, I traveled to Boise, Idaho for a meeting with Governor John Evans and to speak at a state-wide arts conference. I decided to take advantage of the trip to trek and climb in the Sawtooth Mountains, even though it was the middle of January, and the trails were covered with snow and ice. I was too cheap to rent a car, so I walked out of the airport terminal with my back pack and stuck out my thumb. It took five or six rides to get into the mountains, and each driver had a story to tell. A crusty old miner and trapper took me to a stream along the way and taught me how to pan for gold. I even found a few tiny flecks. Another driver took me to Idaho City because he knew Lucy, the owner of the Honey Dew Bakery, was an avid trekker who would be able to suggest the best places to go.

Indeed, Lucy joined me for a cup of coffee and delicious muffins, and she suggested I try to reach and climb on Warbonnet Peak. I did, and she was right. It was spectacular. Leaving Idaho City, a UPS driver pulled up and asked me to walk over a hill so no one would be able to see me get in. (He was not allowed to pick up riders.) Once I was on board the truck, he told me he had very few deliveries to make, so he had plenty of time, and he went far out of his way to get me right to the trail leading to Warbonnet. We had a terrific conversation about living in Idaho compared with Washington, and about politics and people.

The air was bitter cold, but I was well equipped, and my exposed nose was the only body part that froze at night. It was too icy for me to reach the summit of Warbonnet, but the hike and climb in the snow-white mountains was magnificent. On the way out, I noticed steam rising from hot springs, and I couldn't resist the temptation. I needed to get to the road soon, but bathing in a natural hot spring all alone in the Sawtooth Mountains in the middle of January was not to be missed. Like Goldilocks, I tried one and it was too hot. The next one was too cold, but the third one was just right. I stripped down bare naked, slipped into the tepid pool and luxuriated in solitary bliss.

I reached the road in the late afternoon to catch a ride back to Boise. However, I found that cars passed that way about one every thirty minutes. The odds of getting a ride weren't all that good, and I was scheduled to have lunch with the governor the next day in Boise. Time and a few cars passed but no ride. Finally, as the sun was setting, a young couple in a pick-up truck stopped. They told me they would probably be the last car before morning. There was no room in the cab, but they let me ride in the truck bed.

They took me to Idaho City where a big birthday party was underway at Calamity Jane's, the tiny, iconic western town's restaurant and bar. I went in, and they welcomed me as though I lived there, and a young married couple invited me to spend the night with them. They also sent word around town that I needed a ride to Boise in the morning. Fortunately, someone knew someone who was going to the big city; they connected us, and I made it to lunch with thirty minutes to spare—wearing a wrinkled suit, shirt, and tie that had been in my back pack the whole time. I explained my rumpled look to Governor Evans, and he loved it.

We eventually changed the name of the organization to the National Assembly of Local Arts Agencies (NALAA) to embrace a broader concept of our members and their programs. In the arts world, the word community tends to connote not just local, but also participatory— art done by citizens for their own enjoyment and perhaps that of their friends and neighbors, but not necessarily professional quality. Local arts agencies promote participatory community arts, but they also support professional and top quality arts as well. Therefore "local" was the more appropriate and descriptive term.

It was a good move, and the organization managed to survive the fragile first few years under my leadership. However, I was increasingly drawn to canoe and kayak competition, and I couldn't lead a national organization for a growing and demanding community while training and racing all across the country, if not the world. I left NALAA in the hands of Gretchen Weiss who had been my associate director. She handled it ably for the next year or two, and then Bob Lynch, the mandolin player as well as rising star among arts administrators, moved in from Massachusetts to lead the organization. Under Bob's leadership, NALAA grew large, prosperous and strong. It became so powerful that it absorbed the American Council for the Arts, the same organization we had left decades before, and became Americans for the Arts, the premier arts advocacy organization in the country. Bob is still there, just as energetic and enthusiastic as ever.

FIVE RING FEVER

I had a great sense of accomplishment with the new policy of support for local arts organizations, but I had a seriously conflicting ambition. The brief introduction to kayak racing in Cleveland produced a deep desire to see how far I might go with the sport if I ever gave it priority focus. The affliction is known as "five ring fever"—an unreasonable and unrealistic ambition to be an Olympian. The basic athletic drive from my youth was only part of the motivation. The Olympic movement brings people and cultures together in a global celebration of sport and achievement. It is part of the global peace movement, and I wanted to be part of it.

I had joined the Washington Canoe Club (WCC), arguably the premier canoe and kayak racing institution in the country. The WCC had provided all four members of the U.S. team that introduced canoe and kayak racing as a demonstration sport at the 1924 Olympics, and it had produced at least one Olympian in every quadrennial event since then. Helsinki Olympic champion Frank Havens was our inspiration and patron saint. The athletes at the club had become my best friends, and I wanted to be a full part of the family. Some of my Club teammates had qualified to represent the U.S. in the 1980 Moscow Olympics, but their dreams of glory were dashed by the U.S. boycott. Everyone was eager to be in a Team U.S.A. uniform in Los Angeles in 1984. It was an infectious environment.

As a part-time athlete, I was in the Washington Canoe Club, but not part of the inner club of serious competitors. The others were much younger, and they had few distractions. To compete on their level, I had to focus as they did. I could not be both the leader of a national association and a serious kayak racer at the same time. I had to choose.

Perhaps foolishly, I went with the water, the team, rigorous training, racing, and the remote possibility of becoming an Olympian myself. To finance this fantasy, I secured a 9-to-5 job as Director of Government Liaison with the Epilepsy Foundation of America. Bill McLin, Executive Director of EFA agreed to allow me time to train and race so long as I would give EFA extra time and effort during times of special need.

Epilepsy is a serious condition, and it deserved better representation than I gave it, but I was able to build several good contacts in Congress and at the National Institutes of Health. Since this was the Reagan era, there was little hope for increased funding for medical research, so our efforts seemed rather pointless. Our best hope was to minimize the damage, and we did. The highlight was a photo op with President Reagan in the Oval Office. It was a hollow, ceremonial event, but the picture of me shaking hands with Republican deity on my office wall helps win support from conservative donors. Mostly, however, the years at EFA gave me an opportunity to pay the rent while I trained and raced.

Canoe and kayak sprint racing takes place on calm water in long narrow boats over courses of 200, 500, 1,000 and 10,000 meters. At the time, the Olympic events were at 500 and 1,000 meters in singles, doubles and fours. It is not the daring whitewater seen sometimes on TV. Rather, it is straight ahead speed, power, and endurance. It may be a bit dull for spectators, but it is challenging and exhilarating for the athletes. At that time, sprint racing was the only division of canoe and kayak competition in the Olympics. The sport is virtually unknown in the U.S., but it enjoys a devoted following in dozens of countries worldwide. Whitewater slalom competition, the better known version of the sport, returned to the Olympics in 1992.

As soon as I settled into the routine at EFA, I began a serious training regimen at the Canoe Club. We were on the water every morning at six for a ninety-minute to two hour workout, and, we were back on the water at six every evening for more of the same. We were guided by a training schedule provided by the national team coaches, and local volunteer coaches often made adjustments and monitored our workouts. For the most part, however, we were on our own. That environment helped build a wonderful bond among the athletes. We would chart our own path to success, and since we largely created our own program, we believed in it.

I pushed my body to painful exhaustion nearly every day, and the others helped me develop my stroke technique and improve my racing skills. As I grew stronger, and my endurance improved, I actually became competitive with these well trained young athletes. Thankfully there was a wonderful spirit within the Club that welcomed and supported anyone who was willing to pay the price of relentless training.

I was never quite good enough to break into the top level for major international competitions, but I won a drawer full of local, regional and national championship medals, and I brought home two golds and two silvers from the 1982 U.S. Olympic Festival—a domestic version of the Olympics sponsored by the U.S. Olympic Committee. Truth-be-told, however, I won most of these races in team boats because I was able to partner with David Halpern, Dan Schnurrenberger and others who earned positions on the U.S. Olympic team. They pulled me onto the medal stand.

During the Olympic Festival in Syracuse, Joanne Janus, one of my Washington Canoe Club teammates, whispered to me, "Someone in yellow likes you." Our team representing the South wore green uniforms, the Northeast wore blue, and the West wore red. Yellow was the team color for the middle of the country, so I wasted no time scouting the team in yellow. I noticed a particularly attractive blonde woman whom I had not met, and hoped she was the one—and she was. After confirming it with Joanne, I introduced myself to Kay Edwards and found excuses to hang out with or near her for the rest of the week.

I had been divorced since 1977, and I enjoyed being young, fit and single. Kay could fit right in if she lived closer. However, she lived in College Station, Texas, and it was unlikely we would ever see much of each other. I didn't press the matter, but I couldn't get her out of my mind. Several months after the Olympic Festival, I had to attend a conference in New Orleans. College Station was only 450 miles away, so I decided to invite myself to Kay's place to "workout." She welcomed me to visit and stay at her house right on a lake for a good training session. She thought I was serious about the workout, and she put me through a grueling training regimen. Before leaving, however, I made my real intentions known, and she seemed pleased. We started a long distance romance that led to marriage and two fabulous children.

Kay and I were married on Thanksgiving weekend in 1983 in the Chapel on the campus at College Station during the A&M vs. Texas game. Kay's "maid of honor" was her canoe partner Mike Shively. My "best man" was Elizabeth "Boo" Hayman, a dear friend and world champion whitewater kayak competitor from the Washington canoeing community. When you marry well into your 30s, and your parents aren't paying the bill, you can do it any way you want. Kay selected "The Wedding Song," written by Noel Paul Stookey of Peter, Paul and Mary (one of the most beautiful songs ever written), to celebrate our love and commitment. Two decades later, we would become friends with Noel, and we could thank him in person for his musical gift.

We returned to Washington where we trained in miserable weather through the winter with high hopes of making the 1984 Olympic Team. The trials were scheduled for Occoquan Reservoir just south of D.C. in April, and we were determined to be at our best. However, I managed to seriously re-injure my back during an extra long workout about a month before the trials. I could barely walk, and I certainly couldn't compete. (I probably would not have made the team, even at my best. I would have been competitive, but not quite there.) Kay raced and gave it her best, but she also failed to qualify. I was much older than most of the others, and it was a privilege just to have qualified for the trials and to celebrate with the new team.

I managed to recover from the injuries and compete one last time in the national championships held in Lake Placid a few weeks after the Los Angeles Games. Most members of the Olympic Team were burned out from competition, and they stayed home, which gave me a chance to shine. At age 40, I was eligible to compete for the "masters" championship in singles, and I won that race all on my own. I was fortunate enough to partner with David Halpern, the same guy who pulled me to a bunch of medals in the Olympic Festival a few years earlier. He was among the few from the U.S. Olympic Team to attend and compete in Lake Placid. David and I won four races together, so I came home that year with five national championship gold medals—the "masters" championship earned on my own plus four in team boats.

By this time, my aging body screamed, "No mas!" Injuries to my back and shoulder made more serious competition impossible. My racing days were over, but I was satisfied, and I had no regrets. It was a joy to train and compete with so many fine people and exceptional athletes. It felt unbelievably good to be in world-class condition at an age when most have become obese. The sport also introduced me to Kay, so it was all good.

Our sport, however, was underfunded and poorly organized. Most of the leadership came from parents of athletes whose primary objective was the success of their own children. There was, therefore, no incentive to add visibility or to recruit better athletes into the sport. As long as canoe and kayak racing remained obscure there would be little competition, and almost anyone could win at least some medal in some event somewhere. Even the national championships had become a joke. New events and competition categories had been added until almost anyone who could keep a boat upright could win a national championship medal in something. By 1984, the sport was so poorly managed the organizers forgot to order the medals in time. My five golds arrived several months later in the mail.

As athletes, we resented the low quality of the organization, but we had no time to devote to change things. Training and racing, especially on top of a full time job, allowed absolutely no spare time for anything but complaining.

After the national championships in Lake Placid, I was ready to move on with my life and refocus on my family and building a career. My old friend Ralph Burgard had helped create a new arts council in Columbia, South Carolina, and he called to see if I would consider returning to the arts world as their first executive director. Kay was very unhappy with the long cold winters in Washington, and for me the thought of returning to the comfortable and familiar arts environment was appealing, so I accepted the offer from the Cultural Council board. We moved to Columbia.

≈

We had just settled into a cozy townhouse on Lake Murray when I received a call at midnight from David Halpern. He and others from the Olympic team had gone to the annual meeting of the National Paddling Committee (NPC) of the American Canoe Association (ACA) to express their displeasure with the quality of the program. The NPC was comprised of volunteers elected by the members to manage the flatwater sprint racing program. Generally, volunteers might be forgiven for less than professional performance of their responsibilities, but this was pathetic. An Olympic sports organization should operate at a higher level than middle school gym class, but even that comparison insults middle school gym. The dedicated athletes deserved better.

"We have pulled off a revolution," David reported, "And you have to lead it." They had forced the resignation of several of the old guard and filled their seats with a young, energetic new generation who wanted change. "You are the only one with organization management experience," he argued, "You can turn the program around." I had complained as much as anyone about the miserable organization, so I had an obligation to put up or shut up. David assured me it would only require presiding at four meetings each year and attending the national team trials and national championships. I asked who else would be on the new committee with me, and I was satisfied it could be a good group. My heroes like Steve Kelley and Rob Plankenhorn were there along with Leslie Klein, J. T. Kearney and Olympic Bronze medalist Greg Barton. This could be fun. I asked for time to consider it, and David gave me until noon the next day to let him know.

Kay and I discussed it, and with my assurance of only four meetings per year plus a few competitive events, we agreed to give it a try. I gave David an affirmative response with two non-negotiable conditions. First, we would agree on a clear and focused mission for the organization at our next meeting, and second, everyone on the committee would commit to make an Olympic level effort to produce a quality program. They agreed, and my life took another unexpected turn. Instead of moving on from the sport to my family and career, I fell deeply into sports administration—with no pay. Even worse, I found myself in the midst of a colossal controversy that reached the top levels of the U.S. and International Olympic Committees. It consumed at least twenty and often as many as sixty hours every week for the next five years. All of this was my lot as a volunteer while employed more than full time to start a new cultural council in the capital city of South Carolina.

We held true to our commitment at the first meeting. I asked the committee to define—in clear and unambiguous terms—what the purpose or mission was for the National Paddling Committee. The one primary lesson I had learned in business school and in many years of managing organizations was the primacy of mission. A clear, concise and unambiguous mission statement should drive all budget and program decisions. I was convinced that the failure of the NPC to define its mission was the primary reason for its failure. If you don't know what you want to achieve you won't achieve much, and the NPC had achieved precious little.

I indicated that the mission could be to build broad participation in our sport, or it could be to produce Olympic champions. It could not be both at once. With scarce resources, we had to make careful budget decisions, and they had to be based on our mission. If it was to build broad participation, we could allocate resources to clubs to help them acquire equipment and recruit more young participants. If our mission was to produce Olympic champions, we would hire the best coaches we could afford and support the very best of our athletes so they could perform at their peak. We couldn't afford both.

I took no position, but tried to control the debate. It was lengthy and intense. Many wanted to compromise and do both, but I would not allow it. I insisted that a compromise would perpetuate mediocrity and failure at both. We had to decide. I also indicated that once we decided, we must have 100 percent commitment to the mission from everyone on the committee. If you couldn't embrace the mission, you would be asked to resign. It was a tough stance, but it was imperative.

At last, the committee agreed our mission should be to produce Olympic champions. Our parent organization, the American Canoe Association, was responsible for promoting recreational canoe and kayak participation. Our unique role was focused on the only branch of the sport that was in the Olympics, we received virtually all of our funds from the U.S. Olympic Committee, and we should focus on Olympic performance. If we were going to focus on the Olympics, we should do it right and become a world class program—a producer of Olympic champions.

A few holdovers from the old guard objected strenuously, and they were encouraged to resign. Most did. Those who remained made a commitment to work together to fulfill the new mission.

Now that we had a mission, we needed to develop our strategy to achieve it. That meant a new set of standards and a process for hiring the best coaches, more rigorous team selection criteria, and producing high quality team trials and national championship events. We had to become Olympic quality in everything we did.

The transition to build a world class program took time, patience and persistence, but we were on the right path. We hired Paul Podgorski, a Polish immigrant and world class coach, we generated funds to hire a quality professional staff, and with that base we secured a multi-million dollar sponsorship from Champion International paper products company.

I was unprepared, however, for one proposal. An Olympic team member serving on the governing board (I prefer not to identify him) told us, in no uncertain terms, that he knew what it would take to produce Olympic champions. We would have to do what the others do— the East Germans, the Soviets and New Zealand, everyone who made it to the medal podium. We would have to facilitate a performance enhancing drug regimen for our athletes and help them get away with it. We were assured the governing bodies in other sports did it, and we should too. The man making the proposal was in a position to know what he was talking about. No one doubted his word. If our mission was to produce Olympic champions, we were obligated to get into the drug business. "Be there or be square," was the exact phrase.

From my perspective, all-out pursuit of a mission is commendable, but it must also be tempered by values, by rules, by ethics. Too many people and businesses have ruined themselves and those close to them by throwing fundamental principles and values aside to pursue lofty goals. In the end, it isn't worth winning if you have to cheat to do it.

The debate within the committee was every bit as contentious as the previous session to determine the mission. I didn't say so at the time, but I was prepared to resign on the spot had the decision been in favor of drugs. After everyone had expressed their views, and the outcome was still in doubt, I turned to Greg Barton. Greg had won a bronze medal at the Los Angeles Olympics and he was our primary hope for a medal four years later in Seoul. "What do you think, Greg?"

I asked. Greg replied in his usual soft spoken but certain way, "Test me today, test me tomorrow, test me every day. But, test everyone else as well," he added. I looked at the rest of the committee and suggested, "Is that not our answer?" No one could argue with Greg.

We voted to affirm the strongest drug enforcement regimen possible within the Olympic program. We encouraged the USOC to conduct tests whenever and wherever they wished. We wanted to win, and we wanted to win clean. As a result, we took special pleasure and pride in Seoul in the summer of 1988 when Greg Barton won the gold medal in the K-1 1,000 meter race and 90 minutes later he astounded the canoe world with another gold medal in the K-2 1,000 meter event teamed with Norman Bellingham. Both were razor thin victory margins, but the victories were clean, clear and absolutely honest.

The singles race was so close the officials had announced that Grant Davies of Australia won, and Greg was second. I was the head of our delegation at the Games, and Bill Hanson was the official team leader. Bill had the authority to file a protest, and we quickly conferred and agreed a review was necessary. The officials enlarged the photo finish picture three times before they were able to discern a slim difference between the two boats, and they declared Greg the victor by less than 1/100 of a second. I was talking with Grant Davies' parents waiting for the award ceremony when the officials announced the reversal. I had congratulated them on their son's achievement, and now they turned back to me with a touch of disappointment and extended their congratulations to us. Their graceful acceptance was inspiring.

Greg was a finalist for the coveted Sullivan Award that year, and he invited me to be his guest at the banquet in Indianapolis. Others on the podium included the famous runner Florence Griffith Joyner (Flo Jo), swimmer Janet Evans, skater Brian Boitano, volleyball idol Karch Kiraly, and other high profile stars. Just before dinner, Greg looked at the program, leaned over and said, "The only name I don't recognize is my own." Flo Jo won the Sullivan Award that year, but Greg was my champion.

I had met Norman Bellingham when he was a young whitewater competitor from the Washington, D.C. area. His large frame was much better suited for sprint racing than tight maneuvering on a slalom course, so some of us had encouraged him to try our long, skinny, fast boats. Finally one winter evening in 1983 during a winter training session at the David Taylor Naval Model Basin, he wandered away from the whitewater group and asked if he could try a sprint racing boat. I had just finished my workout, so I offered him mine.

He was a bit unstable, and his form was awkward. Nevertheless, even that first time he was already as fast as many of us. We knew right then that if he stayed with it, he could become a champion sprint racer. Indeed, he made the 1984 Olympic team just six months after starting, and four years later, he stood on top of the kayak world as an Olympic champion along with his partner Greg Barton. I have several signed photos of Greg and Norman in which they have expressed their appreciation for my support. My role in their Olympic triumphs was small, but I appreciate having had the opportunity to be part of it. Bellingham is now Chief Operating Officer at the U.S. Olympic Committee.

My responsibilities with the National Paddling Committee grew ever more complex and demanding. The mission decision and the drug battle were minor skirmishes, and they were resolved quickly. The big issue involved money and control—doesn't it always? Two factors converged to drive a wedge in the otherwise placid world of canoe and kayak enthusiasts. First, the American Canoe Association was recognized by the U.S. Olympic Committee (USOC) as the official National Governing Body (NGB) for the canoe and kayak program, with one immensely important caveat. According to the Amateur Sports Act, all NGBs must be single purpose organizations—focused entirely on the sport in the Olympic program. The ACA was a multi-purpose organization responsible for a wide range of canoe and kayak related activities from safety and recreation to a half dozen competitive divisions. Therefore, the Act specifically required the ACA to delegate responsibility for the Olympic discipline activities to an independent committee—the National Paddling Committee. The NPC was part of the ACA structure, but our mandate was to operate independently on behalf of the Olympic sport.

Second, the Los Angeles Olympics had produced a large profit that was to be shared equally among all NGBs—over a million dollars to each. That is, swimming, gymnastics, diving, equestrian, team handball, as well as canoe and kayak would each receive seven-figure checks. With an annual NPC budget of slightly over $100,000, a million dollar windfall was enormous. However, the ACA claimed they were the rightful recipient of the funds, and the fight was on. Should the check go to the ACA—the Governing Body or the NPC, the independent committee responsible for actual governance of and support for the Olympic sport? All other funds from the USOC went directly to the NPC, so, we argued, this should be the same. The ACA, of course, argued that as the NGB, they should receive and control the funds.

The dispute was intense, and it lasted nearly four years. Our leadership team consisted of Steve Kelley, Eric Haught and me. Kelly had been my idol when I started training and racing. He was the best in the country at the time, and *Sports Illustrated* had published a wonderful story about his life. They compared him with Mark Spitz, the multiple gold medal winner with an enormous ego to match. Kelley never won an Olympic medal or endorsement contracts, but he personified the famous Olympic creed: "The most important thing in the Olympic Games is not to win but to take part, just as the most important thing in life is not the triumph but the struggle. The essential thing is not to have conquered but to have fought well."

The ACA's battle team was led by their commodore Merle Garvis with several others in supporting roles. David Mason became their lead attack dog, and he launched a brutal and very personal public assault on my character. Former ACA Commodore Susan Chamberlin, an elegant, eloquent, and wise leader in the canoe community, tried to bring civility and a conciliatory tone to the dispute. She and I met in Colorado Springs with USOC president Barron Pittinger and general counsel Ron Rowan, but the divide was too great for compromise. A few months later, Pittinger, Garvis, and I met for hours in private during an annual ACA meeting while the members of both the ACA and NPC waited for a resolution. We finally reached a compromise on a process to move forward, but no resolution. However, when we stood before the members to announce the outcome, Garvis misrepresented the agreement, suggesting that Pittinger had sided with the ACA. I could not allow him to get away with it as that could have sealed the outcome in his favor. So, with the president of the United States Olympic Committee standing next to us, I took Garvis on and challenged his false statements right in front of the assembly. The divide and mutual hostility increased dramatically as a result, but Garvis had played dirty.

During a particularly bitter stage in the dispute, the ACA Council adopted a resolution banning me, and anyone affiliated with me, from membership and any form of participation in ACA activities. My colleagues took pride in our mutual affiliation, and we all enjoyed our exile. Of course, the ban was meaningless and unenforceable, and everyone knew it.

Eventually Pittinger took the issue to the International Canoe Federation during an International Olympic Committee meeting in Lausanne, Switzerland. In the end, the check went to the ACA, but they were required to establish a permanent endowment with 95 percent of the interest on the principal going to our Olympic sport focused organization in non-Olympic years. The remaining five percent was to be reinvested to assure growth. In the quadrennial Olympic years, 100 percent of the interest would support the Olympic program. Furthermore our absolute independence and autonomy was affirmed. By the time we reached the settlement, we had changed our name and we had incorporated as the US Canoe and Kayak Team (USCKT). With these funds plus sponsorship support from Champion International we were solid.

Many years later, the separation between the ACA and the USCKT became complete with the USOC and International Canoe Federation granting full National Governing Body recognition to the USCKT. The official name has since been changed once again to USA Canoe/ Kayak. In the interim, whitewater slalom canoe and kayak competition had been added to the Olympic program, so the two strongest rivals in the previous struggle over the Los Angeles Olympic funds became partners in the same organization.

Unfortunately, the commitment to produce Olympic champions has waned, funding has declined dramatically, and USA Canoe/Kayak has lost some of its unique spirit and championship results. The ACA, on the other hand, now that it is no longer wasting resources fighting a losing battle with the old NPC, has focused on recreational canoe-ing and canoe safety, and it is thriving. Eventually, the ACA invited me to serve on their advisory board and to conduct a training session for their governing council. When they did, I insisted they first vote to re-scind their ban on my membership. They did, and we are all friends once again.

David Mason, my nemesis throughout the dispute, eventually apol-ogized for his personal attacks. David is a proud son of the segregation-ist South who listens to Rush Limbaugh and despises anything liberal. Being "progressive" may be even worse. Nevertheless, we have moved beyond the old canoe and kayak disputes and politics to become fast— if unusual—friends. While totally wrong on all of the issues, David is extremely generous and community minded. The ACA named Mason as a prestigious "Legends of Paddling" award winner, and he insisted I be present when he featured our friendly/contentious relationship in his acceptance speech. We argue and even shout at each other over po-litical differences, but our confrontations always end in a big laugh and reinforcement of our friendship.

There were dozens of memorable events and encounters during

the years of racing, providing leadership, and officiating in the canoe and kayak program. I served as President of the Pan American Canoe Council for six years, and we successfully lobbied for our sport to be included in the Pan American Games. In addition, I was a representative to the U.S. Olympic Committee and a member of the Racing Committee of the International Canoe Federation (ICF). For the most part, these roles called for endless meetings, tedious budget battles, and debates over arcane policies and rules. The ICF Racing Committee established the rules and operations standards for world championship and Olympic competition, and that presented some serious challenges and conflicts. New boat designs and surfaces emanating from the U.S. and the Soviet block countries pressed the envelope and tested the rules as teams with resources sought advantages based on their access to new technology.

Even though some of the changes might have helped our program, I objected to any team gaining an advantage through technology. I consistently insisted that any new development that might increase hull velocity should be available to all teams before anyone could use it. That posture put me at odds with some U.S. colleagues, but I simply believed the races should be determined on the basis of athletic performance, not engineers, designers, and laboratory performance.

≈

The summer 1991 Pan American Games were scheduled for Havana, and the U.S. Olympic Committee feared the communist government in a small, low income Caribbean island nation would not be able to produce facilities and events that met our lofty standards. The Committee sent a small delegation to Havana in March to inspect the facilities and meet with the organizers. The group included USOC Vice Chairman and New York Yankees owner George Steinbrenner, Olympic champion swimmer Mary T. Meagher, USOC attorney Ron Rowan, a few other notable athletes and officials, and me.

After we had inspected the competition venues and housing facilities, we were escorted to the Presidential residence where Cuba's president Fidel Castro addressed the group in his usual authoritarian but eloquent manner. He raved on and on about Cuba's pride in hosting the Games and he assured us everything would meet if not exceed world class standards. Following the presentation, he welcomed us to a stand-up reception and dinner of fine Cuban cuisine.

As the only one in the group who knew Spanish, I had an advantage, and I spoke at some length with Castro—about sports, not politics or human rights. Castro was dressed in his standard starched and pressed army fatigues, and he drew attention at every turn. His charisma and commanding presence overwhelmed even the superstar athletes and Steinbrenner. During our private conversation, he focused sharply and listened intently to every word, then paused to absorb what I had said, and agreed with some, but then he responded with the authority of the almighty. When he had finished, there was nothing more to be said. Castro had spoken. Move on to the next topic.

Late on the first night in Cuba, I took a long stroll on the Malecón, Havana's famous waterfront avenue. Young couples by the dozens enjoyed romantic embraces along the low wall that separates the road from the sea, and everyone seemed to be in good spirits. Juan, a handsome young man in his twenties, approached, then walked a few paces beside me, and started a conversation in Spanish. I was only too happy to engage with him, as it would be a unique opportunity to learn about this mysterious land from a local resident. He asked where I was from, and he seemed pleased to have connected with a Gringo—a rare find in Cuba. Juan wanted to know more about life in the U.S., but with each topic he proclaimed Cuba superior. "Do you provide universal health care, like we do in Cuba?" he asked. Well, no we don't. "Are there street people in the U.S.?" Well, yes. "Everyone has a decent place to live in Cuba," he countered. "Is education free for everyone all the way through college?" Well no, in fact it is very expensive. "Not so in Cuba. Here it is free." "Child care is also free for every family," he went on with growing confidence and pride.

After this conversation had run its course Juan was satisfied that he had made his case, but he had one more question. "Will you please help me get to the United States?"

"Wait a minute!" I exclaimed. "You have just demonstrated why you believe Cuba is superior to the U.S. in every way, but now you want to leave and come to my country. Please explain."

"Because it's better there," he replied a bit sheepishly. Obviously, I couldn't help him escape to America, but I had learned a lot about life, values and aspirations for at least one Cuban, and I would guess Juan's perspective is widely shared. Like most people almost everywhere, Juan was proud of his homeland, but he is also eager to find his way to a better life.

As soon as I departed the plane in Miami after the trip, I called my old friend Rogelio Tornero (my MBA student companion and a Cuban-American who had been among the first to escape after Castro won his revolution), and told him I had enjoyed an evening with Fidel the night before. His response was instant and emphatic, "And, you didn't kill him?!?" No, Rogelio, I didn't kill him.

A few months later, Kay and I were both in Havana for the Pan American Games. Kay was U.S. Team manager and I was the U.S. Team leader as well as chief executive of the Pan American Canoe Racing governing board. We proudly marched with Team U.S.A. into the stadium wearing red white and blue uniforms and waving our team issue stars and stripes flags. Castro was in a special box in the grandstand, and he stood and greeted the U.S. team with enthusiasm. He also visited our canoe and kayak competition venue to watch the races and cheer. While there, he presented the gold medal to our friend Mike Herbert who narrowly edged out Cuban favorite Ángel Pérez, to win the men's single kayak 1,000 meter event. (The next day, Pérez took the gold over Herbert at 500 meters.) Castro arrived and later departed in an old faded yellow Mercedes with only a driver and one modest police escort.

There was no visible security in the stadium, and he was greeted with wild cheers from an admiring crowd.

I spent much of the time during the games with Cuba's canoe and kayak team coach Miguel Sanchez and their star athletes like Pérez, silver medalist Tatiana Valdés, and others. We had become good friends over the years when they participated in events in the U.S., Latin America and Europe, but this was their opportunity to proudly show off their homeland. The living facilities were comfortable, the food was delicious, the competition venues were superb, and the entire event was delightful.

That same year, I went to Barcelona for a pre-Olympic regatta used to test the course to be sure it would be ready for the real thing a year later. The mayor of Castel de Fels, the site of our competition course, hosted a reception for the officials. Coach Sanchez and I had never discussed politics because we didn't want to let it interfere with our personal relationship. At this reception, however, Sanchez pulled me aside to ask a question that had been bothering him. In Spanish, he asked, "President Bush is a smart man, isn't he?"

We were talking about the first President Bush, so I answered, "Yes, he is very smart."

Miguel followed, "He wants to get rid of Castro, doesn't he?"

"Yes, in a big way," I responded.

"Then," Miguel concluded, "why can't he figure it out? All he has to do is open his arms."

It was another of many confirmations of my firm belief that the U.S. embargo and persistent threats against Castro are the only reason he survived in power for nearly five decades. Castro was able rally his people in proud defiance against the colossal enemy to the North. Had U.S. policy changed, had we opened our arms decades ago, Castro would have been forced to account for his failures, and he would have fallen.

A few years after the Pan American Games in Havana, I answered a call in my Columbia, SC townhouse. *"Don Carlos, estoy aquí."* It was a familiar but unexpected voice.

"Estas donde?" I asked.

"Estoy en Miami," Ángel Pérez replied.

"Porque?" I asked.

"Para vivir, pero necisito un bote." Ángel had defected during a competition in Mexico and made his way to Miami. I asked why and he simply said to live, but he needed a boat. I owned a beautiful sleek mahogany racing craft, but I had retired from racing, so I offered to loan it to him. I never saw the boat again except at races, but Ángel made good use of it. He raced with the U.S. Olympic team twice.

≈

In 1992, Kay and I produced the U.S. Olympic Team trials on Lake Crabtree in Raleigh, North Carolina, and I was selected by the International Canoe Federation as an official for the Games in Barcelona. I believe most people involved with the Olympics over the years agree that Barcelona was among the best, if not the best, Games ever. The setting was perfect. The Mediterranean port city of Barcelona has a glorious and well preserved history, it lives and exudes art and culture in all its forms, and its topography of steep mountains as well as the sea and beaches make it exceptional in every way. The famous Las Ramblas public walkway is alive at all hours with shops, flowers, and caged bird vendors, street musicians, Gypsies, and cafes galore.

Virtually all of the sports venues had unique qualities that paid homage to the great artists with Barcelona connections like Picasso, Miro, and Gaudi. The Opening Ceremonies were unmatched in dramatic and cultural quality. No people or place in the world embodies the celebration of life quite like Barcelona, and it was all on display that glorious night.

The torch lighting ceremony in particular captured the elegance and human drama of the Barcelona Games. The flame was carried into the stadium and circled the field twice before reaching a platform where an archer wearing simple white slacks and shirt waited. The fuel-soaked point of his arrow was lit from the flame that had been ignited on Mount Olympus and circled the globe. The archer drew the string, the bow bent, and he aimed high and far. His fingers released and the flame shot straight and true to the top of the stadium and into the gas-filled cauldron that would be the Olympic flame for the next sixteen days. I was no more than twenty meters from the archer, and my cheap camera captured the moment better than the professional photographers from the world's best journals. That photo is among my proudest possessions.

The Olympic flame—and the Torch Relay that transports it from a Greek mountain top to the grand cauldron at the Olympic Stadium—unites the human family as no other symbol can. Wherever the torch goes, even on remote country roads in the dead of night on every continent, crowds line the route to cheer the flame and the ordinary citizens from anonymous towns and villages in their moment of glory in the celebration of sport and the best of humanity.

The Barcelona Olympic Organizing Committee understood that vision and they incorporated it into all aspects of the ceremony. Nine-thousand, three hundred and fifty-six athletes from 169 nations entered the stadium behind their national flags and wearing uniforms that depict their national colors and cultures. After all of the teams had been introduced and cheered, they gathered on the field. An enormous white flag with the five Olympic rings was unfurled and spread over the entire field and over the heads of all of the athletes. Then the announcer proclaimed, "You have entered the stadium representing your nations. You will leave representing Olympia, all one, all the same." It was a powerful expression of the fundamental value of the Olympic Games.

My role was to be a course umpire in the canoe and kayak racing program. We ride in a powerboat behind the competitors to make sure they do not veer out of their prescribed lanes and that they not ride the wake of another boat to gain advantage. Occasionally, there are close judgment calls, and some officials have been reprimanded for being too strict or too lenient, but it is not a difficult task.

A very bright and engaging young man had been assigned to drive my boat, and we enjoyed working together for the week of preparations and competition. After the Games were over, the Barcelona Olympic Organizing Committee cut the flag that had covered the athletes as a symbol of unity into eight inch by eight inch pieces. They framed each piece and gave them to the volunteers who had made the Games possible and so successful. Months after the Games closed, I received an unexpected package from Barcelona. It was the framed flag, sent to me as a gift from the young boat driver I had befriended. I was tremendously moved with his generosity, and I felt deeply honored to have a piece of that special flag. I put the note from my young friend aside to compose a special response in Spanish to express my gratitude, but somehow I misplaced it. I did not have his name or address; I was never able to thank him, and I have felt guilty about it ever since. But I continue to treasure that special gift.

Our team performed reasonably well in Barcelona, though it was not as impressive as the dramatic success in Seoul four years earlier. Greg Barton won a bronze medal in the 1,000 meter singles event (his fourth Olympic medal), and a few others came close to the medal platform. I had written articles for the U.S. Olympic Committee's magazine, and they asked me to write a chapter about our competition for their official commemorative book for the 1992 Games, which I was happy to do.

Kay and I had been deeply involved with the sport as athletes and officials for decades. Kay served as team manager for the U.S. sprint racing team at the 1996 Atlanta Olympics, and I was the announcer for the competition. After Atlanta, we looked at each other to consider sustaining our commitment through the next Olympiad in Sydney, Australia. Sydney was very appealing, but the work load was just too much. The challenges and struggles had taken a serious toll on our spirits and our finances, and our children needed our full attention, so we agreed to retire and allow others to take over. We had enjoyed it, and we had no regrets. It was a privilege to be part of the Olympic program for so many years. We don't regret moving on either.

LIFE ON THE LINE – THE TRANSPLANTS

Columbia and South Carolina never felt like home to either Kay or me. In fact, she had returned to Texas for a few years, and we sustained a long distance marriage. Grant was born in Texas during this period, and I wasn't even able to get there in time for the birth. We got together every month or two, but I missed too much of Grant's first years.

I did an adequate job of building the Cultural Council into a viable and growing institution, but I was much more interested in the challenges of my unpaid job as Chairman and CEO of the US Canoe and Kayak Team than my paid job with the Cultural Council. The *Christian Science Monitor* newspaper published a full page feature about my dedication to the volunteer position, and some on the Cultural Council board saw it. They were impressed, but not pleased. By 1988, my split loyalty became too obvious, and the Council and I had a moderately amicable parting of ways.

I had long fantasized about the freedom and flexibility of independent consulting, and I had already been hired for several small projects, so this was my chance. I would make a living as a consultant, work my own schedule, and maintain a stimulating leadership role with the US Canoe and Kayak Team. I operated out of our townhouse on Lake Murray for a while, but most of my work was in North Carolina, where I felt much more at home. Eventually, I relocated to a modest rental house on the edge of the Research Triangle Park between Raleigh, Durham, and Chapel Hill.

By the fall of 1991, life was good. Grant was growing, and Kay had come to North Carolina where she worked with Capital Consortium, a fundraising firm in Raleigh. Dambach and Associates, my consulting business, had gained traction and consistency, including a large contract to produce the Raleigh Bicentennial celebration. I was also helping the Piedmont Environmental Center conduct a capital fund drive and several arts councils and chambers of commerce hired me to help with their strategic planning. The US Canoe and Kayak Team selected Raleigh as the site for the 1992 Olympic team trials because Kay and I were there to make it happen, so we were busy and happy.

Kay was pregnant with our second child, and we looked forward to raising two brothers. (Alex had lived with us throughout his high school years, but by this time he had graduated from college and moved out on his own.) Shortly after midnight on November 10, Kay awoke and announced that it was time. We had arranged for our friend Beth Briggs to take care of Grant during the delivery, so we called and woke her with the news. We arranged to meet Beth at a gas station between our house and the hospital to minimize the travel time. Beth was there when we arrived so I pulled up right next to her car. Both car doors opened and our little boy was passed from one car to the other in the dead of night. If anyone had seen it, they would have called the police to report a kidnapping.

Kai seemed completely normal at birth, and the next morning we sent the obligatory announcements with his name, height, and weight and the standard "mother and child are doing well" message to family and friends. Soon, however, Kai became weak and unresponsive, so we took him back to Rex Hospital expecting a quick diagnosis and treatment for some mild virus or another inconsequential malady.

The medical team performed routine tests, and we waited with him in a nondescript room for the results. The phone rang; I answered, and a clear and firm voice on the other end said, "Brace yourself." We were told to prepare for a flurry of activity in our room, and an ambulance would rush our child to the Pediatric Intensive Care Unit at the University of North Carolina Hospital in Chapel Hill. We were to follow the ambulance in our car.

We learned Kai had been born without functioning kidneys, and his life was rapidly ebbing away. Minutes, even seconds were precious. There was no time for questions. Urgent action was all that mattered. Later, we learned his post urethral valves had not opened during gestation, therefore his kidneys never developed. It is a well known but rare condition.

The next forty-eight hours were a sleepless blur of fear, worry, questions, anxiety, exhaustion and profound compassion for our tiny child. He screamed in pain as doctors and nurses injected one needle and tube after another to infuse a complex cocktail of medicines and to extract blood for tests and fluid wastes to prevent toxicity. They did everything humanly possible to sustain his fragile life.

That first night, I called Alex to let him know what had happened. "I'll give him one of mine," he responded immediately. Support from the rest of the family was similar. Everyone should be so fortunate. We asked our Olympic champion friend Greg Barton to be Kai's Godfather, as he would need a strong and determined role model.

Kai spent the next two months in the hospital, and Kay never left his side. I did my best to care for Grant and make sure he knew he was still our special child and that all would be well. I had to maintain my work schedule as best I could. As a consultant, I got paid when I worked, and I made nothing when I didn't. There was no paid vacation or sick leave. Furthermore, we learned all too soon that our insurance had strict limitations on what would and would not be covered. "Usual and customary" costs were covered, but not much seemed to them to be usual or customary. The uncovered tab exceeded $20,000 in the first month, and it grew from there month after month. My annual income was less than $50,000, and Kay had to quit her job to take care of Kai. We were on a fast track to financial ruin while totally stressed about the survival of our child.

So our infant child was clinging to life; Kay was devoting every minute to him and unable to earn a living; two-year old Grant needed special attention to sustain his sense of security and significance in our home; I had to work as much as possible to make enough to cover the rent, food, car and insurance; medical bills were mounting at many times our monthly income, and we were committed to produce the 1992 Olympic Team trials in just a few months. Fortunately, my mother was able to come from Ohio, and Kay's mother came in from Texas at various times to help. Support from friends in Raleigh was fabulous— especially Beth.

Kai survived because of Kay. We have the greatest appreciation for the medical team at University Hospital in Chapel Hill. They were caring compassionate and competent. Nevertheless, without Kay's absolute devotion and determination to monitor everything that was done, Kai would not have reached his first birthday, let alone graduate from high school and move on to college with a bright future. We survived as a family, and we even produced a reasonably good Olympic team trials event. Steve Kelley and others in our canoe and kayak family came in and saved the day. I had not been able to adequately prepare, and I made several stupid decisions. I'll blame it on stress rather than admit to basic incompetence.

Kai required a cocktail of a dozen medicines injected into a gastro tube every hour on the hour, twenty-four hours per day, every day for the first five years of his life. Kay handled all of it, though I did my best to provide support. My primary job was to make absolutely sure Grant received the attention he needed and deserved while trying to maintain my consulting career and sustain sufficient income to avoid a complete financial collapse. It was an incredible struggle.

While most of that period was filled with worry, stress, and sleepless nights, our family grew closer and stronger. I fondly remember an evening when I had been working at my desk on a consulting project as well as preparation for the canoe and kayak team trials. Kay had prepared fried chicken for us, and three year old Grant wanted to bring it to me. He walked into my office, and announced proudly, "Here, Dad, here's your chicken." As he spoke, the plate slowly tipped forward in his little hands, and the chicken slipped off and fell to the floor. He looked down and said calmly, "Oops, there's your chicken." It was one of the few moments of genuine laughter we had enjoyed in months. Grant was a precious and precocious child, and he gave us many delightful experiences and memories. Next to Kay, he is the hero of this story.

That spring, shortly after the team trials, we moved to Maryland as I had taken a job as President of the National Council of Returned Peace Corps Volunteers based in Washington, D.C. With our move, Kai's treatment team switched to Johns Hopkins Children's Hospital in Baltimore. By age two, however, he desperately needed a transplant to avoid dialysis and to stay alive. I proved to be a slightly better match than Kay, so I got to go first. The date was set, and we made all necessary preparations. My mother was to come and take care of Grant; Kay would look after Kai and me, and the board and staff would sustain the office during my absence. However, a week before the procedure, mom was diagnosed with cancer, and she would require surgery in Columbus, Ohio, at exactly the same time as our transplant. Fortunately, Kay's mother was able to come from Texas as a substitute.

The day of the surgery began with a light moment when Kay and I joked with the doctors in the prep room about the possibility of getting two procedures for the price of one. We weren't about to have more kids, so we thought they might give me a vasectomy while I was under anesthesia and they had a scalpel in hand. They discussed it quite seriously, but we didn't have a referral from my primary care physician, so it wouldn't be covered. Nevertheless, it gave everyone a good laugh, and it broke some of the tension.

On the operating table, my left kidney came out just fine, but everything went downhill from there. My kidney was placed in Kai's right abdomen, but there were complications with the connections, and the fluids weren't flowing properly. The prospects of sufficient flow through the graft kidney were dim from the beginning, and the operation was on the brink of failure.

Meanwhile back in Columbus, my mother's husband and my step-father, Gene Good, never made it to the hospital to comfort her. He collapsed and died suddenly and unexpectedly late the night before the dual family surgeries. All of us loved, even adored, Gene, and this loss was both unexpected and devastating. To make matters worse, we couldn't be there to comfort my mother when she needed us. Fortunately, my sister Charlou, who has always been the family glue, was there to care for her. As I emerged from deep sedation, Kay broke both of the dreadful stories to me. I managed to cling to denial in my drug induced stupor as long as I could, but soon the bad dream became all too real.

The medical team at Hopkins did all they could to revive the prospects for the graft kidney, but several procedures failed. Before each one, we were advised of the reasons for the procedure, the probability of success, and the risks of adverse consequences. It seemed to us that the negative outcome was always our fate. The worst was a biopsy procedure to determine the health of the graft kidney. We were advised there was a remote possibility that the instrument used to snip a piece of organ tissue might rupture a vessel and cause internal bleeding. In Kai's case, it hit not one, but two vessels, and it caused a fistula, further weakening the kidney function.

Kay monitored everything the doctors and nurses did, and she prevented inappropriate medications and tests any number of times. Some of them could have been fatal. We know from recent reports that thousands of patients die in hospitals every year due to mistakes. Without Kay's knowledge of medical science and her determination, Kai may well have been among them. My own recovery was delayed by an infection along the incision line. It was not a big deal, but it was yet another in a series of complications, and it delayed my own recovery.

As the week went on, the news of Gene's death, my mother's cancer, and the declining prospects for the success of the transplant settled in. We grew ever more fatigued and distressed. I spoke by phone with my brother George, and he detected instantly that we were in serious emotional trouble. He canceled his appointments and came on the next plane from Detroit. He spent the rest of the week with us, and without his love and support, I fear we might all have collapsed in exhaustion and an all-family nervous breakdown. Having George, the Deputy Dean of the Wayne State University Medical School, in our corner was an added bonus. I am convinced the Hopkins medical staff raised their performance a notch knowing he was there watching.

My kidney provided limited service to Kai's little and vulnerable body for two years, but it was doomed to fail. When it did, Kay had the honor of giving him one of hers. This time, all went well for everyone. Her kidney has been filtering blood and balancing Kai's chemistry quite well for the last fourteen years. He still needs dozens of pills every day, and he has a few side effects from the combination of powerful medicines, but he is alive; he is resilient; he is courageous, and he is happy. We are all grateful to the medical team and to our friends and family who have sustained us. Kay and George saved us.

As for the insurance industry and the U.S. health care system, I have nothing but contempt. I criticize the system, not the doctors, nurses and technicians. They do marvelous work. Not perfect, mind you, but their skills produce miracles. The insurance industry, on the other hand, left us nearly destitute, and they have made Kay's life miserable. They refuse to pay bills that are obviously appropriate, and they make her fight over details. They waste time and impose emotional stress at every opportunity.

Fortunately, end stage renal failure—kidney failure—is covered by Medicare regardless of age. Kai went on Medicare before he turned two. Medicare, government run health insurance, made the transplant and

Kai's survival possible. Unfortunately, however, only the treatments directly attributable to Kai's kidney function are eligible for Medicare. Others are not, so we still have to wrestle with private insurance. Our friends in other countries take pity on us for living in the U.S. with our miserable health care financing system. They are right. Our system is pitiful. I cannot understand why Congress refuses to make Medicare universal. It works, and it costs far, far less than the current dreadful system. Finally, in 2010, we have modest reform in the system. It may protect against the problems we encountered, and it will assure Kai access to insurance when he is on his own. That relieves one of my greatest concerns. The reform doesn't go as far as I would wish, but I'm pleased to see some progress.

We were sinking rapidly into financial ruin, and the stress affected every minute of every day. My former Peace Corps trainer Sam Farr had been elected to the U.S. Congress, and we reconnected when he moved into his Washington office. Sam kept tabs on me and my emotional state, and he offered to conduct a campaign to raise the funds to reduce our debt. I refused over and over, on the basis that others have greater needs than me. Privately, I was embarrassed to admit our need. However, late one Friday evening the phone rang in my office. "Look," Congressman Farr said emphatically, "You have spent your life doing things to help others. When you do it, you expect them to accept it and appreciate it. It's time for you to accept our help and appreciate it." What could I say? Checkmate. I was trapped, but also grateful. With great reluctance, I finally agreed to let him help. It was one of the most difficult decisions of my life, but it was necessary.

Sam enlisted Maureen Orth and Steve Werner, two of the best known and most highly respected Returned Peace Corps Volunteers to help. Maureen had served in Colombia with Sam, she is a prominent journalist known to *Vanity Fair* readers for her rich prose and incisive inquiries into the lives of the rich and famous, and for her high profile marriage to *Meet the Press* host Tim Russert. Steve had been president of the National Council of Returned Peace Corps Volunteers, he was a leader in the Friends of Korea group, and he happened to be the nephew of Vince Lombardi, the Green Bay Packers coach for whom the Super Bowl trophy is named. We had an all-star team on our side.

Sam provided overall leadership and sent dozens of letters. His wonderful administrative aid Rochelle Dornet managed the whole process. Maureen handled the donated funds, and Steve, a seasoned fundraising professional, devised the strategy and built the donor lists. Sam, Maureen and Steve reached out to the Peace Corps community and they found friends from other facets of my life from all over the country. Donations poured in. I hated knowing we had become dependent on the charity of others, but Sam was right. We were desperate, and they pulled us out.

In the midst of the campaign to raise funds for our medical bills, I received the annual solicitation for contributions from the alumni associations at Oklahoma State and the Babcock School at Wake Forest. I had always sent at least $50, if not $100 to each school, and I usually responded to their special fund requests with larger gifts as well. However with others raising funds for us, I felt obligated to guard every dollar in our bank account. I sent a token $25 to OSU, but I sent a letter to Wake Forest's Babcock School expressing disappointment that I would not be able to contribute, and I explained why.

Several months later, we received a check for $2,000 to Kai's medical fund from the Babcock Alumni Association. The school Dean John McKinnon was retiring, and he and the alumni association had agreed that a donation to the fund was the best retirement gift they could give him. Obviously, the Babcock family had absorbed the message Frank Schilagi had taught us back in 1977. There is more to business than profit. I was tremendously moved, and I have been as loyal to the school as possible ever since.

A HIGH PRIVILEGE

Back in the late 1960s, while serving as a Peace Corps Volunteer in Colombia, I envisioned a strong alliance among all of the volunteers when we returned home. We would bring the values that attracted us and the perspective we had gained during training and service back to America, and we would change the world. My false assumption was that everyone else in the Peace Corps shared the same values and perspective, and we would all be motivated to be world changers. I was wrong on all counts.

Volunteers are motivated to serve by a wide range of factors and values. The experiences overseas produce different attitudes, depending on the location and the tasks. Furthermore, returned volunteers fall across the entire political spectrum. The liberal, Birkenstock wearing, tree-hugging, peacenik stereotype does not fit reality. Nevertheless the community of Returned Peace Corps Volunteers is a special and unique club, and I am tremendously proud to be part of it.

A small association of former volunteers had, indeed, been created at about the time I was in Colombia, but its focus was on Vietnam and against the U.S. government—not on overall peace or social and political development for the world's poor. The Committee of Returned Volunteers (CRV) demonstrated against the war in Vietnam—a position I shared—but they also protested the Peace Corps itself—a position I and most returned volunteers opposed. The CRV even invaded and took over the Peace Corps office as a protest. From their perspective, the entire U.S. government was the enemy, and the Peace Corps was part of the government and complicit in America's global imperialist agenda. All of it had to be stopped, according to CRV doctrine.

I couldn't agree with the broader agenda of the CRV group, so I never joined, and it faded away as the Vietnam War came to an end. It took a decade for a new network of returned volunteers to form and much longer for it to gain traction. At the same time, however, local groups had been organized in places like Chicago, Northern California, Washington, and even in less urban places like Iowa and Nebraska. Groups also formed around the countries of service—Friends of Kenya, Friends of Thailand, Friends of Colombia, etc. Re-creation of a national network began in 1979 when leaders of several local and "country of service" groups met in New York and Washington, and established the National Council of Returned Peace Corps Volunteers (NCRPCV). In 1986, a large celebration of the 25th anniversary of the founding of the Peace Corps provided a major boost to the organization.

Unfortunately, however, the organization was poorly funded and it lacked a coherent mission and meaningful programs and services. Eventually, the NCRPCV produced a decent magazine, *WorldView*; it maintained a database of members, and it sponsored an annual conference, but that was about it. I was selected to become the CEO in the spring of 1992, but Board Chair Doug Siglin advised me they had no funds to pay my salary. Membership was low and declining, revenues were low and declining, and morale was low and declining. Furthermore, the organization had achieved too little to justify significant support. I was on the brink of bankruptcy myself due to our medical bills, so taking the job was foolish.

I took the job. Instead of obstacles, I saw opportunity. What could be better than the Peace Corps community? Surely, we could make this work and once again make a difference in the world.

Before I started, Doug conducted a desperate fund drive that generated enough revenue to cover my meager salary and basic operating expenses for a few months. I would have to raise enough to keep it going from there. The challenge was so daunting that I seriously doubted it could be done. I missed several paychecks until enough cash came in the door to sustain us. I came to work on the Metro, and I often looked up to the light at the end of the long escalator at Dupont Circle wondering if it was a light at the end of the tunnel or the proverbial on-coming train.

We set out to boost membership and dues revenue, and build a reliable donor base. To do so, we would have to improve the magazine, strengthen member services, and create meaningful programs that could offer opportunities for Returned Peace Corps Volunteers (RPCVs) to apply their unique skills for domestic and international peace and progress. To do that, we would have to completely change the board structure and discard the established cumbersome operating procedures that handcuffed us. And we had to do it all without increasing expenses.

The board had micromanaged the organization nearly to death, and it had discouraged people with national leadership skills and significant resources from serving. To radically change operating procedures, Doug laid down the law. He announced that no one on the board was to communicate with me in any way shape or form for the first six months unless I asked them for help. This was to protect me from the constant and contradictory intrusions and demands from board members that had caused my predecessors grief and produced the near collapse of the organization. We also developed a new set of procedures that gave me complete control of operations. Fortunately, almost everyone on the board knew they had a serious problem and that a more conventional role for the board—policy, program, and financial oversight, and revenue development, but not intrusions into operations and management—was essential.

We had the benefit of Bob Gale on our side. Bob had been the very first director of recruitment and selection for the Peace Corps, and he was one of the nation's leading experts on nonprofit governance. He was president of the Association of Governing Boards of Universities and Colleges and the founder of the National Center for Nonprofit Boards. Bob knew the appropriate roles and responsibilities of boards, and he knew the NCRPCV board was doing everything wrong—and he told them so.

Bob, Doug, and I developed the new set of operating policies and procedures with help from former Peace Corps Director Kevin O'Donnell. When we presented our resolution to the board, one member of the old guard made a motion to amend the proposal in a way that would, in essence, negate the entire intent of our proposal. Doug politely looked at the board and asked if there was a second to the motion to amend. There was a long pause. He asked again if anyone cared to second the motion. Bob, Kevin, Doug and I glanced at each other with a slight grin, as Doug announced, "The motion to amend dies for lack of a second." The motion to approve the new policies and procedures was then approved with only one dissenting vote.

Without those changes, it would have been impossible to function, and I would have been forced to resign. With it, we had a chance of getting things done. It took several years to make all of the changes we wanted, and resources were always tight, but we were remarkably successful. We persuaded the Peace Corps to allow us to adopt a much more effective name, the National Peace Corps Association (NPCA). The new name indicated that we welcomed former Peace Corps staff, families and friends and not just former volunteers. It was also shorter, and it was easier to remember, to say, and to understand.

The office was on "S" Street in a row house just north of Dupont Circle, my favorite Washington neighborhood. As I recall, there were five of us on the staff, and we were stressed with financial pressures and conflicting demands from the members and the board. My first hire was Maria Nazareth, a remarkable young lady who had recently moved to the U.S. from Goa in India. I never understood the complex immigration rules, but for some reason she needed to work without pay for three months in order to qualify for a work visa. I was more than willing to hire a competent finance manager who wouldn't be paid for a few months.

Maria was a godsend. The organization had so mismanaged past grants from the U.S. Agency for International Development (USAID) that we were prohibited from applying for more. Maria re-created all of the records and accounting entries for those past projects; she found the people who had done contract work; got them to sign time sheets; submitted amended reports to USAID, and she enabled us to regain our contract eligibility. She also brought Vic Zapanta, a dedicated CPA from the Philippines, in as our auditor and financial advisor. Together, we developed a solid financial management system.

≈

Our only hope for financial stability was to increase membership and to generate significant donations from financially successful returned volunteers. We launched a major membership development campaign that produced thousands of new members and tens of thousands of dollars in new revenue, but it was not close to sufficient for us to survive, let alone thrive. I proposed a new level of giving that had never been considered—a special "Director's Circle" for donors of $1,000 or more. Historically, the largest individual donations had been a few hundred dollars, and the combined giving of all board members the previous year had been less than $500.

Most members advised against such extravagant expectations. Having worked in the arts, however, I knew what real philanthropy was all about. Thousand-dollar donations are actually very modest. Five-figure donations are expected for small town cultural institutions. Why would we not seek at least four-figure donations for a national organization seeking to have a significant impact on peace and the quality of life in developing countries?

In spite of the objections, we established the "Circle" and nearly seventy people joined in the first year. We gave each of the founding members of the "Circle" a copy of the *National Geographic World Atlas* with the Director's Circle name and logo embossed in gold leaf as a special gift. Ron Tschetter, a very successful businessman from Minneapolis, was among the first to join, and he eventually became NPCA board chair, and then he was appointed Peace Corps Director for the last three years of the Bush Administration.

My next task was to help the organization re-define its mission and to give returned volunteers, former staff, and others a reason to join and support the organization. I believed we had to be more than a repository of addresses and phone numbers and a facilitator of periodic pot luck dinners for former volunteers to indulge in the strange but delicious cuisine of our countries of service.

WorldView magazine was NPCA's primary membership benefit, and it helped build our identity. Unfortunately, the board had never embraced the publication and it had been under-funded. Several articles and stories were of high quality, but its appearance was thin and unimpressive. I believed it could be a vital resource, and that it must have a solid look and feel as well as quality content.

I had corresponded with David Arnold who was working on a journalism project in Kenya through the Fulbright program, and I was impressed with his background and skills. I'm no genius, but hiring David to revitalize the magazine was a stroke of genius. It took several years, but we turned *WorldView* into a solid publication with a unique and vital perspective on the people, places, and issues of the developing countries of the world. Eventually, Jim Collins joined our team to sell advertising, and *WorldView* became a real magazine worthy of newsstand exposure. Unfortunately the audience for magazines about the third world is very limited, so it never became a large seller or profitable. Nevertheless, I will always be proud of our contribution to a broader knowledge of and appreciation of the least known people and cultures in the world.

The "third goal" of the Peace Corps is to bring our experiences home to help Americans better understand and appreciate the people and cultures of remote parts of the world. Approximately thirty percent of all Returned Peace Corps Volunteers pursue careers in education. That meant more than 30,000 teachers with Peace Corps experience in the schools of America's towns and cities. We felt we could form a network of RPCV teachers to help them bring a global perspective to their students. The myopia, and lack of global knowledge and understanding among Americans of all ages, is well known and documented. Perhaps we could have a meaningful impact on thousands of young people who might become adults with an appreciation of and respect for other people and cultures.

We called it Global TeachNet, and I hired Anne Baker to run the program. We never reached as many teachers as we would have liked, but the program remains in place fifteen years later, and tens of thousands of students are better informed because of it. Anne is still there as Vice President of the organization and she is a model of intelligence, quality leadership, and stability.

≈

The Peace Corps had been in existence for over thirty years, but no returned volunteer had ever been appointed by the President to be the director. Virtually the entire RPCV community felt slighted and insulted. We were determined to force the candidate elected in November 1992 to appoint an RPCV, and my job was to make it happen. We found people in both parties with strong connections with the candidates, and we pressed them as hard as possible.

Elaine Chao was the Peace Corps Director at the time, having been appointed by President George H. W. Bush. I got along well with Elaine, but everyone knew she was not the right person for the job. Even Elaine knew it. She had no concept of the unique qualities of the agency or the motivations and values of the volunteers. She and I talked about it on several occasions, and I became convinced that she would never understand why anyone would voluntarily spend two years living in a strange land under poverty conditions just to be helpful and to learn more about their people and cultures. Elaine herself would never do such a thing. She had always put herself on a fast track to power. She left the Peace Corps even before the 1992 election to become President of United Way of America, and I was one of her references for the job. Later she became Secretary of Labor for all eight years of the George W. Bush Presidency.

Candidate Bill Clinton was our primary target to ensure that the next Peace Corps Director would be an RPCV. Several of our members had connections to his campaign, but none were stronger than Maureen Orth. Maureen had served in Colombia, and she was a famous journalist married to Tim Russert, the host of Meet the Press. Maureen had clout. We were told by people who know that Maureen cornered candidate Clinton at a very "chic" reception at the home of George-town's premier hostess Pamela Harriman shortly before the election. Maureen demanded and secured a promise from Clinton that the next Peace Corps Director would be an RPCV. Finally satisfied that Clinton was sincere, Maureen let him go.

After the election, we felt confident we would succeed, but we took no chances. I met with every Member of Congress who had served in the Peace Corps or on Peace Corps staff or had strong connections with the agency. Every one of them agreed with our position, and they promised to let the Clinton transition team know. Congressman Jim Moody had been the original Peace Corps country director in Pakistan, and he had aspirations of becoming the Peace Corps director himself, so he wanted to be sure we would accept a former staff member. I indicated we were determined to have an actual RPCV, but his credentials made him a strong candidate—just not one we could support at this time. I doubt any non-RPCV could have been confirmed without our consent. *Washington Post* columnist Al Kaman (also an RPCV) wrote about the influence of the "powerful National Council of Returned Peace Corps

Volunteers."

At the same time, we began to hear rumors and read newspaper stories that Kathleen Kennedy Townsend, daughter of Robert F. Kennedy and the rising political star among her generation of Kennedys, wanted the Peace Corps Director position, and she was campaigning vigorously. Mary McGrory, the brilliant and esteemed columnist for the *Washington Post,* was covering the story, and she seemed to enjoy the emerging confrontation between a Kennedy and the former Volunteers. I had admired McGrory from afar for decades, so I felt quite privileged when she called to ask for my opinion. She asked the right questions, and she told the story to the American people accurately and forcefully.

As the story was gaining intensity, Kathleen called. She told me she had been meeting with Members of Congress to generate support for her candidacy for Peace Corps Director, and that everyone told her the same thing: she would have to secure my approval before they could endorse her. She asked if we could meet.

I had been inspired by President Kennedy to be active in civic life and to join the Peace Corps. Those of us who served in Latin America at the time were affectionately called "hijos de Kennedy" sons or daughters of Kennedy. It was a strong and powerful connection that I revered. Furthermore, I had never met a Kennedy, and out of loyalty to the memory of the fallen President, I felt an obligation to respect everyone in the Kennedy family. I would grant her request to meet, but not her appeal for an endorsement. From the moment Kathleen called until I met with her, I thought about little else. How would I face President Kennedy's niece and tell her no?

I finally developed the exact words to use, and I practiced them many times. Kathleen came to my shabby office, and we had a pleasant get-acquainted chat. Then she popped the question. What would she have to do to secure my support? With practiced timing, pacing, and intonation, I replied, "Join the Peace Corps; return in two years, and you will have my support."

Kathleen was visibly taken aback. I think she expected me to offer some kind of deal that would make it possible for her to be nominated, but my terms were clear and firm. "You mean it?" she asked, and I simply said, "yes." We talked a bit longer and she left.

We had planned a reception for the leading candidates in conjunction with a board meeting, and I had extended an invitation to Kathleen even before our encounter. About a week passed after we met, and it was a few days before the reception when Kathleen called. "I have thought about what you said, and I have discussed it with Sarge (Shriver) and others, and I have to admit you are right. The next Peace Corps Director should be an RPCV, and I am withdrawing my candidacy. But can I come to your party anyway?" I was relieved and extremely pleased. I told her we would love to have her attend. She did, and we all enjoyed the evening.

The Clinton transition team asked us for a list of preferred candidates, and we provided them with two lists. When they wanted my assurance that everyone on the list was an RPCV, I knew our campaign had succeeded. One long list had the names of all of our members who had indicated that they wanted the position. Not wanting to offend any of our dues paying members, we included everyone in alphabetical order. The short list, the one the transition team took seriously, had ten names, and they were priority ranked based on our perception of qualifications and leadership skills. Donna Shalala and John Garamendi would have been at the top, but both deferred. Shalala was in line to become Secretary of Health and Human Services, and John became Deputy Secretary of the Interior. John wanted his wife Patti on the list, and she was. Shalala highly recommended her friend Carol Bellamy. Carol had been President of the New York City Council and she was known to be a prominent FOB—Friend of Bill (Clinton). We made it clear that anyone among the top ten would be a solid choice. Clinton selected Bellamy, and she was nominated and confirmed. Thus, she became the very first Returned Peace Corps Volunteer to be appointed Director of the Peace Corps.

Patti Garamendi became the Director of Volunteer Recruitment and Selection for the Peace Corps, a position held by our dear friend Bob Gale back in the very beginning of the agency in the early 1960s. Chuck Baquet, former ambassador to Djibouti, became deputy director, and several other friends moved into senior positions. I often reflect on the extraordinary privilege of a direct association with the leaders of the Peace Corps, possibly the best instrument ever created to advance the relationship between the people of the U.S. and the people of the rest of the world. (My good friends with the Fulbright Scholars program and the International Visitors program would argue that point, but we all agree that the combination of the Fulbright, International Visitors and Peace Corps programs have been essential for positive global relations.)

≈

We held the 1994 NPCA annual conference on the campus of the University of California, Berkeley. The opening session had far too many speakers, but we had to accommodate a long list of dignitaries from the university and the local group. By the time I was to speak, we were already two hours overtime. I gave the best speech of my life, or at least the one most appreciated by the audience. I had prepared a 15 to 20 minute report on our progress and my vision for the future, but instead I stood before our members, and announced, "I know this has gone on far too long. You will see and hear more from me throughout the conference. So I will close my remarks now so we can move on." I received a thunderous standing ovation.

We had just changed our name to the National Peace Corps Association, and our members were still getting used to it. However, I had failed to take advantage of the conference to build new-name identity. One of our members who specialized in marketing noticed the oversight, and called it to our attention. A special session was on the agenda that could attract national television coverage, and we didn't even have our new name and logo on the podium. To my mind, it was too late to do anything about it, but our innovative board chair, Doug Siglin, went to work.

Early in the morning, I walked past a quick copy shop, and noticed Doug at the copy machine bare from the waist up. He had taken off his t-shirt that had our name and logo on it. He photocopied it in color onto a large sheet of paper, and then framed it for placement on the front of the podium.

Shortly thereafter, I stood before a packed auditorium to introduce a video of President Clinton addressing our members followed by addresses by Secretary of State Warren Christopher, Senator Harris Wofford and Congressman Sam Farr. Our name and logo were proudly displayed on the podium for the audience and the television cameras. Only Doug and I knew how it had been made. When Doug retired from the board, we gave him that framed masterpiece as a gift.

The president said nice things about us and about me, but that was expected. After all, I wrote his script. My first draft said nothing about my own work, but the speechwriters in the White House insisted I include something personal, so I did. President Clinton said, "I want to thank Chic Dambach for his tireless efforts to build this organization into the powerful force it has become." I have the tape, and maybe someday my grandkids will appreciate the reference to grandpa by the President of the United States.

I also worked with Secretary Christopher's speech writers, but it was a frustrating experience. They wanted him to talk about the major issues involving the geopolitical powers, but our audience would want to know about policies for third-world development and combating violence, hunger, and poverty. One draft after another would come in for my review, and I would send back language to insert about the world where Peace Corps Volunteers serve. They finally accepted some of my language, but it was limited and grudging. We were disappointed to learn from this experience that this President and this foreign policy team were not serious about our priority issues. Wofford and Farr, on the other hand, knew us and our issues thoroughly, and they spoke to them with profound understanding and commitment.

While I am the world's biggest fan of the Peace Corps, I have always been troubled by the inability of the agency and the volunteers to do more for peace. We call it the Peace Corps, but volunteers receive no training in conflict resolution or mediation, and many countries with years of Peace Corps Volunteers serving in the villages remain among the most violent in the world. Places like the Congo, Ethiopia, Sri Lanka, Colombia, and even Nepal come to mind.

At the same time, I know and appreciate the reason the Peace Corps must stay out of the politically-sensitive arena of violent conflict. The Peace Corps only serves where and when it is invited by the host country. If we were to become entangled with conflict issues, we could be expelled never to return. However, former Volunteers, the NPCA constituents, are not constrained by U.S. government policies. We are free agents, and many RPCVs have developed remarkable skills in problem solving, diplomacy and conflict resolution.

Ambassador Chris Hill, for example served in the Peace Corps before becoming the extraordinary diplomat who has helped ease tensions with North Korea, and now represents the US in Iraq. I am told by colleagues who work for peace in Iraq that Hill has changed the tone tremendously and the prospect for a positive outcome has improved beyond anyone's dreams. Michael Lund, who served in Ethiopia, is another peacebuilding RPCV of special distinction. He is known and respected worldwide as a leading expert on violence prevention. These two and many, many others are among the world's leading peacebuilders.

RPCVs have several unique advantages over anyone else who would attempt to intervene in violent conflicts in far off places. First and foremost, we have credibility because the Peace Corps is admired worldwide. Furthermore, we know and respect the people, culture, language and terrain of the countries where we serve better than almost anyone. We know how to listen. Most diplomats, foreign aid workers, missionaries, and business people who live and work in other countries spend most of their time in U.S. and English speaking enclaves—ghettos separate and apart from the local population. Peace Corps Volunteers, on the other hand, become totally immersed in their communities—most live hours from the nearest American. We embrace and live the local language, food, music and dances. I still consider myself to be part Colombian because of my experience in Bogota and Cartagena.

≈

In April 1994, the unspeakable genocide broke out in Rwanda. I followed the tragic story through the news services with deep concern and disappointment that neither the U.S. government nor the UN intervened to prevent or stop the carnage. Within the span of 100 days, the Hutu majority killed 800,000 Tutsi and Tutsi sympathizers with machetes and small arms in a well planned and efficiently implemented slaughter. A few weeks after the attacks started, Steve Smith called from San Francisco to see what the RPCV community would do about it. Steve had been outraged by the indifference to genocide expressed by U.S. citizens calling in to talk radio shows. Coming out of World War II and the Holocaust, we as a nation had declared, "never again" to genocide. We and the rest of the world community had promised to step in and prevent or stop genocide wherever and whenever it might happen. Yet, when it has happened, we have done nothing—not in Guatemala, not in the killing fields of Cambodia, not in Timor-Leste, and, most remarkably, not in Rwanda. The belated intervention to stop the Serbian attacks on Muslims in Kosovo may be the only exception.

Steve and I decided we would do whatever we could, even if our government refused to act to prevent or stop the killing. Obviously, we couldn't fly to Kigali and yank machetes out of the hands of the *genocidaires*. We could and did, however, mobilize a small group of RPCVs (mostly people who had served in Rwanda) to go back as soon as it was reasonably safe to help establish stability and begin reconciliation and reconstruction. Rick Barton, the head of the newly created Office of Transition Initiatives at USAID, recognized the unique value of RPCVs in this desperate emergency environment. He and I reached a hand-shake agreement that USAID would cover the costs for our initiative. There was no time to plan. We needed to get there, determine what was needed most and start doing it. That was the operating plan, and there was no budget. There were no words or numbers on paper, just a mu-tual commitment to a vital mission. We would do whatever needed to be done to help achieve stability and security for the survivors.

I informed the NPCA board about our initiative, and many were horrified. I can't blame them. We were in serious financial distress, we were understaffed, and we had never even considered taking on a project like this. It was absolutely irresponsible from an organizational standpoint. Yet, from a moral standpoint it would have been unspeak-ably irresponsible to do nothing. I told the board I was committed to the project, and if it failed, they would have my resignation. Reluctantly they gave their assent.

Steve, along with John Berry and his wife Carol Pott Berry flew to Kigali and returned with their report. They arrived in Washington at about 5 pm, and gave me a quick briefing. At 9 pm we found ourselves at the State Department providing an analysis of the situation and rec-ommendations for immediate action for the Africa Bureau and US-AID officials. Establishing safety and security for the survivors was the first priority, and the UN had recruited and deployed over fifty human rights monitors for this purpose. However, they had not been trained, they had no plan of action, and they were holing up in a hotel accom-plishing nothing. We agreed to develop a training program and action plan for them. Many, if not most of the top human rights experts in the U.S. were RPCVs, and we brought them together to provide training and develop a plan. After meeting in my office, the team of experts flew off to Kigali and carried out the project.

We also linked over a dozen of our members with relief and development agencies such as CARE and the International Rescue Committee for desperately needed services. The former Peace Corps Volunteers were particularly valuable because they knew the language and culture. For them, Rwanda was a second home. They would get off the plane and go right to work.

At the same time, the UN's Rwanda relief mission based in Geneva was badly understaffed and inadequately equipped, and they asked us for help. We recruited five RPCVs who had served in or near Rwanda who would be able to help coordinate the UN's work with thorough knowledge of the country. All of them had other jobs in various parts of the country, but they quit their secure jobs or arranged for extended leave for this vital project. They did not know each other, and they had no idea what they would be expected to do. They just knew something had to be done, and they were willing to do it. We arranged for them to fly to Washington in the morning for a brief meeting before departing in the afternoon for Geneva.

The day before their departure, we received a call from the UN's Rwanda mission control center in Geneva telling us they desperately needed the help, but they had no computers for our people. Computers would be absolutely essential for the project, but it would take weeks or even months to navigate the UN procurement process. I knew an RPCV in Chicago who owned the largest computer retail store in the city, and I called him to explain the situation. We needed five notebook computers with basic Microsoft software as well as networking and internet capacities by 10AM the next day. I told him I thought he would be reimbursed with USAID funds, but I couldn't guarantee it. If we were paid, he would be paid. If we weren't; he wouldn't. He checked his inventory and told me, "You'll have them in the morning."

The next morning our team members arrived one by one between 9 and 10 am, and a big box with five notebook computers was delivered by FedEx right at 10. We had just a few hours to organize, distribute the computers and get them back to Dulles airport to depart for Geneva. We also had to at least boot up each computer and load the software to make it appear they were not new so they could pass through customs as personal property—not new machines for resale at the other end. Someone in our group remembered they would need adaptors for European power outlets, so we sent our staff on an emergency mission to purchase five power adaptors. We introduced everyone, completed testing of the computers and software, acquired the adaptors, and explained, as best we could, how the whole operation would work. At the curb outside our office, we flagged down two cabs, pushed our colleagues in, and off they went to help avert a return to violence in a far off land few Americans had ever heard of and even fewer cared about.

Building on our initiative, John and Carol Pott Berry worked with CARE and gathered 100 genocide survivors to reflect on what had happened and why. The report on that group catharsis is documented in a powerful book, *Genocide in Rwanda*, edited by John and Carol. It is the story of Rwanda told by Rwandans from their perspective. It is both chilling and insightful.

I wasn't there, so I can't describe in any detail the work our team did in Rwanda. All I know is that it was exceptional. About a year later I attended a reception for Congressman Tony Hall, and I overheard a conversation between Gene Dewey, executive director of the Congressional Hunger Caucus, and another reception guest. "You should have seen what those former Peace Corps Volunteers did in Rwanda," he said. "They were responsible for saving hundreds of thousands of lives." A moment later, Gene saw me there and introduced me to others as the head of the Peace Corps organization that had orchestrated the highly important and effective initiative in Rwanda. It was a powerful independent validation of our effort.

Rick Barton was true to his word. We kept him and his very able deputy Mike Mahdessian informed at every step, and with few exceptions, they approved and agreed to fund every new initiative on the spot. We actually worked within the USAID bureaucracy quickly and efficiently. People in the international development field know that is rare—perhaps unprecedented. The NPCA was reimbursed for all expenses, including the computers, plus a modest amount for overhead. I did not have to resign, and I have been grateful to Rick ever since. We have sustained contact and we collaborate on ideas and plans regularly. Rick has become a frequent guest on major national news programs providing insight into the most difficult and complex foreign policy issues, and President Obama appointed him as the U.S. Representative on the Economic and Social Council of the United Nations, with the rank of Ambassador.

Our project received no publicity and very few RPCVs ever knew it happened, but I will always believe it was the finest thing ever done by our community. Steve, John, Carol and the people who sacrificed their careers to implement the program deserve all of the credit. They are unsung heroes of the highest order.

≈

The Rwanda project demonstrated the value of RPCVs responding to special needs. Based on that experience, we created an Emergency Response Network (ERN) with a database of RPCVs who were prepared to take time and respond to special needs throughout the world. The primary use of the ERN turned out to be monitoring elections in volatile regions. The International Foundation for Electoral Systems found our members to be among the best available. In most cases, our people knew the language and culture wherever they were assigned, and they were comfortable living and working under adverse conditions. Many others who tend to volunteer for such assignments expect the comforts of home and have difficulty adapting. Not RPCVs. Living without a comfortable bed or hot shower just reminds us of the good old days.

The Clinton administration was determined to make its mark on national service, and it created a new program called AmeriCorps. I was all for the new initiative even though in reality it simply created a variation on the well established but little known Volunteers in Service to America (VISTA) program. Harris Wofford was the lead Senator drafting the bill authorizing the new program, and Clinton's friend Eli Segal, a very successful businessman from Boston, helped create the agency. Segal became the first director.

Senator Wofford and Segal consulted with me frequently on the mission and structure of AmeriCorps, and they wanted to know how to make sure AmeriCorps Volunteers would maintain a lifelong identification with the program and commitment to service—something the Peace Corps had not done. I urged them to build the lifetime of service concept into every component of the AmeriCorps experience from recruitment and training through to the end of service. I also urged them to create an AmeriCorps alumni organization from the beginning. Indeed, the prevailing theme of AmeriCorps is, "I will carry this commitment with me this year and beyond!" Furthermore, AmeriCorps Alums is a strong and effective network promoting lifelong service.

An umbrella agency, the Corporation for Community and National Service was created to manage all volunteer service programs including AmeriCorps, VISTA, RSVP, CCC, etc., and the Clinton administration wanted to incorporate the Peace Corps into the new structure. We had been down this road before when the Peace Corps was subsumed into an umbrella service agency called ACTION during the 1970s, and it almost killed the Peace Corps. We would have none of it, and we let Segal and others in the administration know, in no uncertain terms, we would move heaven and earth to oppose it.

Peace Corps Director Carol Bellamy was a powerful force in opposition, and Senator Wofford was on our side as well. Former Peace Corps Director and Republican Senator from Georgia Paul Coverdell also intervened on our behalf, so it was an easy victory. However, after the bill passed, the public relations people in the White House created the brilliant idea of a ceremonial torch passing from Peace Corps Volunteers to AmeriCorps Volunteers. Carol and I were outraged. It would suggest the Peace Corps had run its lap and AmeriCorps would carry on. The Peace Corps was not finished, and we weren't about to allow an image of passing our baton to anyone. Once again, we prevailed, but we were also proud to participate as supporters at the White House celebration of the launch of AmeriCorps—without a torch.

≈

With the fall of the Berlin Wall, U.S. funding for anything international declined substantially. It was known as the "peace dividend". The Pentagon budget was reduced dramatically by the Bush administration, and the Clinton administration followed suit. Unfortunately, funding for diplomacy and international development dropped even faster—over 50 percent between 1985 and 1995. Those of us who believed in building a more integrated and cooperative world and in helping the poorest of the poor find a way out of absolute poverty were appalled. We felt part of the peace dividend should be invested in building a better world, not in isolation from the world. The U.S. government missed a great opportunity to build positive relations with the global community, and we have paid a dear price for that negligence.

Tex Harris, President of the American Foreign Service Association (the trade association for diplomatic professionals) was the lead champion for investment in diplomacy, but he needed help. Tex and his colleague Harry Blaney approached me to see if the Peace Corps community and the diplomatic establishment could join forces to lobby Congress for the entire international affairs budget—diplomacy, development assistance, education exchanges, arms control, the Peace Corps, the UN, etc. I was skeptical at first. Peace Corps Volunteers tend to maintain maximum distance from the embassy and the foreign policy establishment. The priorities and cultures of the Peace Corps and the diplomatic community are very different. Yet, when it comes to the funding, all international affairs institutions are in the same account.

We rise and fall together, so we needed to pull together. I agreed to work with Tex and Harry, and we created the Coalition for American Leadership Abroad (COLEAD).

Tex was the founding chairman; I was vice chairman, and Harry was the volunteer president who would run the day-to-day operations. We attracted dozens of members the very first year, and we built strong relations with members of Congress and key staff members. Tex stepped aside after the first year when his term as President of AFSA ended, and I became COLEAD Chairman. With the exception of two years when Garber Davidson and later Sherry Mueller took the lead, I have served as COLEAD board chair ever since.

Harry worked full time and then some without pay, and we built the membership to fifty of the most important international affairs organizations in the country. The United Nations Association, the Stimson Center, the Fulbright Association, the Academy for Educational Development, Partners of the Americas, the National Center for International Visitors as well as the American Foreign Service Association and National Peace Corps Association all joined forces to convey an overriding message to Congress—America must sustain its global leadership role through diplomacy, exchanges, development assistance, and respectful engagement in and support of international institutions, especially the United Nations.

I wrote an essay and PowerPoint presentation called "No Time to Retreat" to make the case against abandoning active engagement in global affairs and for positive investment in diplomacy and development. Variations on that basic theme have been incorporated into almost everything I have written or spoken since. Presidential advisor David Gergen saw it and requested a copy to help him shape his own thinking on the subject.

At the time, the entire U.S. foreign affairs budget was barely one percent of the Federal budget. That included every penny for embassies, the UN, development assistance, education exchanges, and arms control. Furthermore, the U.S. government's contribution to social, political, and economic development in underdeveloped countries was the smallest, not the largest, among all developed nations. This, of course, ran absolutely counter to the public perception. Most Americans believe foreign aid alone consumes 15 percent to twenty-five percent of the Federal budget and that the U.S. alone carries the burden of foreign aid. It is a myth. Our task was to inform members of Congress who were badly misinformed, and to make the case for a more reasonable commitment to global engagement and development.

We have operated COLEAD on a miniscule budget of less than $10,000 per year contributed by our members, but we gained substantial credibility and recognition. Key congressional staff members have told us we made a significant difference in funding for America's diplomatic and development assistance capacity. We sponsored annual breakfast meetings on Capitol Hill that attracted virtually all of the key foreign relations staff as well as several members of the House and Senate. It gave us an opportunity to present the case and build support. We sponsored weekly meetings among our members to share information, develop strategies, and mobilize group presentations to congressional leaders and their staff. We also built a solid relationship with the Department of State, and we co-sponsored national "town meetings" to connect private citizens and NGOs with foreign policy makers. As chairman, I usually delivered the welcome remarks, and the Secretary of State would provide a significant address at the events, and the assistant secretaries and other top officials spoke and engaged in dialogue with participants. C-SPAN often broadcast the sessions nationwide. We have been told our initiative was unprecedented and that the diplomats ensconced in Foggy Bottom had never connected with the public in such a meaningful way. The international affairs budget is still miniscule, but the free-fall has stopped, and it has even grown—largely in response to the new threat from extremist elements.

I was also deeply involved with the International Development

Conference, a fifty-year-old institution that brought the global development community together every two years to share information and ideas and to explore strategies to more effectively overcome hunger and poverty worldwide. The brightest people in the development field served on the board and in leadership positions, and my heroes Bob Berg and Andy Rice were the primary leaders. I looked forward to board meetings just because it put me in direct contact with the very best people in the field. I became vice president of the board and program chairman for the 1998 conference, and it proved to be one of the very best in IDC history. Our plenary speakers included Treasury Secretary Robert Rubin, Carnegie Endowment President Jessica Mathews, Organization for African Unity President Salim Salim, and other world renowned experts.

The IDC operated on a tight budget, and we depended on sponsors and conference registration income to survive. We usually had to commit funds up front and then count on revenue at the time of the event. We were particularly vulnerable approaching the January 2002 conference when the tragedy of September 11, 2001 took place. Visas for international participants became almost impossible to obtain, and sponsors were not inclined to commit to an event that might not happen. Our obligations greatly exceeded our resources, and there was no hope of reconciling the difference. For the first time in my life, I learned the difference between chapter 7 (liquidation) and chapter 11 (restructure) bankruptcy. We were chapter 7, beyond hope of recovery. Fortunately, board members were not held personally liable for the expenses, but the demise of this great institution was tragic and very hard to accept.

≈

Elizabeth Radcliff, a retired California school teacher and activist had been bothered by the predominance of monuments to war heroes and the absence of tributes to peacemakers in Washington. Most of the famous squares and circles are adorned by men on horses carrying guns and swords. If a nation is defined by what it honors, she concluded, America is a land of warriors.

Elizabeth felt there should be at least one major tribute to peace-makers, and she persuaded the Congress to designate a plot of national park service land for the honor. Radcliff had even conducted a national design contest for a National Peace Garden, and it would occupy ten acres at the tip of Haines Point, a lovely, if somewhat obscure, location right on the Potomac River, a long walk and short drive from the Jefferson Memorial. The budget for the project was a mere $12 million—a pittance in comparison with similar capital projects. Yet, valuable as the project appeared, raising the funds had been extremely difficult.

Elizabeth wanted the garden to honor the Peace Corps as a major part of America's contribution to world peace, and she asked if the National Peace Corps Association would help. I took it to the board, they agreed, and Kelly Brest van Kempen and Ginny Kirkwood were designated to represent us on the Peace Garden board. Bob Gale joined the Peace Garden Board as well, and Ginny, Bob, and I traveled to Atlanta to meet with former President Jimmy Carter to solicit his advice and endorsement for the project. Carter shared insight from his struggle to raise the funds for the Carter Center, and he offered moral if not financial support.

We assembled a solid board for the National Peace Garden, we hired a top level fund raiser, and did everything any successful capital campaign should do. But the money just wasn't there. Donors weren't interested in building a monument to peace. John Garamendi was Deputy Secretary of the Interior with responsibility for the National Parks at the time, and we reported our difficulty to him. He suggested we simply go out to Haines Point, put up a "National Peace Garden" sign and declare it so! It was a great idea, and it might have sent a message, but we decided against it. Unfortunately, the National Peace Garden in our nation's capital never happened.

At about this time, I received a letter from Gordon Radley, a famous name in Peace Corps circles. Gordon's brother Larry, along with David Crozier, had been the first two volunteers killed in service. They were on a DC-3 flying over the Chocó region in Colombia when the plane crashed. The site was so remote that it has never been found. The Chocó has dense rainforest with the world's highest rainfall at over 400 inches per year. The Peace Corps training site in Puerto Rico was named Camp Radley in Larry's honor. (Gordon has tried to organize an expedition to locate the crash site, but it has not yet been possible.)

Radley had seen an article in the *San Francisco Chronicle* about Radcliff and the Peace Garden, and he wanted to know if I knew anything about it. I did, and I gave him the details as I knew them. Gordon had been interested in establishing some special recognition for all Volunteers killed in service, and he saw the Garden as a possible venue for the tribute.

I manufactured an excuse to fly out to the Bay area to meet with Radley to discuss the Garden and the other NPCA initiatives. Gordon was President of LucasFilm Ltd. with an office at Skywalker Ranch in Marin County. I wasn't about to pass up an opportunity to see the home of *Star Wars* and meet the guy who runs the company that makes all of the movies, video games, books, and toys happen.

Skywalker Ranch is located on Lucas Valley Road, but the road had been named long before George Lucas bought the land. It is secluded and quiet, the very converse of glitzy Hollywood. I visited Radley at the Ranch a few times every year until he retired, and we still meet up when he comes to Washington. He became a member of the board of the National Peace Garden; he joined the NPCA's Director's Circle, and now he is on the Alliance for Peacebuilding's Advisory Board. We asked Gordon to be the speaker for the awards luncheon at a National Peace Corps Association luncheon and he delivered an address that was stirring, challenging and memorable. He likened the Peace Corps experience to Icarus testing his wax wings and learning to fly and explore. Icarus, however, got carried away and flew too close to the sun where his wings melted and he fell into the sea. The joy of the Peace Corps is that all of us learned to fly. Most Volunteers manage to stay far enough from the sun to avoid disaster, but the risk is always there, and we are better for having taken the chance. When he finished Peace Corps Director Mark Gearan leaned over to me and said, "After all these years, it is hard to say anything new and significant about the Peace Corps, but Gordon just did." Gearan knows a good speech when he hears one. He had been director of communications for President Clinton.

In 1997, George Lucas created a nationwide sensation when he re-released the *Star Wars* films for theater showings. I had scheduled lunch with Gordon at the Ranch on the first day the film would be shown, so I called to see if he needed to change the date. "No, not at all," he said. He wanted to meet. I drove a rented car past one movie theater after another with lines of fans who had camped in place for days just to get a good seat. When I got to Skywalker Ranch, all was just as serene as ever. Gordon and I went to their onsite café and enjoyed a relaxed two hour lunch talking about the Peace Corps and the National Peace Garden. I asked repeatedly if he didn't need to be doing something about the opening, and he calmly repeated that everything was under control, that he had done all he could do, and that he really wanted to talk about the Peace Corps.

A year or so later, when Lucas was about to release *Return of the Jedi* for a second round, Gordon called, "We're doing a special preview screening at the Uptown Theater in Washington for members of Congress and their staff, and I want you and your family to be there." The event was the next day, and a courier delivered four tickets to my office that morning. We arrived early and found the whole cast greeting the guests. My kids, ages seven and five, (and their star- struck parents) got to meet the world's most famous interplanetary personalities—complete with heavy breathing Darth Vader, C-3PO, R2-D2 and Chewbacca.

Every time Gordon and I got together, he would look at me and say,

"I want to do what you do." He wanted to run a nonprofit that does good things in the world. He especially wanted to be a peacebuilder. I invariably looked straight back at him and said, "I want to do what you do!" We would both chuckle, but we both meant it. Nevertheless, I think he meant it more than I did. I'm not sure I really ever wanted to run a large company, not even one as delightful as LucasFilm Ltd. Gordon, on the other hand, genuinely wanted to run a nonprofit that did good things for the planet. He told me he had a few more projects to finish at Lucas, but he planned to retire and do what I do as soon as possible.

A few years later, while I was working at BoardSource, Gordon called to say, "I just gave George my letter of resignation. I am retiring, and now I can do it." He wanted my advice on ways to connect with the nonprofit world. He took a few months off to decompress, and then he aligned himself with a small organization that is helping protect the environment in the South Pacific. He had been a Peace Corps trainer in Samoa, and he had become attached to the beauty and the people of the Pacific island nations. Now, he could do what I do—devote himself to his passion.

≈

In the summer of 1995, Peace Corps Director Carol Bellamy was selected to become the new director of UNICEF, the United Nations agency to support children worldwide. Her departure presented a new challenge for the community of returned volunteers. We still wanted assurance of another RPCV as director, but our case was weak. Prior to Carol, we could argue vigorously that there had never been an RPCV director. That was no longer true. We also tried to argue that any RPCV would be better than anyone who did not have on-the-ground overseas volunteer experience. However, we knew it wasn't true. Carol was a superb Peace Corps director, but no one would say she was the best ever. In fact that title was shared, in nearly everyone's view, by the first director Sargent Shriver and President Reagan's appointment, Loret Ruppe.

Ruppe was a pleasant surprise to the Peace Corps community. We feared and anticipated the worst when she was named. Reagan had demonstrated little regard for the Peace Corps, and Loret Miller Ruppe had no relevant experience. She was an heiress to a share of the Miller brewing fortune, her husband Phil was a conservative Republican congressman from Michigan, and she managed the Reagan campaign for the state. Yet, her warm personality, genuine compassion for people living in poverty, commitment to peace, and her absolute devotion to the mission of the Peace Corps and the volunteers was unparalleled. She defended the agency from hostile budget cutters and ideological opponents within her own party. She made the case for and actually won modest increases in funding, and the stature of the agency grew far more under her leadership than it had during the supposedly Peace Corps friendly Carter years. (By the way, Phil and the entire Ruppe family are among my favorite people.)

We notified Members of Congress and the White House personnel office that we were just as determined as ever that the new director should be an RPCV, and we provided a solid list of candidates. At the top of our list, however, was a former Peace Corps staff member, not a former volunteer. Senator Harris Wofford had been part of the Peace Corps from the very beginning. He and Sargent Shriver had set up shop in the Mayflower Hotel in early 1961 to create this new agency for President Kennedy. Wofford, along with Shriver, Senator Hubert Humphrey and a few others created the agency, and they established its unique character and quality. Wofford became the first Peace Corps country director in Ethiopia, and he is revered by everyone who knows him.

Wofford had won a special election to the Senate from Pennsylvania, and he was our strongest ally in the U.S. Congress. A note on my desk on my first day as President of the NPCA welcomed me to the job and invited me to lean on him whenever I wished. It said, "I am your personal Senator," signed Harris Wofford. He was true to his word, and we met regularly to solve problems and advance our respective causes.

In addition to the Peace Corps, he was a passionate advocate for health care reform. He knew of our family's experience with private insurance carriers, and he saw our struggle as an example of the consequences of the dreadful U.S. health care finance system.

Unfortunately, Wofford was among the Democratic victims of the 1994 election. His race against Rick Santorum was so close it was not decided until 3 am. I stayed up watching the news until the final count clinging to a glimmer of hope for a positive future if Wofford could retain his seat. When he fell, I fell into deep despair.

On a Saturday shortly after Bellamy's departure, Harris called me at home, "I just heard from the White House, and I am on my way to meet with the President," he said. "I expect he wants to discuss the Peace Corps position," he and I both surmised. A few hours later, the phone rang again. "Well, I met with the President," he began, "and it's not the Peace Corps." Clinton wanted Wofford to help rescue the Corporation for National and Community Service and its AmeriCorps program that was seriously threatened by Newt Gingrich and the Republican dominated Congress. That's what he did, and he did it extremely well. The Corporation and AmeriCorps survived, and it now enjoys strong bipartisan support.

So the Peace Corps director question remained on the table. We had heard rumors that President Clinton wanted to name his communications director Mark Gearan to the post, but we didn't take it seriously until we learned Wofford was not the choice. Immediately, the Gearan possibility loomed large, and we had to respond. Just as before with Kathleen Kennedy Townsend, the press smelled a confrontation between a President who was popular with much of the Peace Corps community and the appointment of a Peace Corps director who would not be acceptable. *Newsweek* was on the story, and they called my office daily in search of an explosive statement. I let them know it might come to that, but that we were not ready to pull the trigger. We needed more information.

Gearan called and invited me to meet with him in the White House. He knew the NPCA would be the tallest hurdle between his White House post and the Peace Corps director job. Calling from the White House gave him a distinct advantage, but I had gained strength and courage from my encounter with Kathleen. I was ready. At the same time, I knew we couldn't make the same rock-solid case we had before, and the NPCA leaders agreed we should not close the door completely. We knew we couldn't insist that all directors had to be returned volunteers. Furthermore, Gearan was very close to the President, and he might be able to advance the Peace Corps agenda more effectively than any of our RPCV candidates.

Instead of declaring absolute opposition, we developed a set of conditions Gearan would have to meet to gain our reluctant support. We wanted to be sure he would take full advantage of the Peace Corps experience of others, so we insisted he retain the services of and listen carefully to the advice of Jack Hogan who had been acting director during the transition before Bellamy started. Jack had been a volunteer in Venezuela, and he had held about every position imaginable in the agency over the years. No one knows the Peace Corps better than Jack Hogan. We also insisted Gearan promise to surround himself with other RPCVs in leadership positions. (Some directors in the past had actively rejected former volunteers in the executive suite.) We wanted a commitment to do everything possible to help rebuild the agency toward the well established goal of 10,000 volunteers, and we wanted a promise to serve two years or more. Many Peace Corps directors had stayed on the job for less than a year, and the typical longevity (not counting Shriver who served five years and Loret Ruppe who served eight years) was barely a year. I also insisted he be open to interaction with the Returned Peace Corps Volunteer community. Many of our members would oppose his selection on grounds he had never served as a Volunteer. He would have to be willing to meet with them directly and make his case face-to-face.

Gearan greeted me in the West Wing, showed me around a bit, and led me to his impressive office. We chatted to become acquainted at a personal level, and then I outlined our conditions. He wanted details and he probed to understand the rationale for each one. Then he asked for some time to consider my offer. If he accepted our conditions, we would support him. If not, there would be a very public struggle. By the time I left, I was convinced this would be a good choice for Peace Corps Director, even if he didn't meet all of our demands. Mark is a very smart and articulate leader, and he would be able to elevate the profile of and build support for the agency. A few days later he called and promised to fulfill all of our conditions. When the *Newsweek* reporter called, I told him there would be no war between the White House and the Peace Corps community. There was no story.

A month or so later, Mark went before the subcommittee of the Foreign Relations Committee for his hearing prior to confirmation by the full Senate, and I was there to testify on his behalf. My prepared testimony began with a declaration that I would prefer an RPCV, but short of that standard, Mark Gearan was an ideal candidate and he had the full support of the National Peace Corps Association. Prior to the hearing, I had a brief discussion with two members of the committee, and both expressed enthusiasm for the Peace Corps and for Mark. One was Ted Kennedy, of course. The other was Jesse Helms, the famous right wing firebrand who ferociously opposed anything and everything with the slightest hint of liberal ideology. Helms was chairman of the committee and his surprising support was tremendously important.

Senator Chris Dodd of Connecticut, the only RPCV in the Senate, pulled me aside to ask if our community was prepared to support Gearan. My affirmation was good enough for him. I was never asked to provide an oral statement at the hearing because Mark's confirmation was already sealed. They just asked him a few perfunctory questions and voted approval. I provided the written endorsement for the record, but I doubt anyone anywhere ever read it.

One of Gearan's first and most enduring acts was the creation of the Peace Corps Crisis Corps. I had told him about our Emergency Response Network and the project in Rwanda. He liked the idea, he looked into it, and he wanted to appropriate it into the agency. He had the decency to ask permission to use the concept, and I had no choice but to grant it. We were barely able to sustain the data base, let alone manage the program without special funding—which we didn't have. The Peace Corps would be able to ramp up the program and make it viable on a much larger scale. The Peace Corps Crisis Corps (now known as Peace Corps Response) is thriving, but very few people in the agency know its origins. I was invited to attend a celebration of the 10th anniversary of the Crisis Corps, and the literature completely missed its true genesis. Only a few of us know the real story.

≈

March 1, 1996 would be the 35th anniversary of the Peace Corps, and we planned a special celebration with a gala dinner at the Mayflower Hotel and a program at George Washington University. The Mayflower was the logical location because Shriver and Wofford had designed the agency in one of its rooms. Some RPCVs thought it was a bit pricy and elegant for the Peace Corps image, but historical significance carried the day. We charged $250 per person, which again we were told was too pricey. Bob Columbo, president of Friends of Colombia, my country of service group, was particularly vociferous in protest. Yet, Friends of Colombia was the first group to fill a table, and they filled a second one as well.

We agreed to use the occasion to honor Sargent Shriver, the first Peace Corps director, and Loret Ruppe, the longest serving director. There were two other, more compelling reasons to honor Loret, but they couldn't be expressed publicly. Many, if not most of us believe Loret, along with Shriver, was the best director ever. After all, she saved the agency during the Reagan years, and she made it stronger. Everyone, regardless of political affiliation loved and admired Loret. After the

Peace Corps, the first President Bush appointed her U.S. ambassador to Norway, and from there she was a major advocate for peace throughout the world. The other reason to honor her at this time was that she was dying, and this would be our last opportunity to thank her in public. Loret had been diagnosed with cancer two years before, and she had done everything possible to live as long as she could, but she had already entered the palliative phase. It would soon be over, at age 55.

Loret had become a dear personal friend and a strong supporter of the NPCA. I knew I could count on her for wise counsel and for a morale boost anytime. Her cancer diagnosis came shortly before Kai's first transplant and our distressing experience, so we often shared health stories and concerns. She had radical surgery at about the same time as Kai's first transplant. When Kai and I were well enough to get out, our family went to her home to visit and wish her well. Loret was in bed, and when we entered her bedroom, two-year-old Kai seemed to sense that she had just been through the same medical trauma as he. He went straight to her, climbed into bed, snuggled up, smiled, put his head on her shoulder, and settled in. Loret put her loving arm around him, and we talked like that for almost two hours.

We sold out of tickets for the banquet honoring 35 years of the Peace Corps and our champions Shriver and Ruppe, so it was a significant financial boost for the organization. Our board chair Ron Tschetter would welcome the crowd and introduce Donna Shalala to emcee the program. Shalala had served in the Peace Corps in Iran, and she had been President of Hunter College in New York and then the University of Wisconsin before becoming President Clinton's Secretary of Health and Human Services.

We had agreed to recognize every Peace Corps director from the very beginning, and I had the challenge of writing the script for Shalala to present. I knew personally every one of the directors except Carolyn Payton. Payton had not enjoyed a positive experience as director during the Carter administration, and she did not attend Peace Corps events. She was teaching at Howard University, so I went to the campus to meet with her. I hoped to persuade her to attend the banquet, but she would not. She expressed sincere appreciation for my visit; however, she felt she had been ignored by the Peace Corps community over the years, and she was right.

I managed to learn enough about each of the directors to write something positive about their respective contributions to the agency. In addition to the featured guests, past heroes of the Peace Corps and the Kennedy administration agreed to speak. Public television star Bill Moyers had been the first Deputy Director at age 27. He had remained a loyal supporter ever since, and he was happy to participate in the event. Ted Sorensen was Kennedy's speech writer and special advisor. His daughter had served as a Volunteer, and I had been able to call upon him for advice from time-to-time. It was a coup to attract him to speak.

So, we had an all-star cast for a very special night. I was exhausted from the preparation, but excited as the day arrived. However, late that afternoon my mother called in distress. Kai seemed to be growing weak. Kay was out of town for one of the very few times in his entire life that she left Kai's side, and my mother had come to take care of him. She said I must come home immediately. I did, and it was obvious Kai was in serious trouble. We rushed him to the Johns Hopkins Emergency Room, and they confirmed our fears. It was a serious emergency. In Kay's absence, I had allowed Kai to indulge in too many potato chips (his favorite snack), and he had potassium poisoning. His compromised system couldn't process so much of the alkali in the chips, and it could kill him. The medical team went to work injecting needles to pump medicines in and others to suck blood out for testing. Kai screamed in pain as I helped hold him down for the torture. I was totally concentrated on him and almost forgot the grand event I was missing.

Fortunately we had a terrific team managing the Peace Corps celebration, and my only official role that night was to say a few words and meet and greet the dignitaries and guests. It came off flawlessly without me. Furthermore, it was broadcast live on C-SPAN, and I was able to watch much of it—in between treatments for Kai—in his room.

After a lavish introduction that I had written and Shalala delivered, Loret took the podium. This would be her last speech before cancer took her life, yet she looked strong and absolutely radiant that night. She thanked the Peace Corps community for the love, prayers, and support she had received. Then she grew more serious and said, "You all know that Chic is not here tonight because his son Kai has taken a turn for the worse. He is struggling for his life at Johns Hopkins. Tonight he is the one who needs your prayers and support." She asked the audience for a moment of silence for Kai. This was to be her night, but she gave it to Kai. I was able to watch it from Kai's room in the hospital. I cried openly and without shame. Her speech was humorous as well as powerful, and it is a lifetime treasure for everyone who experienced it.

A dozen years later, during the 2008 Christmas holidays, C-SPAN broadcast highlight programs from its archives, and the Peace Corps 35th anniversary program was included. I happened to catch it, and Kai (by then 17 years old) was able to see it, including Loret's tribute to him. The emotion of that long night came back with full force, and I cried all over again.

Kai survived the night, and the medical team released him at 5 am. Neither of us had slept a second the entire night, but we were happy to be going home. Another emergency and threat to his survival had come and gone. I took Kai home where my mother was waiting up while watching Grant. I took a shower, dressed, ate a quick breakfast, and drove back to George Washington University for the rest of the Peace Corps 35th anniversary celebration. Madeleine Albright, U.S. Ambassador to the UN and soon to be Secretary of State was our keynote speaker, and Peace Corps Director Mark Gearan was to give an update on the agency. My responsibility was to introduce Albright and give our own State of the National Peace Corps Association address.

I made it in time, but I suffered a near breakdown just before going on stage. The fear that we might have lost Kai, along with complete exhaustion caused me to collapse. My close friend Joseph Permetti was with me in the green room, and he gave me the moral support I needed. After sobbing for several minutes, I was able to pull myself together, puffy eyes and all, and pull off a pretty good presentation. It is all on tape, and no one would be able to tell I was a total basket case. The next week, Mark Gearan gave me a very large framed photo of Secretary Albright at the podium speaking with me seated behind her. It hangs in my office as a constant reminder of that extraordinary experience.

≈

Later in 1996, we received a small grant from the Ford Foundation to enable me to fly to Cape Town, South Africa for a conference on volunteerism and to meet with Peace Corps Volunteers and local hosts in other parts of the continent. Cape Town has a pristine beach and Table Mountain with a clean, vibrant city in between. The image is too perfect. Just beyond the prosperous comfort of the city, "townships" of endless shanties built of scrap wood and metal accommodate a million of the world's poorest people. I toured Khayelitsha with our group from the conference, and came away fearful that the new post-apartheid government would never be able to overcome the deeply entrenched inequity between the prosperous and well-educated whites in the city and the desperately poor, uneducated, and dispossessed masses in the townships.

From Cape Town, I flew to Nairobi, Kenya, a bustling city that seemed to have better prospects. In spite of incompetence and corruption under President Daniel Arap Moi, there was much better balance and growing opportunity for everyone. It lifted my spirits after the depressing tour of the South African townships.

In Rwanda, I met many of the people our RPCV team had worked with to learn more about their work and to better understand how the country was recovering two years after the genocide. Since I was a member of the CARE Board of Overseers, I stayed in their guest house.

The lady responsible for meals and cleaning had a deep scar across her face. She had survived the attack, but her husband had not. Every time I saw her, the reality of the genocide pierced my protective armor, and it hurt. One after another, aid workers and Rwandan government officials expressed appreciation for the RPCVs who had returned to help. While Kigali was a city without joy, there was a palpable sense of purpose and a determination to recover and overcome the dreadful past. I was inspired.

I went on to Ghana where I got to meet many Peace Corps Volunteers at their sites far into the bush. Their villages, living conditions and bright optimism took me back to Albornos and my experiences of thirty years before on another continent. It was exactly the same, and I loved every minute of it, even the minimal overnight lodging conditions and bumpy roads.

Abidjan in Cote d'Ivoire was Africa's Paris, complete with wonderful cafés and an urbane cultural climate. The concept of savoir-faire came to mind as I walked the streets of this charming city. (Sadly the good life and stability of Abidjan was shattered by civil war a few years later.) A few years before this trip, I had met Alice Dear, President Clinton's nominee for the U.S.A. Executive Director of the African Development Bank based in Abidjan. However, North Carolina's Jesse Helms, who took pride in his reputation as "Senator No," planned to exercise his power and block the nomination. I had a very good relationship with Georgia's Republican Senator and former Peace Corps Director Paul Coverdell, so I asked him to intervene with his colleague. He did, and Alice was confirmed. She took me to a wonderful resort beachfront hotel for lunch to express her appreciation and to discuss social and economic development on the continent.

The last stop on the Africa tour proved to be the best. Bamako is the capital of Mali in West Africa on the Niger River. Mali is a hot, dry and predominantly Muslim country in the southern Sahara. When I arrived, the city had just opened a marvelous new marketplace built in

the fascinating architectural tradition of the great Mosque of Djenne—
made of adobe and wood, and entirely rounded shapes. Many of the
women wear brilliantly colored caftan dresses with billowed sleeves,
and men dress up in magnificent dashikis. The sight of these beautiful
women and handsome men in such elegant garments walking in front
of the splendid architecture was breathtaking.

I first met Mahamane Baby on that trip. Mahamane is from Tim-
buktu, but he was living in Bamako at the time. He created and was
managing the Mali Volunteer Corps, and more recently he served as
the United Nations Volunteer Program director in Niger. Mahamane
is one of the rising stars in African politics with a firm commitment to
end corruption and build peace and progress for a people who have endured too much hardship. We have become like brothers, and every few
years he comes to spend time with my family. I taught him to fly fish,
and we may even turn him into a Baltimore Orioles fan. He teaches me
about Africa, Islam, and brotherhood. He taught my kids some super
soccer moves as well.

≈

That fall, I received an invitation from the government of Taiwan to
be part of a ten member delegation to visit and learn about their emerging democracy and thriving economy. Prior to the trip, my impression
of Taiwan was based on the dictatorial Chiang Kai-shek. I never held
Mao in high regard, but I saw little difference between the two dictators, so I had little sympathy for the small island nationalist government
that wanted to be recognized as the official government of the entire
massive mainland nation of China. However, I couldn't pass up a free
trip in the company of several very prominent American foreign policy
experts.

The new government of Taiwan, however, had shed the authoritarian past, and it was embarking on a bold new experiment with freedom.
They wanted more American leaders to see it first-hand and to share the
story. However, terms of the agreement to recognize the government

in Beijing, dating back to the Nixon era, prohibit U.S. government officials' travel to Taiwan. Therefore Taiwan invited high level officials from nongovernment think tanks and from the political party not currently occupying the White House. They knew these people would return to policy making positions in future administrations, and they were making an investment that would reap rewards later.

I was included because the government of Taiwan held the Peace Corps in high regard. Current Peace Corps officials couldn't go to Taiwan, but I could since the NPCA was not a government agency. Others in the group included Larry Korb who had been Assistant Secretary of Defense in the Reagan Administration. Korb had become a high-profile commentator on military matters on the major news networks. Ann Thurston, the ghost writer of the famous and controversial book, *The Private Life of Chairman Mao*, officially written by Mao's personal physician, Dr. Li Zhisui, was in our group. Jerry Glenn, co-founder and director of the UN's Millennium Project and executive director of the American Council for the United Nations University, was part of the delegation as were several former sub-cabinet officials in the Reagan and George H. W. Bush administrations.

We met with the very top leaders in the new and independent political parties, and we had substantial interaction with several key business and government officials. We attended the elaborate and reverential celebration of the 2,547th birthday of Confucius, and we flew into the Northeast section of the island to tour the magnificent Taroko National Park. I was impressed with everything I saw, and I was converted from a Taiwan skeptic to an enthusiastic fan.

We had become aware during the trip that our hosts had ranked all of us in order of their perception of our status or importance. Larry Korb, of course, topped the list. However, to everyone's surprise, the Peace Corps guy was second. Wherever we went, Larry was introduced first and given the prime seat. I was introduced second and given the next seat. The final event on our trip was to be the equivalent of a state luncheon at the Foreign Ministry. Korb had to leave the day before, and that left me as the top ranking delegate to represent and speak for the group. I was seated directly across a large round table from the foreign minister, and the equivalent of their chairman of the House and Senate foreign relations committees sat on my left and right. Other dignitaries were interspersed among our delegates around the table.

At first, the luncheon conversation focused on our impressions of their country, but soon the foreign minister Fredrick Chien turned the conversation to me and the Peace Corps. He asserted that from his perspective the Peace Corps is the best thing the U.S. has ever done in the world, and he wanted to know how the Republic of China (Taiwan, not the People's Republic of China on the mainland) could do something similar. Others in the U.S. delegation were experts in economics and trade, diplomacy and international institutions, but the Foreign Minister wanted to focus on the Peace Corps. Obviously, I was thrilled, and I engaged in a lively discussion about the core values of the Peace Corps. I emphasized the concept of mutual respect and mutual learning between Peace Corps Volunteers and their host country counterparts. At the end of the luncheon, we were given a toast by the Foreign Minister, and I thought I was to give one in return. However, they moved immediately from his gesture to another presentation, and I barely found room for a very brief and poorly presented expression of gratitude for the opportunity to visit and learn so much about their splendid country.

Taiwan officials met with me several times back in Washington after that trip, and I gave them my thoughts on what they might do. Currently there is a small Taiwan Root Medical Peace Corps program that may have emerged from those discussions, but I cannot confirm it.

≈

The National Peace Corps Association along with our Washington, D.C. affiliate organization, marched in the Presidential Inaugural Parade carrying flags of each of the 139 countries where we have served. In 1997 we had arranged for Sargent Shriver (the first Peace Corps Director) and Mark Gearan (the Director at the time) to be with us. Shriver was recovering from knee replacement surgery, so we arranged for him and Gearan to ride in a convertible at the head of our group.

We assembled at our designated place on the Mall, and by coincidence Congressman Sam Farr, my friend since our "huelga" in Bogota, was there as well. A high school band from his district was marching immediately behind us, and he wanted to greet them. When the time came for us to start moving there was no sign of Shriver or Gearan, so the convertible was empty. I yelled out, "Sam, jump in the car!" He looked puzzled and resisted, but I insisted. "Just get in. I'll explain on the way." So, Congressman Farr and I rode together seated high on the back of the back seat of a white convertible and waved at the crowd as we moved down Pennsylvania Avenue toward the White House. However, when we neared 4th Street and the Canadian Embassy, we saw Gearan with Shriver hobbling along behind him rushing toward the car. Since Sarge was in some pain, they had decided to wait for us in the Embassy. Sam and I jumped out and lifted Sarge and Mark in with the car still moving. We walked beside them the rest of the way thoroughly enjoying the whole experience.

With President Clinton's close friend Mark Gearan running the Peace Corps, the agency had the best access to the White House since the first five years when President Kennedy's brother-in-law Sargent Shriver was the director. Clinton referred to the Peace Corps often, and when he devoted one of his Saturday morning radio addresses to national service, we were invited to attend in person. We invited a few key board members and John Schelp from the North Carolina RPCV group to participate.

I had been in the White House on several occasions for meetings and ceremonial functions, but it is always special, especially when you get to see the President in the Oval Office. We were joined by Harris

Wofford and several officials with the Corporation for National and Community Service, and Kathleen Kennedy Townsend was there as well, so the whole group was familiar. Some of us were interviewed by the media after the address, and then Gearan asked if we wanted a private tour of the White House. He took us to rooms the public never sees, including his previous office space. The tour included the White House pressroom, where reporters and camera operators were relaxing while waiting for the next story to develop. Schelp managed to get his camera from his car, and we thought it would be fun to have our pictures taken behind the familiar podium and White House logo used for press briefings. Each of us took our turn pretending to address the media, and members of the press corps enjoyed participating in our faux news event.

We left the White House and went together to a neighborhood restaurant for lunch, but we decided to drop the film off at a one-hour photo shop so we could see the pictures right away. All of us looked forward to showing our families and co-workers the photo proof that we had been there. John started to rewind the film in his camera to give it to the clerk, but as he wound and wound, nothing happened. His face grew increasingly concerned, and finally he realized there was no film in the camera! We were all disappointed, but we also got a good laugh, and John will never live it down.

≈

I always make it a point to befriend the cleaning staff wherever I work. Ersel Coats was the head of the crew that cleaned our offices. Ersel was a large, loud, proud, and delightful African American lady who bowed to no one for any reason in any place. She was a devoted Dallas Cowboys fan, and we loved to argue about the Cowboys and Redskins. It was always worth working late just to end the day in a discussion—or argument—with Ersel. No matter how bad the day had gone, if I got to see Ersel, it ended well. Her crew included Guillermo Silva, a very quiet and shy immigrant from El Salvador. Guillermo gave me a good opportunity to practice my Spanish, and I gave him an opportunity to learn some English and to better understand our culture and customs.

Many evenings Guillermo would enter my office and pause to watch me work on the computer. Finally, one evening, he asked if I would help him buy a computer. I had been down this road before—loan a friend some money, and they betray you and ruin the relationship. So, I put him off. But week after week, Guillermo brought the subject back up.

Finally, I decided to try to help him find a way to save enough to buy it, but I was determined not to loan him a penny. I opened an Excel spread sheet on my computer and asked him how much he made. He shared the information without hesitation. It wasn't much, but by combining his two jobs and his wife's two jobs, they seemed to have enough. Then we went over his fixed expenses, including sending a substantial amount to his extended family in San Salvador. I subtracted his expenses from his income and found he had several hundred dollars left over each month. Unlike me, he had no debt, so he was doing better than I was.

"Guillermo," I said, "You could save enough in a few months to buy a computer."

He said very gently, "I know. I have already saved the money. I just don't know which one to buy. It is for my son who is going to college next year, and he needs one. Can you help me pick the best one?"

I was ashamed. I had assumed that he, an uneducated, low-income immigrant laborer from El Salvador was looking for a loan that he would never repay. Yet, he was the responsible and honorable one. I never bought a computer with cash. I always did it on credit. But he did—on a very modest income while supporting an extended family.

I spent the next few weeks looking for the best buy I could find for him. I owed it to him. When the Office Depot near our office dropped the price on a very good model to make room for new machines, I told Guillermo to bring his money the next day, which he did. At the store, we made the same unfortunate discovery we all make when buying a computer. You can't get just get the computer. You also need software, a printer, cables, disks, etc. And there is sales tax.

When the checkout clerk tallied it all up, Guillermo was crushed. The total was $20 more than he had. He told the clerk to cancel the order. "NO!" I protested loudly and pulled out my wallet. "Here's the other $20. Buy the computer." Guillermo refused, and we argued in Spanish right there in front of a very confused clerk.

Finally, I convinced Guillermo to let me cover the difference— on condition that I let him pay me back. The next day, Guillermo arrived early, and he came straight to my office with a $20 bill and a lovely shirt he had purchased as a gift. This wonderful man had demonstrated personal character and values we rarely see in our arrogant, every-man-for-himself and get-away-with-whatever-you-can society. Whenever I hear Lou Dobbs or anyone else denigrate immigrants, I think of Guillermo and I boil with indignation at their ignorance and outrageous conceit. America is a better place because Guillermo Silva lives here.

$$\approx$$

By the fall of 1998, I was exhausted and deep in debt. The pressure to satisfy our members, maintain our programs, and raise funds had taken a toll. Furthermore, my modest salary at the NPCA was not sufficient to cover basic living and mounting medical expenses. I needed a change. I wanted something with less pressure and more money. I found both with the Museum Trustee Association, and I signed on to become their CEO.

Before moving on, however, I was invited to give a keynote address to the Congress of Student Government Associations at their annual conference held in College Station, Texas. After my experiences at Oklahoma State, I couldn't resist this opportunity. I was able to reflect on our activist era in the 1960s, and I urged this new class of student leaders to embrace their opportunity to influence the current generation of national leaders—to challenge my generation. We made a difference back then, and likewise they could bring fresh ideas and energy to the problems we face today.

I told them the story of our battle against "thought control" and for free speech on campus. I concluded, "In those days, controversial speakers were barred from college campuses because our parents and administrators feared we might succumb to bad influences. We just wanted a broader perspective. We wanted to look at the other side of the coin...We forced changes in those rules." A few days later someone called and asked permission to use that quotation from my speech. I wasn't sure who it was, but I said go ahead.

It turned out to be the Center for Campus Free Speech, and they were assembling significant quotations related to free speech to post on their web site. The others quoted on the same page were: Thomas Jefferson, John F. Kennedy, Salman Rushdie, Kerry Brock of Freedom Forum, the UN Declaration of Human Rights, and Kurt Vonnegut, Jr. I keep a framed copy of it on my wall. I may fail at everything I ever do again, but at least I made it into rarified company this one time.

Just as I was leaving the NPCA, I was invited to participate in a symposium at the Kennedy Library in Boston on the theme, "... Ask what you can do for your country." Participants included members of the Kennedy administration and family, leading political figures, academics and journalists.

When I looked at the attendance list I was reminded of the comment Greg Barton had made when he scanned the list of Sullivan Award nominees, "The only name I don't recognize is my own." Caroline Kennedy was the host, and Senator Ted Kennedy was there along with several other members of the family including Kathleen—the only one I knew well. My heroes Ted Sorensen and Harris Wofford were the only participants from the President's administration I knew personally. Daniel Schorr and Elizabeth Drew brought a journalist's perspective, and the presidents of Harvard, Chicago, Stanford and a few other prestige schools added a scholarly flavor. My old friend Brian O'Connell, founder and long time president of Independent Sector, helped organize and lead the event. I was there to represent the people who had served in the Peace Corps—the living essence of the Kennedy challenge to serve.

We spent the day discussing the current state of the nation. The Library asked us to explore the culture of service and community as compared with a nation based on greed and individual domination. They wanted our thoughts on where the America of 1998 fit on that scale. As I recall, the verdict was quite mixed. We were no longer dominated by the Reagan era when greed was deemed the ultimate good, but we were far from the service oriented culture inspired by the Kennedy years.

Between the day-long work session and the gala dinner, we toured the museum portion of the Library. My favorite exhibition in the museum is a small black and white television showing Kennedy's famous inauguration address, the very theme of our event. It had special significance that day. Brian O'Connell, Ted Sorensen and I stood together watching the small screen, and when the speech ended, I paused for a moment to absorb the significance of being there. Then, I looked to Sorensen and inquired, "Who wrote the speech?" Sorensen had been asked many times before, and his answer was just as perfect as was the speech, "Ask not," he said. "When the President speaks, it is the President's speech." I accepted the answer, but I also knew I was standing with the man who wrote the immortal words that inspired my generation.

Serving as President of the National Peace Corps Association was the very highest honor I could imagine. Many years before, I had aspired to be an Olympic athlete. However, given a choice between winning an Olympic gold medal and representing the Peace Corps community, I would choose the Peace Corps every time. It was a rare high privilege, and I will always cherish the memories. At the same time, it was frustrating and exhausting. I am absolutely thrilled to have done it, and it opened doors to wonderful new opportunities. I was ready to move on.

TO STOP A WAR

My background with arts organizations and managing associations qualified me for the Museum Trustee Association CEO position, even though museum trustees didn't quite fit my style. The job met the basic requirements I was looking for after an exhausting and underpaid stint with the NPCA. It was low pressure, and it paid well. I helped turn an adversarial relationship between the MTA and the American Association of Museums into positive collaboration; we produced some reasonably good conferences, and we added a few new members, but I can't point to any significant accomplishments for the museum world. I delivered what I was paid to do, but little more. I promised to stay at least two years, and I left on my second anniversary and never looked back. At the same time, the low expectations and minimal responsibilities enabled me to expand into other realms with my newfound free time.

In the spring of 1999, John Garamendi called and said, "Chic, my friends are killing each other, and we have to do something about it." John had been a Peace Corps Volunteer in Ethiopia, and war had broken out between Ethiopia and its neighbor Eritrea. Fifteen years earlier, John and his wife Patti had returned to Ethiopia to help his old friends cope with severe drought and famine. Now, he felt compelled to do whatever he could to put an end to this dreadful war. "I have no idea what we can do," I replied, "but let's give it a try."

I asked David Arnold to join us for the meeting. Like John, David had also served in Ethiopia, and he had been a vital source of reason and information when we worked together at the NPCA. While meeting with John, we speculated about several options, but we also knew our ability to be helpful would depend entirely on the will of both of the adversaries to welcome, respect, and respond to our engagement.

John had spent the previous few years as Deputy Secretary of the Interior in the Clinton Administration, and he had just returned to the private sector to pave the way back into California politics. (John had also been an All-American football player for Cal Berkeley during the same time I was at Oklahoma State. He had an opportunity to play in the NFL, but he chose the Peace Corps instead.) John was a remarkably skilled politician, but far more importantly, he was absolutely genuine in his concern for the people of Ethiopia and Eritrea. His stature as an important member of the Clinton administration also gave him instant credibility with foreign leaders. John called his former counterpart Stobe Talbot, Deputy Secretary of State, to inform him of our intensions and to make sure we would not be opposed by the State Department. Talbot encouraged us to do all we could.

We called Ambassadors Semere Russom of Eritrea and Brehane Ghebre-Christos of Ethiopia to express our concern and offer to help. Both were eager to see us, and both said the same thing, "We have found ourselves in a terrible war that should never have started, but we don't know how to bring it to an end. We trust you. Please help us." They trusted us because of their enormous respect for the Peace Corps and because we made our intensions absolutely clear. They respected the Peace Corps because both ambassadors, both foreign ministers, and both heads of state, Meles Zenawi of Ethiopia and Isaias Afwerki of Eritrea, had been taught by Peace Corps Volunteers. Our mission was very clear and direct—to help the leaders of Ethiopia and Eritrea find and pursue a mutually acceptable strategy to end their war and build their pathway to lasting peace. We wanted to help end the violence, killing, and destruction—period.

We were not interested in determining who might be right or wrong. We didn't care who started the fighting. We had no position on where the border should be. Nor did we have any interest in supporting or opposing the position of the U.S. government. We were totally independent. We simply believed the resolution to all of the issues in dispute could and should be determined through honest and impartial fact finding, negotiation, and mediation. It should not and could not be settled on the battlefield.

With this invitation from both countries to become engaged in finding a path to peace, John and I agreed to build our team, and go to work. As much as I liked David Arnold and would have liked him on the team, it was impossible because of his role with the NPCA. He would not be able to devote enough time, and as a journalist and editor of *WorldView* magazine, he had to be an observer and reporter, not a participant.

The NPCA's "Friends of Ethiopia and Eritrea" group had started its own initiative to try to help end the war, but we felt they were on the wrong track. They had offered to have RPCVs manage the disputed territories during a ceasefire until the actual legal ownership could be determined. It was a worthwhile idea, but both sides had already rejected it. We were willing to encourage the governments to reconsider the "Friends" proposal, but we took a different tack. We wanted to listen to the two governments, build a mutual trust relationship, ascertain what might help them find a path to peace and help make it happen.

We built our own team with people who would work well together, who would bring special skills, and who would add stature to the group. Mike McCaskey is Chairman and part owner of the Chicago Bears NFL football team, and an RPCV who served in Ethiopia. Judge Bill Canby had been a Peace Corps regional director based in Asmara and then country director in Addis Ababa. He served on the 9th Circuit Court of Appeals, having been appointed by President Carter. Mel Foote was a volunteer in Asmara, and he runs the Constituency for Africa, an NGO promoting business development throughout the continent. I was the only member of the group who had not served in Ethiopia or Eritrea, but I brought a global Peace Corps and RPCV perspective to the group. John was the group leader, and I, in essence, served as unofficial chief of staff. I set up most of the meetings, maintained communication with the group, and I did most of the writing. John and I met regularly, often daily, and we brought the whole team together whenever necessary.

While the group shared a common bond through Peace Corps service, the project was not connected with the Peace Corps, which is an agency of the U.S. government. Travel expenses for the group were covered, in part, by a grant from the William and Flora Hewlett Foundation channeled through the National Peace Corps Association. Beyond that we did everything as unpaid volunteers and without formal connection with any official organization. We were simply a group of people who had served in the Peace Corps who cared enough to make a commitment to make a difference.

Over 3,200 Americans had served as Peace Corps Volunteers in Ethiopia and Eritrea. They lived with the people, learned the local languages, shared in the local customs, provided new educational opportunities, and established lasting friendships. Tens of thousands of Ethiopians and Eritreans had been taught by Peace Corps Volunteers— including the leaders of both countries and their respective ambassadors to the United States. Furthermore, each Peace Corps Volunteer had been taught by, and their lives have been enriched by their friends in Ethiopia and Eritrea. Therefore, the relationship between Returned Peace Corps Volunteers and Ethiopian and Eritrean citizens and leaders was based upon mutual understanding and respect.

Eritrea was part of Ethiopia until 1993 when Eritrea was granted independence. The separation followed a bifurcated process of overthrowing the dictatorial rule of the Marxist Mengistu government on one hand, and a three-decade struggle for independence on the part of Eritreans on the other. The overthrow of Mengistu was carried out by Ethiopians and Eritreans working together under the leadership of the men who now lead their respective countries. In that struggle, they were partners and friends.

Perceptions of the achievement of Eritrean independence, however, differ between the two nations. Ethiopians believe they willingly granted Eritrean independence and that Eritrea should be grateful. Eritreans, on the other hand, believe they won a long and bitterly contested struggle, and that their achievement of independence was won by their strength, strategy, sacrifice, and resolve. Regardless of the genesis of Eritrea's independence, both nations enjoyed peace and substantial progress from 1993 to 1998. The leaders of both countries worked together on trade and economic development issues. Ethiopia even reduced its military strength dramatically during this period.

The world community was tremendously impressed with the relationship that seemed to have developed between the countries, and they were viewed as emerging models for African peace and prosperity. In early 1998, President Clinton visited the region and expressed his support for and confidence in both leaders.

However, the borders between the countries were never marked, and tensions over the boundaries, as well as economic and trade policies, eventually developed. In May of 1998, Eritrean militia and Ethiopian troops confronted each other and engaged in brief but deadly combat in Badme, a tiny, dusty border town. Eritrea reported that its people were unarmed and that several of them were killed. Ethiopia reported casualties on both sides. Regardless of the actual events and provocations, open warfare began at that time in that remote place.

Subsequently, the conflict spread to other areas along the border, and there were significant incursions into each country. Casualty estimates vary widely, but by the time the fighting finally stopped in the late summer of 2000, up to 100,000 people had been killed, and over a million had been displaced. Landmines had also been planted in conflict zones, and enmity between the countries had become pervasive.

Eritreans were convinced that Ethiopia planned to conquer Eritrea and reclaim it as a part of Ethiopia. At a minimum, they believed Ethiopia intended to capture and control the Red Sea port town of Asab. While several factions in Ethiopia expressed these objectives, the government denied them. Ethiopians, on the other hand, believed Eritrea had become an international outlaw state seeking to expand its boundaries through military conquest. Sovereign control of Ethiopian land was their central issue. In the eyes of Ethiopian officials, Eritrea had to be stopped and taught a lesson. Eritrea countered that its initiatives simply enabled them to occupy their own land as designated by the treaties between Ethiopia and Italy in 1900, 1902 and 1908.

Living standards in both countries had stopped improving, and they declined during the war. In addition to the debilitating impact of the war, drought threatened both countries with massive famine. Furthermore, both countries were engaged in disputes with other neighbors. Ethiopia had experienced violent conflict with Kenya and Somalia, and Eritrea had engaged in territorial skirmishes with Yemen and Sudan. On top of that, both countries had built alliances with opposing clans in Somalia.

The war had raged for nearly a year by the time our RPCV team became involved, and dozens of private and official efforts in the search for peace were under way. Some had already given up in frustration. The U.S. Government had dispatched several missions led by Anthony Lake and Assistant Secretary in the Department of State Susan Rice. The United Nations and the Organization of African Unity (OAU), and a number of other countries actively pursued mediation of the dispute. These missions had made significant progress, culminating in the December 1998 OAU framework for a peace agreement. The eleven-point plan, and subsequent clarifications, had been accepted by both countries. Yet, the plan had not been executed, and the war continued because the countries could not agree on implementation steps.

Based upon meetings at the embassies of both countries and several meetings with expatriates from both countries, we believed opportunities were available to facilitate communication between the people and the governments of the countries and that a new, citizen-based initiative might be effective. Our mission, then, was to help the leaders of both countries turn their attention from strategies for combat to strategies for peace. Our objective was to find ways for each side to take the steps that would enable the *other side* to reach agreement.

We were engaged in the process continually from the spring of 1999 through the signing of the peace agreement in December of the next year. We met frequently with diplomats from both countries, and we met privately and in public gatherings with individual Ethiopian and Eritrean nationals. We shared information with U.S. Government officials in the State Department and the White House, and we maintained contact with interested members of Congress and with journalists. At the invitation of the leaders of both countries, we traveled to Asmara and Addis Ababa to meet with the leaders and with concerned citizens, and whenever the leaders visited the United States, members of the team met with them in Washington.

During this process, we adopted a central theme that was repeated at every opportunity. The contrasting conditions for resolution as expressed by both leaders were important but not insurmountable. The terms for peace, as indicated in the Organization of African Unity framework, were fair, reasonable, and appropriate. The final result would be the same today, or months or years from now. Battlefield outcomes would have little or no impact on the final resolution. Therefore, we repeatedly pressed the leaders with a moral imperative. How many more lives would be lost before the agreement would be accepted? Why not declare a cease fire today?

During April and May, 1999, we held several key meetings at the embassies which led to invitations from the leaders to meet in person in Asmara and Addis Ababa. The expressed purpose was to explore alternative paths to peace directly with President Isaias Afwerki of Eritrea and Prime Minister Meles Zenawi of Ethiopia. In addition, we planned to meet with prominent business, academic, religious and civil society leaders in both countries to promote public support for the peace process and to help build a foundation for reconciliation at the citizen level.

In preparation for the trip, we met with officials of the U.S. Department of State, the National Security Council, and the Ambassadors from Eritrea and Ethiopia. We also convened a forum at Howard University with community leaders and academics from both countries living in the United States. These meetings were designed to provide the team with ideas and suggestions for getting on the path to peace, which we would pursue during the course of our mission. The forum at Howard attracted a large and vocal crowd. While partisans on both sides vigorously defended their countries, virtually everyone agreed the war must end and a reasonable resolution was well within reach.

When I checked my car out of the garage to drive to Dulles Airport to depart for Africa, I asked the chief parking attendant Muluneh Lema what he would like me to bring him from his home country. I knew Muluneh was Ethiopian, but I had never mentioned our involvement with the war. I expected him to request some food or artifact that would remind him of his homeland, but he responded instantly, "Peace. Please bring me peace." I replied, "That's why I am going." Muluneh called out to the other garage attendants, all of whom were from the Horn of Africa—Eritreans and Ethiopians—to gather and hear what I had to say. I described our group and the purpose of the trip, and they as much as bowed in reverent appreciation. They were from the opposing countries, but the war had not separated them. Quite the contrary, they were united in their opposition to the war and to the leaders who had dragged their people into it. They even organized a unified group of Ethiopians and Eritreans, Christians, Muslims and Animists to pray for our success.

We visited Asmara, the capital of Eritrea, first. Following a preliminary meeting with the Deputy Foreign Minister, Amdemichael Kahasi, we held a three-hour meeting with the Head of State, Isaias Afwerki. President Isaias presented his analysis of the origins and causes of the conflict from his perspective. In his opinion, the purpose of the war was to stop aggression by Ethiopia and to establish the principle that a country has the right and obligation to protect its sovereign land, and that no nation can change international boundaries by the use of force. President Isaias expressed his desire to end the war, and to accept the OAU framework agreement as it had been clarified. The ultimate goal was a neutral demarcation of the border according to colonial treaties and international law, with the result to be respected by both sides. It was clear President Isaias believed the United States should play a significant role in the peace process and he would attend a peace conference, if one were called by President Clinton or the UN.

We reviewed dozens of issues still in dispute and explored possible concessions President Isaias might be prepared to make. We also analyzed how far we felt his counterpart in Addis Ababa might go to reach an accommodation. Isaias was remarkably willing to modify his stance in order to find a reasonable middle ground and end the fighting. Before leaving, we confirmed each and every policy concession with the President to make sure we would not misrepresent his position. He gave us permission to express his desire to end the war and to indicate very specific concessions on his behalf. We knew we had a very substantive set of proposals to share with Prime Minister Meles when we went to Addis Ababa.

We also conducted meetings with 34 business leaders, and with the leaders of the Coptic, Muslim, Catholic, and Lutheran faiths. We participated in a community forum with 125 academics, leaders of community organizations and others to discuss how the country could get on the path to peace. Informal meetings were also held with representatives from the U.S. Embassy in Asmara. Prior to departing Eritrea, we held a live national press conference, and the team met with a group of former Peace Corps Volunteers who were living and working in Asmara. Our visit was covered wall-to-wall by Eritrea's television and print media. Every Eritrean everywhere in the world knew all about our initiative.

≈

We had to fly by way of Sana'a, Yemen to travel from Asmara to Addis Ababa because all direct routes had been cancelled due to the war—nearly a thousand miles of travel to go just over 400 miles. We arrived at the VIP lounge at the Asmara airport in plenty of time for our scheduled departure on Yemen Airways, but the flight was delayed by an hour. Since we were to leave at midnight for the one hour flight to Sana, and since we would have to depart Sana'a at 8 the next morning, and since we were already weary, the delay was not welcome news, but we couldn't complain.

Our companions in the lounge included Yemen's Ambassador to Eritrea. We had encountered extreme difficulty obtaining visas just to spend the night in transit in Yemen, and the ambassador had personally intervened to help. This gave us a chance to express our gratitude in person. The Russian ambassador to Eritrea was there as well to see his friend off, but he was inebriated almost beyond control. We listened in mild amusement as he railed against the U.S. and our foreign policies, but he was gracious to us personally.

We arrived in Sana'a at 2 am, and tried to pass through customs quickly to get to the hotel for a precious few hours of sleep before returning early the next morning to fly to Addis Ababa. However, the customs agent refused to accept our visas. He claimed they had not been processed properly. We envisioned a sleepless night in the spare airport customs room and uncertainty about our departure the next day. Fortunately, however, the ambassador had been on the flight with us, and he noticed our predicament just as he was about to leave the airport. He returned and engaged in a loud, vigorous argument with the customs officer. After all, the ambassador had processed our visas himself.

We finally passed customs, gathered our luggage and went to find taxis. Immediately after I stepped out of the terminal, a young man grabbed my luggage and ran toward a cab. I was sure it was a thief, but he was simply an aide to one of the drivers and he was trying to make sure I went with his preferred driver. All of the drivers and others passing time in the late night—or early morning—hours wore the jambiya, a short dagger, in their belts. They were also high on khat, the narcotic enjoyed by many if not most men in Sana'a. Khat (or chat or quat) is an amphetamine that causes excitement, euphoria, and delusions of grandeur. It may feel good, but it is not recommended to mix with driving.

Since there were five of us, we split into two cabs. Mike McCaskey and I shared one cab and the other three went in the other one. Our driver peeled rubber and sent gravel flying as he pulled away from the curb, and we knew we were in for an exciting trip. At one point, the cab sped and skidded around a corner barely missing a parked police car. Mike and I turned to face each other with eyes wide and a look that said, "This is it. Here we will die." Somehow the cab avoided a collision and the police did nothing, so we arrived shaken but whole at the Sana'a Sheraton Hotel, in time to sleep for two hours and take a cold shower before returning for the early morning flight.

Fortunately, the morning cab drivers were not yet intoxicated with khat, so the trip was uneventful. At the airport, however, the official responsible for checking luggage for explosives and contraband was thoroughly drugged. His eyes stared into the distance, and he missed every other bag as he tried to affix stickers that indicated the bags had passed inspection. We assumed this was normal, so we proceeded to the final counter with some bags stamped and others not. However, we were refused entry until every piece was marked. As the others presented our tickets and passports, I took the unmarked bags back to our friendly agent, and demanded stamps. He seemed to be a bit irritated with me, but he finally complied, and we were permitted to board the Ethiopian Airlines flight for Addis Ababa.

Unlike Asmara where we had a complete itinerary in advance indicating our schedule, we had no advance notice of the schedule or whom we would see. All we knew was our hotel, because we had made those arrangements ourselves. When the plane landed, it remained stopped on the tarmac, but the door didn't open. We looked out the window and noticed a group of well-dressed officials waiting at the bottom of the ramp, so we assumed some important people must be on the flight, and we would have to wait for them to depart.

In a few minutes, the stewardess came to us and announced, "They are ready for you now." We were the important dignitaries holding up the departure for everyone else. We were tired from the lack of sleep, but we also knew things would go well in Addis Ababa. We were greeted at the bottom of the ramp by high level officials from the foreign ministry and taken to the VIP lounge to be oriented and given an itinerary.

We were taken by our assigned drivers to the hotel, and after time to rest, we were given a private tour of the Ethiopian National Museum with Emperor Haile Selassie's throne and the amazing cast replica of Lucy, the recently discovered oldest humanoid bones ever found. Lucy had lived in the Afar Triangle region of Ethiopia 3.5 million years ago. The actual skeleton is not on display, because it is too fragile, and it is being studied in the Paleoanthropology Laboratories of the Museum.

The Ministry of Foreign Affairs was a gracious host, and they had arranged a remarkable set of high level meetings. We started with the Minister of Foreign Affairs, Seyoum Mesfin, followed by a very serious and penetrating two-hour meeting with Prime Minister Meles Zenawi. The Prime Minister presented his analysis of the origins and causes of the conflict from his perspective. In his opinion, the purpose of the war was to stop aggression by Eritrea and to establish the principle that a country has the right and obligation to protect its sovereign land, and no nation can change international boundaries by the use of force. He expressed his desire to end the war, and to accept the OAU framework agreement as it had been clarified. It was clear that Prime Minister Meles believed the United States should play a significant role in the peace process and Ethiopia would attend a peace conference if one were called by President Clinton or the UN, if certain pre-conditions were met.

Prime Minister Meles' analysis, perception, and explanation for the war and its resolution was a mirror image of his counterpart and adversary President Isaias. Both identified the same issues and objections to the other. Both firmly believed they were right and the other was wrong. During the meeting with the Prime Minister, we perceived a special opportunity to advance the peace process. President Isaias had agreed to many concessions on the major points in contention, and he had authorized us to share the information with Prime Minister Meles. Meles expressed surprise and appreciation for the progress we had made. He had not anticipated any concessions from Isaias. We encouraged him to accept the concessions from Isaias and make appropriate ones of his own. He did. Point-by-point, we seemed to be able to reach a mutually acceptable accommodation.

It appeared we had found resolutions to each contentious issue save one—who would administer the disputed territories between the beginning of a cease fire and the final resolution of the boundary issue? Meles refused to allow anyone other than Ethiopia to administer Badme or any other territory they had claimed prior to the onset of the war. Eritrea insisted it should administer the land they claimed, but they would consider allowing a neutral body such as the UN to provide temporary control.

Aside from this fundamental issue of temporary control, both sides agreed on all other points. An independent commission should use international law and historic treaties to determine precisely where the actual border should be, and it should be demarcated accordingly. They agreed to allow UN Peacekeepers to monitor the cease fire, and they would allow other independent commissions to determine who was responsible for starting the war. Independent commissions would also determine who should make reparations to whom and arrange for the exchange of prisoners.

In addition to meetings with top government officials, we met with business leaders, with religious leaders, and with academics at Addis Ababa University, as well as representatives of the Inter-Africa Group. We had requested meetings with citizen groups because we wanted to understand how the public felt about the war, and we wanted to do all we could to help build popular support for a peace process. The business leaders wanted peace because the war was ruining the economy. Academics and civil society representatives wanted peace because they wanted to be able to interact with their intellectual friends and counterparts to the north.

All of the meetings went extremely well, with one surprising exception. We were invited by His Holiness Abune Paulos, Patriarch of the Ethiopian Orthodox Church, to meet with him and the other top religious leaders in the country. The head of the Catholic, Lutheran and other Christian denominations were there along with the leaders of the Jewish and Muslim congregations. John spoke for our group, explaining the purpose of our trip—to help both sides find a path to peace. When he finished, we looked forward to an expression of appreciation from our religious hosts and a discussion of strategies to achieve peace. Patriarch Paulos thanked us for our efforts, but he then raised his voice to express his disdain for Eritrea for insisting on independence and for starting the war. Ethiopia, he said, must defend itself and its honor. "Therefore, there must be war! There must be war!" he roared shaking his large ceremonial cross in our faces.

We were appalled. John had not been feeling well, and he was sleep deprived, and he nearly lost his temper with the holiest man in Ethiopia if not the entire African continent. John did his best to counter the patriarch, but it was useless. Patriarchs don't debate or argue. They proclaim. As we were leaving, most, if not all, of the other religious leaders came to us quietly to assure us that the patriarch did not speak for them. They wished us well and offered their support.

We knew the patriarch was a close ally of Prime Minister Meles, and we had to assume he felt he was defending his friend and colleague, but it was a very disturbing experience. I have read reports in which the patriarch is given credit for helping build bridges between the religious communities in Ethiopia and Eritrea and advocating for peace. I hope that is true, but we saw a very different man that day.

Our team also met to share ideas and strategies with Sam Ibok, head of the Organization of African Unity's Conflict Resolution Center. (The OAU has since been reorganized as the African Union to give it more authority.) Ibok was intimately involved in the coordination of the OAU's efforts to resolve this conflict, and he deserves much of the credit for framing the final resolution. We also met twice with U.S. Ambassador David Shinn to keep him and the Department of State informed of our activities, ideas and progress. We maintained our independence from US foreign policy, but we also kept the State Department and President Clinton's envoy Tony Lake informed of any major new developments.

Because of the significant progress, we were determined to push for a final solution before leaving. All of the parties agreed that if interim control of the disputed territory could be resolved, peace would be at hand. Additional meetings were held with Ethiopia's Foreign Minister Mesfin, his deputy and other senior staff. Direct contact with Asmara was not possible because all phone lines had been cut, so we established communications with Eritrean leaders through Haile Menkerios, Eritrea's ambassador to the UN.

We met with the Ethiopian officials in their offices, then retreated to our hotel to call Menkerios in New York with new proposals, questions, and suggestions for possible resolutions. Menkerios called Isaias to relay the messages, then he called us back with the response. We would return to the foreign ministry with the latest information. It was a cumbersome process, and we had limited time. We went through three rounds of these interactions, and each one clarified and narrowed the difference in positions. It seemed we were near a final resolution, but time ran out, and we were not able to achieve a breakthrough on the last intractable issue of administration of the disputed territories. Neither side would budge, and we had to catch our plane to return home. We were prepared to extend our stay if we had seen a crack on either side, but it just wasn't there.

≈

Our message had been consistent in both capitols—the killing could and should end now. The war had become a stalemate with neither side capable of achieving a military victory. Too many lives had already been lost, economic and social progress had been arrested and set back, and further chaos and conflict could engulf the entire region. Ultimately, we argued, Ethiopia and Eritrea must live together and get along peacefully because they are locked in a symbiotic relationship dictated by geography, economics, and culture. The solutions to end the conflict were the same then as they would be in six days, six months, six years, or 60,000 more dead. The issues separating the leaders were no longer insurmountable. We strongly recommended face-to-face meetings, facilitated by a third party, between representatives of the leaders and then between the leaders themselves.

Unfortunately, more than a year would pass before Isaias and Meles would look directly at each other, embrace, and sign the final agreement—an agreement virtually identical to the one on the table at the time of our trip. Tens of thousands of soldiers died and one million civilians were displaced to change absolutely nothing of consequence.

Following the trip, we wrote to both leaders to express appreciation for the opportunity to meet, to indicate extreme disappointment that the war was continuing, and to urge them to continue looking for opportunities to end the conflict. We also expressed our continued commitment to help wherever and whenever possible. In addition, John and I reported on our observations and impressions to U.S. officials, interested NGO leaders, and the media. John took advantage of a private meeting with President Clinton to share his impressions and recommendations. He urged the President to use his personal relationship with President Isaias and Prime Minister Meles to press them to take the final steps toward peace.

Based on our discussions with both ambassadors and with the foreign ministers and occasional direct contact with Meles and Isaias, we were convinced that a resolution could be achieved if the U.S. government were to exert the right pressure. International affairs reporter Steve Mufsin picked up the story and published an article in the *Washington Post* that in essence chided the Clinton Administration for its inaction. The article also quoted Susan Rice, then Assistant Secretary of State for Africa, accusing us of being naïve and ill informed. Immediately after the story appeared, I went straight to both embassies. I feared the criticism from Rice would undermine our credibility and weaken our position. I was wrong. Both ambassadors gave the exact same response: "Now, we know we can trust you!" They also affirmed our contention that the right pressure from Washington could force both sides to agree to end the fighting. Unfortunately, the pressure never came, and the war went on for another year.

Throughout the process, we tried to ascertain precisely where each side believed the actual national boundaries to be. We reasoned that if each side would independently indicate their concept of the border, and if the differences proved to be less consequential than imagined, a breakthrough might be possible. Responses to questions about the actual border had always been vague. Both sides produced their own maps to prove their points, but the maps were imprecise and incompatible. No one, including the U.S. government, seemed to have detailed maps that could be used to determine the perceived boundaries in a meaningful way. Action-oriented John obtained a very large and detailed map of the border area from the U.S. Mapping Agency. With the map in hand, John and I met with visiting top level officials from Eritrea to draw a line on the map designating where they believed the applicable treaties indicated the boundaries to be. (We used a clear mylar film overlay to keep the map clean for Ethiopia.) They did so.

Then we met with officials in the Ethiopian Embassy and asked for a similar indication on a clean overlay of the same map. The Ethiopian officials declined the invitation to draw a line on the map, but they produced a list of villages that, in their view, belong within Ethiopia. Unfortunately, however, it was never possible to reconcile the line on the map drawn by Eritrean officials with the names of the towns and villages provided by Ethiopia in a way that would help determine if serious boundary issues actually existed. It was a worthy effort, but we were foiled.

≈

In February 2000, the Center for Strategic Decision Research sponsored a panel discussion at the Stanford University Law School on the conflict. The governments of both countries were invited to participate, but they declined because they would not appear together. Therefore, the speakers were intellectuals and activists from both countries who presented sharply contrasting analyses of the causes and possible solutions to the war. Our RPCV team was invited to present a moderating overview, and I represented the group. The room was filled with hundreds of students and others from both countries as well as Americans who were interested in the issues. While the debate ignited passions, it was clear that all participants, particularly those in the audience, wanted the war to end, and the differences did not warrant further casualties.

By early March, Eritrea had agreed to apply the *status quo ante* principle to the administration of disputed territories during a cease fire. Ethiopia would administer Badme and other places it controlled before the war, and the same would apply to Eritrean land. However, now negotiations over technical arrangements for implementation of the OAU framework appeared to break down. The central issue this time was the sequence of events in the implementation process, the modalities. Having tried and failed to get the two sides to draw lines on the map, our group tried a new tactic on a similar theme. The OAU framework called for a neutral commission to demarcate the border. This, however, was to take place after several other steps in the process, and neither side liked the sequence. Why not, the group asked, agree to allow the commission to demarcate the border as the first step in the process. If both sides would agree to hold their fire in place until the border had been determined, and if both sides would agree to abide by the decisions of the commission, then the war could end. Both sides agreed this approach seemed logical. However, neither trusted the other to abide by it, and the war continued.

In April, President Isaias Afwerki once again visited the United States, and we hosted a reception for him at the Cosmos Club in Washington. My good friend and colleague Bob Berg is a member of the Club, and he served as a well-informed and effective host. Bob is one of the leading American experts on Africa, and his wife Vivian Lowrey Derryck was head of the Africa Bureau for USAID. Their presence and engagement with us added to our credibility. The event gave President Isaias an opportunity to meet and address a substantial group of invited guests from leading NGOs and the U.S. government. The event also provided our team with yet another opportunity to try to help the President find ways to respond affirmatively to the issues that remained unresolved.

At that time, Eritrea's military held substantial territory within Ethiopia. I feared it gave Ethiopia an excuse to mount a devastating counter invasion. With its larger army and support from both Russia and the U.S., Ethiopia could inflict serious damage. We had picked up intelligence from several sources that Ethiopia was about to launch a major attack, but Eritrea remained resolute. We urged Isaias to voluntarily redeploy his troops back to the original border as a declaration of commitment to a reasonable resolution. The Ethiopian assault might be averted, and the peace process might be revived with this bold initiative, we argued. The merits of the case for re-deployment were apparent, and they were appreciated by the Eritrean leaders. However, Isaias and his staff believed they were entitled to the territory they occupied based on the Colonial Treaties, and they were convinced they needed to hold the additional occupied land for military and security reasons.

A few weeks later, on May 12, I called Haile Menkerios at the UN to once again urge an Eritrean redeployment out of Ethiopian territory, but he assured me Ethiopia would not attack, and that Eritrea had to hold the captured land or it would sacrifice a strategic advantage. Precisely as we were speaking, Ethiopia began a massive offensive that drove Eritrea's forces out of all occupied Ethiopian territory and far back into Eritrea. It profoundly changed the dynamics.

The next morning, Haile called to express his regret that he and his government had not heeded our warning. I believe it was the only time I was right and Haile was wrong, but I wish I could have been wrong this time. The invasion caused extensive casualties on both sides, and Ethiopia's occupation of and extensive deposits of landmines in fertile Eritrean land caused severe long term suffering. Ethiopia occupied nearly a quarter of Eritrea's prime agricultural land, and 650,000 people were displaced.

The battles raged for months, and Ethiopia drove further into Eritrea. The power positions were reversed. Ethiopia now occupied Eritrea's sovereign land. Many in Eritrea believed the invasion proved that Ethiopia's ultimate objective was to overthrow the Isaias government and to take the port city Asab. Rhetorical flourishes by leaders in Ethiopia promising conquest gave credence to those fears.

≈

Finally, in July, an OAU Summit appeared to produce an agreement that would end the war. Newly elected OAU President Abelaziz Bouteflika of Algeria was to lead the mediation "alone and with others." The *New York Times* headline read, "Peace Deal May Be Near for Ethiopia and Eritrea". President Bouteflika did, indeed, lead a vigorous effort, but peace remained elusive.

In August, Eritrea's President Isaias visited the United States for the annual Eritrea Festival which attracts thousands of participants. During the visit, he met with our team, and the issues were reviewed yet again in great detail. President Isaias indicated his conditions for peace, and the group expressed appreciation for his efforts, but also urged him to find new ways to be flexible and end the war.

The fighting took a major toll on both militaries and civilians as well. Eritrea lost an entire growing season in its primary agricultural region. At last, however, the fighting subsided. High level talks were underway, and both sides held their fire in place, just as we had urged a year before. John and I went back once again to see President Isaias' close friend Ghebre (Gabe) Selassie Mehreteab who would arrange a call to his friend, the President of Eritrea. (We had been meeting with Gabe on a regular basis from the beginning of the process. He was closer to the President than even the ambassador, and since he was not obligated to adhere to the official government position, we were able to explore options freely with him.)

We had been assured by Ethiopia that the war could be over if only Eritrea would agree to a modest change in the proposed sequence of steps, the modalities, to implement a ceasefire. We wanted to encourage Isaias to accept the change. As we spoke on the phone, it was obvious Isaias resented having to be the one to make the last concession. It was one more assault on his pride. Yet, it was also an opportunity to challenge his adversary to live up to his word and end the war. Reluctantly, Isaias gave us a firm, absolute commitment to accept the change.

I jumped into a cab and went straight to the Ethiopian Embassy. Ambassador Brehane was not there but his Deputy Chief of Mission Fisseha Adugna was, and he received me immediately. I asked him to confirm the word we had from Ethiopia that the war would be over if Isaias would make the specified changes in the sequence in the ceasefire modalities. Fisseha reaffirmed the commitment, but expressed confidence that Isaias would never agree. "I just spoke with President Isaias, and he just did," I informed him. "I don't believe you," Fisseha replied with a look of surprise. "Have I ever misled you?" I declared, a bit impatiently. "No, but I just can't believe it," was all he could say.

I pulled my cell phone out of my pocket and offered to call the Eritrean Embassy to confirm it. "You can't do that!" he insisted. Both countries had absolutely prohibited their envoys from communicating with each other. He wouldn't even let me use my own cell phone to call the enemy embassy while on his property. "Okay," I said, "I know the rules. But please convey the message to your Prime Minister."

The second I stepped off the curb from Ethiopia's embassy, I reported the conversation to Eritrea's ambassador Semere Russom. Semere and I had become good friends in large part because he had also attended Oklahoma State, and we enjoyed sharing stories from our experiences in Stillwater. Semere and I discussed the complications of communication between the embassies, but we shared confidence that we had reached the end. We both felt the message would reach Ethiopian Prime Minister Meles, and we hoped he would not raise any new obstacles to the final resolution.

Two weeks later, Prime Minister Meles visited the United States, and we offered to host a reception for him, just as we had for President Isaias earlier in the year. Instead, the Embassy invited John, Mel Foote and me to have breakfast with the Prime Minister in the Ambassador's residence. As we settled in at the table, Meles leaned forward and said, "I want you to know the war is over, and I want to thank you for helping make it happen." He proceeded to provide details of the peace agreement that was still in the process of being written. We also discussed essential steps to restore relations between the two countries and to rebuild the economy of the area. I had trouble concentrating on the rest of the discussion. The war was over. I wanted to celebrate in the streets, but no one else would have understood.

In November, President Isaias called his friend Gabe with the announcement that the war was, indeed, over and that the agreement would be signed on December 12 in Algiers. President Isaias asked Gabe to be sure the Peace Corps group would be there to witness the event. Shortly thereafter, a formal invitation was extended by the Eritrean government. The Ethiopian government was equally enthusiastic about our participation in the ceremony.

≈

John, Mike, and I flew to Algiers to represent the group. While there, we discussed the war, the difficult road to peace and the final resolution with Secretary of State Madeleine Albright and with President Clinton's special envoy Tony Lake. Susan Rice was also there, and we had a very brief conversation with her about the resolution. There had been some differences between the official U.S. negotiators and our team during the process, but our respective roles and contributions were understood and appreciated by everyone in the end.

Prime Minister Meles greeted us warmly prior to the ceremony, and again after it had concluded. John, Mike, and I retreated to the hotel bar after the ceremonies thinking we would relax, go to bed and leave the next day. However, a member of President Isaias' staff found us and invited us to meet with the President and his delegation. President Isaias expressed his deep appreciation for the work of the group, and he indicated again that our efforts had been extremely important to the process. The meeting lasted well into the night, as we explored issues relating to building a firm foundation for lasting peace and for economic recovery.

The following morning, Seyoum Mesfin, Ethiopia's Minister of Foreign Affairs, hosted us for breakfast. His message of appreciation was similar to that of President Isaias the night before. The group reflected on the lengthy meetings we had held in Addis Ababa eighteen months before, and we lamented the death and destruction that had occurred during the intervening period. However, Mr. Mesfin assured us that in spite of the death, destruction, and animosity, the peace would last. Most of the meeting focused on opportunities to rebuild relationships between the countries and restore economic progress.

Shortly after the ceremony in Algiers, Prime Minister Meles wrote a letter to John with this message: "I write to you and to your colleagues to express my profound appreciation for your friendship, and for all the concern you have demonstrated during one of the most difficult periods for our country... I can assure you, though you did not draft the Agreement that was finally signed, your contribution was indeed invaluable for creating the momentum and the spirit which made this historic achievement possible."

We knew from the beginning that we would not and could not draft the formal agreement. That was the role of the lawyers and official diplomats. Rather, our role was to persuade both leaders with logic and moral conviction to find a way to put their differences aside for the sake of peace and for the sake of their people. Our group sought to provide momentum toward a path to peace and build a spirit of reconciliation. The process took far longer than anticipated, and the price paid by the people and the economies of both countries was extremely high. In the end, however, the mission was accomplished.

Immediately upon my return from Algiers, I went to visit Muluneh Lema and his Ethiopian and Eritrean colleagues in the parking garage, and they treated me like a national hero for both countries. They had followed our efforts through news reports from their respective countries. We had become celebrities in Eritrea. While the press coverage was less prominent in Ethiopia, we were well known there as well. I was grateful for their expressions of appreciation, but I felt inadequate, and saddened that it had taken so long.

On January 3, 2001, shortly after the ceremony in Algiers, the following article by Lewis Dolinsky appeared in the *San Francisco Chronicle*:

How Africa's Forgotten War Finally Ended

On a stage in Algiers on Dec. 12, in front of dignitaries and guests, Ethiopian Prime Minister Meles Zenawi and Eritrean

President Isaias Afwerki signed the treaty that ended their war, which began in May 1998. Algerian President Abdelaziz Bouteflika, sitting between Meles and Isaias, encouraged them to shake hands. They did, coldly and perfunctorily. Secretary of State Madeleine Albright and U.N. Secretary-General Kofi Annan witnessed the treaty. Then Meles and Isaias shook hands again. This time there were little smiles, pats on the back and an embrace. Tension was broken.

For three private U.S. citizens in attendance—Chic Dambach, John Garamendi and Michael McCaskey—this was the true end of the war, a moment they had prayed for and worked for as friends of both sides. Former Peace Corps Volunteers talking to leaders who had studied under Peace Corp teachers, they had offered proposals, nudged whoever was recalcitrant, and asserted privately and publicly that the terms available in June 1999, when they visited both countries, would be the terms whenever the fighting stopped. They were right.

The Boundary Commission will determine the disputed borders based on colonial maps and "applicable international law." Both sides agreed to abide by its ruling, and the three Americans are sure they will. In Algiers, both Ethiopians and Eritreans seemed happy and relieved.

The disputed territory—a few barren miles—never meant much. Ethiopia has proved that it is mightier and that Eritrea cannot change the status quo by force; Eritrea has shown that it may bend but it will not break. Normal life can return. But even before the devastation and the spending of precious capital and lives, these were two of the world's poorest countries.

For efforts not always appreciated by the State Department,

PHOTO ALBUM

Chick Dambach above works in and around Cartagena forming a Coop which will help local fisherman get out to sea in boats instead of using dynamite and throwing the "atarrayas" (which he demonstrates above) from the shore. (See feature, page, 6).

The cover story in the November/December, 1968 issue of *Porvenir*, the Peace Corps, Colombia (Cuerpo de Paz, Colombia) newspaper.

Washington Canoe Club's K-4 Team: David Halpern, Dan Schnurrenberger, Grant Niskanen and Chic Dambach on the Potomac River in the early 1980s.

With Barry Goldwater and David Block
at OSU in 1966.

Peace Corps 35th Anniversary celebration in 1996. UN Ambassador (and future Secretary of State) Madeleine Albright
honors former Peace Corps Director Loret Miller Ruppe.
L-R Maury Sterns, Ruppe, Joseph Permetti, Albright, Ron
Tschetter (NPCA Board Chair and future Peace Corps Director), and Chic Dambach.

With Peace Corps Director Mark Gearan and the first Peace Corps Director, Sargent Shriver.

With Brian O'Connell and Ted Sorensen at the Kennedy Library in Boston in 1999. Asked who wrote the famous words, "Ask not what your country can do for you..." Sorensen responded, "Ask not. When the President speaks it is the President's speech."

With John Garamendi and Mike McCaskey, exchanging gifts with HE Meles Zenawi, Prime Minister of Ethiopia, in 1999.

With John Garamendi, Mike McCaskey, and HE Isaias Afwerki, President of Eritrea, in 1999.

With President Ronald Reagan in the Oval Office in 1983.

With President Bill Clinton in the Oval Office in 1996.

With former President Jimmy Carter, Ginny Kirkwood and Bob Gale at the Carter Center in 1995.

With Vice President Dick Cheney and Jim Click in Phoenix in 2007.

With Congressman Sam Farr and Peter Yarrow in Farr's office in 2004.

With Peter Yarrow (background) and Judy Collins after the Operation Respect "What Works" conference banquet in Washington, D.C., in 2005. Collin's husband, Louis Nelson, is at the far left, and *Stagebill* chairman, Fred Trater, is at the far right.

At the Global Symposium of Peaceful Nations, November 1, 2009, with Harriet Fulbright, presenting a Most Peaceful Nation Award to Van Chuong Pham and Hong Quang Nguyen of Vietnam. Photo by Dakota Fine Photography.

With Aaron Voldman, Eric Ham, Congressman John Garamendi and Julia Simon-Mishel at Peacebuilding Policy Days, April 15, 2010.

these three Americans and two other Peace Corps alumni (of the five, all but Dambach once served in the region) were invited to Algiers by Isaias and encouraged to come by the Ethiopians.

They were embraced and thanked by both leaders. They met with Isaias for an hour and with Meles' foreign minister, Seyoum Mesfin, for longer, and got similar messages: Help us rebuild. They said they would, and they can. Dambach has ties to nonprofits; McCaskey, chairman of the Chicago Bears, has extensive business connections; Garamendi is a former California legislator and insurance commissioner and former deputy secretary of the interior.

In turn, they emphasized the need to tone down rhetoric and quickly re- establish road and air links, communications and ties between business and academia in the two countries, which are related by blood, culture and language. Bitterness and estrangement must be overcome sooner rather than later.

The three Americans give high marks to Bouteflika, who remained as mediator months after Algeria ended its term as head of the Organization of African Unity, and to Anthony Lake, President Clinton's special envoy. (In appreciation of the administration's work, Isaias told Clinton he wanted to wind this up before Clinton left office.)

Under the terms of the treaty, a panel will determine who started the war. Dambach thinks there are lessons for Africa in this conflict and its slow resolution. He hopes someone will write a book, or thorough analytical article.

Even partisans acknowledge that this war should never have started or widened or dragged on. What little press coverage it received often focused on how little press coverage it was receiving: "Africa's Forgotten War." People talk of tens of thousands of deaths, but no one really knows. Ethiopia probably paid dearly for its final thrust into Eritrea and would have paid more had it tried to press on.

Maybe when a history is written, these American amateur diplomats will be mentioned and their conduct evaluated. Did they help or were they just naïve intruders? Dambach would like to know.

Implementation of the agreement has been slow and problematic. Investigators concluded that Eritrea was responsible for starting the war, but the commission determined that Badme, the small town that was in dispute and the site of the firefight that lit the fuse, belonged to Eritrea. That came as a surprise to many observers, and it was an unacceptable conclusion for Ethiopia. After all, they had fought a costly and brutal war on the premise that they were protecting their territory—Badme—from the invader Eritrea. Now, the independent and balanced border commission said they had been wrong. Nearly a decade later, Ethiopia has yet to redeploy its troops from the Eritrean side of the border, and both sides maintain forces poised to fight. The hostile stalemate continues to consume enormous resources. Both countries need each other for social and economic progress, but pride and hostility continue to trump reason and the public good. Nevertheless, there has been no fighting, death or destruction for many years, and there is still reason to believe a permanent resolution is possible. As before, patience and persistence can produce results.

Several months after the trip to Algiers, I stopped for a hot dog at the kiosk at the corner of 18th and L Streets in Washington. The lady in the small aluminum mobile store had the distinct look of an Eritrean, so I asked her where she was from.

"Eritrea," she replied proudly.

"I thought so," I said and added, "I know your President Isaias Afwerki."

She stopped putting mustard on my lunch dog, and looked straight at me, almost through me. "Who are you?" she wanted to know.

"I'm Chic Dambach." Her eyes widened, and her face filled with joy.

"I know you! I know who you are! You brought peace to my country!" She bounded out of her tight space and gave me a big hug.

Yeshu Habitegioris Woldemicael and her family had followed the story of the Peace Corps team through news from Asmara from the very beginning. She and thousands of others in the Horn of Africa Diaspora had been our silent cheering squad all along. Yeshu and her family and I have been dear friends ever since. They always come to our annual Christmas party in full traditional Eritrean clothing, and they are the highlight of the event.

While we built strong relationships with the embassy staff and the Diaspora from both countries, the Eritreans have gone out of their way to reciprocate. We are invited to the annual Eritrean Festival every year, and we go whenever possible. Freweni Abraham and Tsehai Habtemariam of the embassy staff have also become treasured friends, and I have built a positive relationship with each new ambassador.

Unfortunately, however, my relationship with President Isaias and his government have become strained. He had promised to implement democratic reforms, guarantee political freedom and protect human rights as soon as the war ended. But instead, he has become authoritarian, abused human rights and obliterated the free press. UN Ambassador Haile Menkerios and fourteen other high level officials wrote and signed a statement challenging his behavior and they have paid a severe price—they have been charged with treason. I had met several of them, and I had developed a personal friendship with Menkerios. When I heard that the offenders were in prison, I feared for their fate, especially my friend Haile.

≈

Almost a decade later, in August, 2009, the seat next to me on the Metro from Dupont Circle to Union Station became vacant, and a very nicely dressed and attractive young lady took it. I noticed she was reading *A History of Modern Ethiopia 1855—1991*, a book I had studied to better understand the country. It had been recommended to me by Fisseha Adugna, the Deputy Chief of Mission at the Embassy, and the man to whom I had delivered the message that Eritrea was prepared to accept the final terms to end the war. I asked if she was from the Horn of Africa, and she responded with surprise that anyone on the train would even know where the Horn is. "Yes." She said proudly, "I'm from Ethiopia." I told her I had been there, and a friendly, even enthusiastic, conversation ensued. As our discussion developed I told her more about my experiences, and she told me her father had worked for the Ethiopian government.

Finally she asked, "Do you know Fisseha Adugna?" The man I had come to know and admire when he was Deputy Chief of Mission for the Embassy of Ethiopia was her father. For a moment, we just stared at each other in disbelief that we had met by chance on the Metro. I gave her my card; she took it to her dad, and now we have reconnected and renewed our friendship under much more relaxed and enjoyable circumstances. Mitty Fisseha is studying international relations at Duke, and my guess is she will become the first female Prime Minister of Ethiopia by age 45.

ROME, ARABIA & PERSIA

While with the Museum Trustee Association, I spent more time on international affairs and my favorite causes than on museums and their trustees. Since I worked very long hours, the association members got their money's worth from me, but they did not get my commitment or anything extra. In addition to devoting time to the Ethiopia and Eritrea peace process, I used another week of annual leave to spend a fascinating week in Rome as part of the U.S. delegation to the World Food Conference of the UN's Food and Agriculture Organization (FAO). Patti Garamendi held a senior position in the U.S. Foreign Agricultural Service, and she persuaded Agriculture Secretary Dan Glickman to appoint me as a delegate based on my expertise on the role of nongovernment organizations (NGOs) in international development.

The FAO had been the least willing of the UN agencies to incorporate an official role for NGOs in the formulation of their policies and programs. However, early in the conference the new council chairman acknowledged the fifty or so observers from NGOs, even though they had no recognized status. I was part of the official U.S. government delegation, which gave me a unique advantage. I had one foot in the official delegate camp, but the other foot was firmly planted among the NGOs. My primary purpose was to advocate NGO interests. The chairman reserved a special room for the NGO people to meet and develop a proposal for consideration by the council. Patti agreed I should participate in the NGO session while she and other members of the U.S. contingent attended to other matters.

The nongovernment observers from at least twenty countries gathered with no designated leadership, no agenda, and no plan. Some knew each other from previous FAO meetings and their work in the field, but most were complete strangers. I knew a few of them, but barely. Nevertheless, we organized ourselves in no time, selected leaders to preside at our meeting, set an agenda, and went to work determining our recommendations. I was selected to preside at the meeting and to lead the presentation team.

In short order, we agreed to acknowledge that our role relative to official FAO policies and positions was to provide information and policy recommendations. We should be a voice but not a vote at the table. Some of the official delegates had feared we would demand a vote in addition to a voice. They also feared we wanted to organize street demonstrations, mount a coup, and take over their official responsibilities. Yet, we were seasoned professionals who knew better. We respected the fact that the government representatives had official standing to make policy, and we did not. We just wanted a voice to provide vital information and to make the case for policies and programs that could be effective. As long as that basic principle could be respected and honored, we might gain access to the process. We took the power and confrontation issues off the table from the outset.

Nongovernment organizations bring a unique perspective to international policies and programs. Since we do not represent governments, we are free to focus on the needs and priorities of the people we seek to serve—the people who go to bed hungry and sometimes die from malnutrition. The data is sketchy, but UNICEF reports 26,000 children under the age of five die each and every day due to malnutrition, unsafe water, and related diseases. We know them, we know their needs, we see the causes of their hunger, and we can be their voice in the halls of power. We manage on-the-ground programs designed to alleviate hunger through both agricultural development and food distribution. We know what works and what doesn't. We also know that all too often the suffering is caused by—rather than alleviated by—governments and their policies. That is why the NGO voice is absolutely essential.

A small leadership team drafted our set of proposals, gained the support of our group, and we presented our report and recommendations within three days. The FAO took them under advisement, but we feared they would be buried in a bureaucratic junk pile. I went on to other endeavors, and did not follow up to see what became of our initiatives. However, a few years later I was invited to give a speech in Oklahoma on world hunger policies. In the process of my research, I discovered that our recommendations had been adopted, almost verbatim, and that NGOs are now invited to participate as a recognized and respected source of information and policy recommendations. Mission accomplished.

≈

The controversial 2000 election took place that fall, and as a vigorous Gore advocate, I thought the Florida fiasco was a national disgrace. I became particularly agitated when Bush spokespeople objected to a manual recount. They tried to argue that the scanners were more accurate, and that a hand count would be neither necessary nor appropriate. The Democrats, however, were doing a miserable job of explaining their position to the public. They used arcane legal language while the Republicans spoke in plain, persuasive English.

To me, the problem with automatic scanners was no different than the experience of middle class shoppers living in the heartland every time they go to the grocery store. Most of the time, the checkout scanners work just fine, but sometimes the machine fails to read the code. When that happens, the clerk stops scanning, visually reads the numerical code, and manually types it into the register. That's what a manual vote recount was all about. If the Democrats would explain the problem as similar to a grocery store scanner failure, and the solution as visual verification and manual correction, the public would understand, and the public relations battle might shift.

I called John Garamendi and told him how badly I thought our side was losing the public relations battle, and I suggested using the grocery store scanner analogy. John agreed and promised to convey the recommendation directly to the Gore campaign leaders. That very night, Vice Presidential candidate Joe Lieberman was on *The Larry King Show*, and he told King and the public, "It's just like going to the grocery store and the scanner fails to read the code. The clerk holds up the item, reads the code and manually enters the correct information." The next day, Gore said much the same thing, and campaign spokesmen used the analogy from then on. My small input didn't change the election outcome, and we suffered eight years of flawed domestic programs and foreign policy disaster as a result. At least I played my own small part in the effort to place the man who actually won the 2000 election in the White House.

≈

Bob Gale, my friend from the National Peace Corps Association board, was the founder of the National Center for Nonprofit Boards (NCNB), and he liked the materials I had developed for consulting. As a result, he encouraged me to associate with NCNB because he knew it would be a much better fit than the MTA. I had already become friends with Judy O'Conner, the NCNB president, and with Sandy Hughes, the senior consultant on their staff. I had known Sandy when she was CEO of U.S. Rowing, the governing body for the Olympic rowing program. The headquarters offices for rowing and canoeing were on the same floor of the same building in Indianapolis, and we shared competition venues during most major international events, so we worked closely with them. I had several friends in the rowing community, including Sandy.

With these special connections with the founder (Gale), CEO (O'Conner) and senior consultant (Hughes), it was easy to slide from the MTA into NCNB. I joined the staff as a senior consultant to work along with Sandy, Berit Lakey and Marla Bobowick. (They really needed a guy to achieve token gender balance!) We provided consulting services to nonprofits throughout the country and worldwide, and we brought the lessons we learned from those experiences back to the Center. We were the eyes and ears of the organization to help develop new and creative intellectual frameworks and concepts to advance the practice on nonprofit governance. Over my objections, NCNB changed its name to BoardSource shortly after I arrived.

Our consulting team wrote articles for *Board Member* magazine, and we wrote and edited books. I wrote one small book on *Structures and Practices of Nonprofit Boards*, and I co-wrote a *Business Professionals Guide to Service on Nonprofit Boards*. A few years later, BoardSource asked Melissa Davis to combine my book with one on leadership roles written by Bob Gale. The result is a vastly superior *Structures and Practices of Nonprofit Boards* with three co-authors. I am particularly honored to have my name associated with Bob as a co-author.

My consulting clients included Special Olympics International, several United Way agencies, the Red Cross, Keep America Beautiful, Junior Achievement, Fleet Financial in Boston, and many others. My favorite was also the most intimidating. Phi Beta Kappa, the fraternal organization for the best liberal arts and sciences students in the country, had tried unsuccessfully to produce a strategic plan to help the society adapt to a changing academic and social environment. They asked me to help them try again. Since, as a student, I had been far from qualified for Phi Beta Kappa membership, I feared my lack of intellectual capacity would be apparent to the brilliant minds on their board, but it actually went remarkably well. They adopted the plan, they still use it, and I remain friends with their Secretary (CEO) John Churchill.

≈

Shortly after I started at BoardSource, Sherry Mueller, President of the National Center for International Visitors, arranged for the two of us to spend a week in Saudi Arabia on a State Department sponsored trip to help members of the Royal family develop the country's civil society. Sherry and I had been officers on the board of COLEAD from its inception, and she served as chair during one of the few years when I relinquished the title. I was vice chair during her term as chair, and we had become close friends as well as professional colleagues.

Sherry was to meet and work with the Saudi women, and I would work with the men. Saudi Arabia's Princess Adela served as the host and primary point of contact for Sherry, and Prince Sultan bin Salman was my host. The Princess was well-educated, cosmopolitan, progressive, and astonishingly beautiful. Prince Sultan bin Salman had become famous as the Saudi Astronaut Prince because he had flown in the U.S. Space Shuttle two years earlier as an expression of solidarity between the U.S. and the Saudi Kingdom. He was also well educated, cosmopolitan, progressive (by Saudi standards), and astonishingly handsome.

In the paternalistic Saudi society, members of the royal family had taken care of the needs of the people with their petroleum wealth through multiple charities. But times were changing. The family's resources were becoming dispersed as each generation added to the population of royals. Furthermore, many non-royals had become quite wealthy and active in the leadership structure. It was time to build a more diverse system, and Sherry and I were there to learn about their system and offer them some guidance. I met with a wide range of Saudi organizations from educational institutions to programs for disabled children, the national museum, and the World Alliance of Muslim Youth—a Saudi version of the Peace Corps but with a distinctively religious bent.

Sherry and I were well aware of Saudi rules and customs before the trip, so we knew what to expect. Women are prohibited from moving about in public alone or with any man other than their own father, child, or husband. Since Sherry and I wanted to see the sights together, we decided to get "married". That is, we would present ourselves as a married couple if anyone from the notorious morality police should stop us. We enjoyed a week of marital bliss (without the normal meaning of that term) and then declared ourselves divorced upon departure. Ever since, we have enjoyed introducing each other as ex-spouses. It has delightful shock value, and it gives us a chance to tell the story of our trip.

Saudi Arabian society is further removed from the modern world than any I have seen anywhere. The architecture is futuristic, but mores are atavistic. The society is structured and stratified with royals in one universe and everyone else in another. Furthermore, the segregation of sexes is incomprehensible to anyone from the West. The men all dress entirely in white, and the women all dress entirely in a black "abaya". The men all wear the red and white checkered "gutrah" head scarf with a black "ogal" holding it in place, and the women cover their heads and most cover their faces as well with the "hijab". Men move about freely, and they may take several wives. Women don't. A few women are educated and hold professional positions, but that is rare.

McDonalds has invaded Saudi Arabia, and customers queue up to the counter just as they do all over the world, with one exception. A dividing wall separates one side of the store from the other. Men stand in line and order on one side of the divide, and women queue on the other side. There is no opportunity for physical connections or even for eye contact.

Sherry and I spent most of the week in Riyadh, but we were able to visit Jeddah as well. Riyadh is prosperous, but ultra conservative. There were modern shopping malls, and the traditional souks where hundreds of shops selling gold were dazzling. Jeddah is much more relaxed, and it even displays a marvelous collection of whimsical, oversized outdoor sculptures spread over several miles along the Red Sea coast.

We addressed a national conference of civil society leaders in Riyadh at the end of our visit. It was held at a hospital because that is the only facility where men and women could meet together. Even there, however, the auditorium was absolutely segregated with women seated on one side and the men on the other. I've given many speeches to a wide range of audiences, but this one was the most disorienting, by far. As I looked out from the podium, I saw a sea of pure white with red and white checkered head scarves to the left, and a dark sea of black from head to foot on the right.

To be honest, I felt relieved as we boarded the plane to depart. I have loved virtually every place I have been all over the world, and that includes many predominately Muslim countries. I found Saudi Arabia fascinating, and the people were wonderful. Nevertheless, the Wahabi version of Islam has produced a repressive society with few liberties and an abundance of prohibitions with draconian punishments attached. The customs card we completed upon landing in Riyadh warned in bold red type right on top, "Death to drug dealer." The punishment for stealing can be removal of a hand, and the death penalty can be applied to most sexual transgressions as well as drug dealing or murder. Hand amputation and the death penalty—beheading—are imposed in public in "chop-chop" square in Riyadh. I was happy to leave without having committed a transgression, or at least without having been caught.

≈

Sherry and I were on separate return flights as she went on to visit friends in Sweden. I flew from Riyadh to Frankfurt where I was to change planes for a direct flight to Baltimore Washington International airport. I had been on the same Lufthansa flight before as it originates in Addis Ababa, stops in Riyadh and continues to Frankfurt. I was seated next to a young man from Canada who was serving in the military as part of the UN Peacekeeping force on the border between Ethiopia and Eritrea. I told him of my role in the peace process, and he seemed to appreciate it. He said his job was quite boring as there was no action. I was pleased.

While waiting for the connecting flight from Frankfurt, I noticed an absolutely beautiful young lady waiting for the same flight with olive skin and jet black hair, wearing a bright red sweater. I allowed myself to glance her way a few times during the wait. Why not appreciate the scenery, I rationalized. When I boarded the plane, I noticed the lady in red once again as I moved toward my seat, and when I arrived at my row, she was there. The assigned seat right next to her was waiting for me. I had won the lottery. I introduced myself, as I always do on airplanes. If my traveling companion wants to talk, I am happy to do so. If not, I keep to myself.

Shahrzad was flying to Baltimore to meet a man she had encountered on the internet. I was unimpressed, to say the least. But the conversation quickly changed and grew into an intense discussion of personal stories, then to philosophy, theology and ethics, cultures, politics and international relations. Once we started learning about each other and moved on to discuss important issues, we connected on a deep personal and intellectual level. We talked non-stop throughout the entire eight hour flight. There is nothing I enjoy more than in-depth conversation about important issues and ideas with intelligent, well informed, and articulate people. I never enjoyed a conversation with anyone anywhere more than this one.

Shahrzad was born in Tehran, Iran to a prosperous family. Her parents had been active in the resistance to the Shah, but the opposition that brought down the Shah produced the wrong revolution. Her family wanted a uniquely Persian democracy with respect for human rights, religious freedom, and social and economic opportunity for everyone in the country. Instead, Iran became saddled with religious extremists who imposed intolerable social, political, and religious restrictions.

Her parents became part of the resistance to the new government, and her father had been taken prisoner and executed. Her mother was also at risk. When she received notice that she had been targeted, she took her two teenage daughters and escaped. The mother and sisters traveled on foot for six days and nights across the mountains into Turkey. It was a perilous escape with several close calls, and they bribed smugglers to help them slip across the border. Once in Turkey, they hid from authorities and mercenaries who would have returned them to Tehran and certain imprisonment if not execution.

Again, with the help of smugglers, they were able to board a plane to Germany and attain refugee status to avoid repatriation. They settled in Frankfurt seeking to build a new life. Shahrzad went to school with the full support of the German government, and she was pursuing a career in web-based marketing.

I learned more about Iran and its cultural history on that flight with Shahrzad than I had over all of the years previously. I knew nothing of Zoroastrian philosophy and values, and I had little appreciation of the powerful differences between the Persian people and Arabs. I knew they were different, but I likened it to differences between the U.S. and Canada. Shahrzad let me know, in no uncertain terms, that these two cultures share Middle Eastern geography and identities but little else.

Shahrzad had no use for organized religion and she held deep contempt for leaders who cite the divine as a source of wisdom and authority. She had seen theocracy at its worst, and she rejected it. She did, however, embrace the Persian traditional values enunciated by Zoroaster—think good thoughts, speak good words, do good deeds. Based on Zoroastrian principles, the Persian emperor Cyrus the Great had proclaimed religious freedom and prohibited slavery even in the territories he conquered over 2,600 years ago. It took us here in the West a long time to catch up with his enlightened philosophy.

We stayed in touch by email, and eventually I arranged an internship for Shahrzad with BoardSource. She used the Anglo name Sherry while in the U.S., and within two weeks of her arrival, everyone in the building seemed to know her by name, and by the end of the month, dozens of people called to her whenever she walked down the street. I have known many charismatic and friendly people, but Sherry was extraordinary. Her beauty certainly drew attention, but her warmth, grace, generosity, and genuine interest in other people and their lives captured hearts at every turn.

Shahrzad left Washington the day after the U.S. invaded Iraq, and I had a few opportunities to discuss the situation with her. Her intense reaction to the invasion helped deepen my resolve to oppose the invasion and seek to influence US policies. "Don't you dare invade my country," she said with eyes like daggers piercing me and my country. "I despise the government of Iran, but if you invade, I will return home, and I will wear the uniform of our army, and I will kill every invading soldier I can." She went on to say Iran has dreadful problems, but that the Persian people will solve them, not outside forces. It will take time, it may take more than her lifetime, but it will happen. She welcomed our moral support to strengthen the resistance, but change must come from Persians themselves.

I wish the neo-con intelligentsia that believes America can and should impose our "superior" ways on other people and cultures could have seen and heard Shahrzad that day. They might change their thinking. We can, and we should help other people overcome tyranny, human rights abuses, and violence, but we cannot impose it.

≈

I had joined the International Platform Association (IPA) while with the National Peace Corps Association to keep in touch with the field of my undergraduate studies. I had great appreciation for the dying art of elocution—live, in-person public speaking—as a means of civil public discourse. The IPA had been created in 1831 by Daniel Webster and Josiah Holbrook as the American Lyceum Association sponsoring lectures by intellectuals and political leaders throughout the country. It had survived the advent of radio and television, but the Internet added yet another form of competition for the time and attention of the public. Fewer and fewer people were willing to leave their homes or offices just to hear a speech. So, the IPA was clinging to a sinking tradition.

Nevertheless, the organization still sponsored an annual event that attracted many of the world's leading public figures to address a well informed and appreciative audience. In addition to preserving the art of elocution, the IPA conference served as a showcase for speakers on the lecture circuit. I was invited to speak at the 1998 conference, and in 2001, I was invited back not just to speak but also to receive the IPA's "Global Coalition Peace Award" for my work in the Horn of Africa. I had come to know Peter Yarrow, and the annual Peter, Paul and Mary concert was scheduled for Wolf Trap the night after the award presentation. Since Peter would be in town anyway, he offered to speak and sing on my behalf at the awards program. Peter gave a moving tribute with a medley of his best peace songs. I poured my heart and soul into that speech, and later IPA president Luvie Owens sent a letter indicating that, "You were at the top of our audience poll...You are an inspiration!" The silver bowl is in our small display case along with awards given to Kay and my father.

That night, we settled into the best seats in the house at Wolf Trap, the exquisite amphitheater in a pastoral setting in Virginia, just 30 minutes from downtown Washington. Peter had invited us to be his guests for the Peter, Paul and Mary concert that had sold out every year for decades. After intermission, each member of the trio did a brief solo piece. Peter came first, and he dedicated his song to someone he admired for his courage and perseverance. As Peter described the object of his esteem, Grant leaned over to me and said, "It's Kai, isn't it?" And it was. The great Peter Yarrow shared Kai's remarkable story with 6,000 folk music fans that night, and he dedicated the song "Day is Done" to him. I had always cherished that song, but now it has extra meaning for all of us.

Day is Done
Peter Yarrow

Tell me why you are crying, my son
Are you frightened like most everyone

Is it the thunder in the distance you hear
Will it help if I stay very near, I am here

And if you take my hand, my son,
All will be well when the day is done
And if you take my hand, my son
All will be well when the day is done
Day is done, when the day is done
Day is done, when the day is done
Day is done, when the day is done
Day is done

So you ask why I'm sighing, my son
You must inherit what mankind has done
In this world full of sorrow and woe
If you ask me why this is so, I don't know

Why are you smiling, my son
Is there a secret you can tell everyone
Do you know more than men that are wise
Can you see what we all must disguise,
Through your loving eyes

TO STOP ANOTHER WAR

I was absolutely exhausted after devoting so much time and emotional energy to the Ethiopia and Eritrea project, and I promised myself to never again make such a large commitment—especially without pay. I had given every day of vacation time to the peace process. For two years, I worked sixty to eighty hours every week to maintain my day job and work for peace. I needed a break. However, within months of the Algiers signing ceremony, Steve Smith, the same guy who got me involved in Rwanda in 1994, called and asked if John and I would be willing to try the same thing in the Democratic Republic of the Congo. My first inclination was to decline, but Steve was persistent, and it seemed that if we could once again have a meaningful impact on a war and help save lives, we should do it. John had much the same reaction. He had moved back to California, and he would not be able to devote as much time to the Congo as he had the Horn of Africa, but he would provide leadership for the team and participate in person as much as his schedule would allow. With John on board, I would do whatever I could to help.

Steve promised to take the lead in handling the coordination and logistics that had consumed so much of my time before. He also agreed to allow John to serve as the leader of the group so we could have the value of his wisdom and leadership skills. I would be an advisor and actively participate whenever needed. We added Rob Ricigliano, a conflict resolution specialist from the University of Wisconsin—Milwaukee and Marik Moen. Marik had served as a Peace Corps Volunteer in Gabon, and she was fluent in French. Her original role was to translate for the three of us who did not know French, but she contributed greatly to the substance of our work as well. We could always count on her for a fresh perspective.

With John's help, we were able to secure a modest grant from the Gordon and Betty Moore Foundation to cover travel expenses and a stipend for Steve since he would be doing the daily management of the program. Rob also received a fee as the professional conflict resolution consultant for the project. The rest of us volunteered our time.

The Congo civil war has been described as the most deadly since World War II. Direct combat casualties numbered in the hundreds of thousands, while collateral deaths due to starvation, untreated disease and exposure of displaced populations reached five million. It was a complex war with several rebel factions fighting against each other as well as trying to overthrow the government of Joseph Kabila in Kinshasa. Rwanda supported the Rally for Congolese Democracy (RCD) rebel group led by Azarias Ruberwa and based in Goma. The RCD was determined to take control of the Congo and destroy the "Interahamwe"—the Hutu militia who perpetrated the Rwanda genocide and escaped into eastern Congo after they were defeated in Rwanda. President Paul Kagami of Rwanda feared the Interahamwe were refortifying themselves and planning to return to Rwanda and reignite the genocide. Kagami and the RCD accused the Kibila government in Kinshasa of complicity with that plan.

Uganda backed the Movement for the Liberation of Congo (MLC) rebel group based in the Northeast of the country and led by Jean-Pierre Bemba, a very successful, but corrupt businessman from the Northern province of Equator. Bemba's chief lieutenant Olivier Kamitatu was a well educated and charismatic figure who would turn against Bemba and for peace later in the saga.

The government of Joseph Kabila was weak and incapable of managing the immense and complex set of challenges including corruption, regional and tribal conflicts, limited infrastructure, and enormous national debt accumulated under the all-time world champion of corruption, Mobutu Sese Seko. Kabila's father had orchestrated the overthrow of Mobutu (after the U.S. had no further use of him) only to be assassinated by one of his own body guards over a personal grudge. The younger Kabila demonstrated positive values and instincts, but he was uneducated, inexperienced, and controlled by the same corrupt and belligerent cabal that had surrounded his father.

Steve knew several of the leaders in the government and the rebel groups, and he persuaded them to meet with us at Airlie House near Warrenton, Virginia in the spring of 2001. He convinced them that John and I had been successful in helping end the Ethiopia and Eritrea war and they should give us a chance to see what could be done in the Congo.

We spent the first day getting acquainted and listening in order to develop our understanding of the dynamics of the conflict from the perspective of each of the belligerents. We went out of our way to respect each one and to build a trust relationship. Our primary objective was to learn what they wanted to achieve in hopes that we might be able to help them find a way to reach their objectives without further violence. Each gave us a similar vision for the Congo. If they were to prevail, each one told us, they would end corruption, establish democratic institutions, build roads and schools and health centers, and the Congo would become a model nation. There were, of course, variations on that theme, and the RCD certainly included their determination to defeat the Interahamwe and end the threat to the Tutsi and Rwanda that was festering in the East.

The similarity of their stated objectives gave us an opening. We indicated to each of them that we appreciated their positions and their concerns. However, it was obvious the violent path they had taken would never achieve their objectives. The war path would further destroy the country they claimed to want to help, and it would foment ever deeper hostility among the people and sharpen the regional and ethnic factions. At the end of the day, one or another of them would prevail and occupy the presidential palace, and the others would be dead or in exile. Furthermore, as soon as the victor took his seat of power, someone else would start coming after him, and the cycle of violence would continue. If, on the other hand, they would be willing to abandon their hostility, lay down their weapons, and work together for the good of the country, everyone's objectives could be met.

We made it clear we had no power or authority to offer them anything or to take anything away. All we could offer was our goodwill, and our unwavering commitment to help them find their way out of violence and into peace. Their only incentive to work with us was to do the right thing, and the only reward would be peace and hope for their country.

Our guests from the Congo came to Airlie House as enemies determined to conquer each other and take control of their country and its rich mineral resources. Yet, we had asked them to cease their hostility and become partners for the good of the whole country, not just themselves and their loyalists. I've been called idealistic for my approach to peacebuilding, and this was about as naïve as it could be. Yet, they took our challenge seriously.

They literally went for a walk in the lovely woods at Airlie House to talk about the possibility of collaboration rather than brutal combat and conquest. John, Steve, Rob, Marik and I sat on a bench and waited for them. I have no idea how long we waited. It seemed to take hours. We didn't know if they would walk out in peace or if we would have to go into the woods and handle a violent confrontation. At long last, they emerged and walked across the lawn engaged in friendly conversation. "Let's give it a try," was their collective response to our challenge. They would seek to find a way to work together to end the massive killing and build their country.

This was the beginning of a long and extremely difficult process, but it was a turning point. That quiet and secret meeting in Virginia set in motion a remarkable transition that eventually changed the course of violence in the Congo, but it took time. The leaders we met with faced strong opposition from their followers who had risked their lives for their version of a revolution. The concept of compromise and participation in a coalition government was completely alien. Months of brutal fighting continued as the leaders of the principal rebel forces and the government in Kinshasa argued. Positions and alliances changed as each leader or group searched for a superior position. But now, they were also seeking a path to a peaceful resolution. Finally, in the spring of 2002, the long delayed Inter-Congolese Dialogue (ICD) took place in Sun City, South Africa, hosted by South Africa's President Thabo Mbeki, and facilitated by Ketumile Masire, former President of Botswana.

Our team had no official standing at the ICD, but all of the major participants insisted that we be there to provide an outside and unofficial track for dialogue, consultation, and mediation. Steve, Rob, Marik and I made the trip, and we set up our operation in the Palace of the Lost City Hotel. We were separate from the ICD's official hotels, which gave us a unique advantage. We had established our expertise and our neutrality. Delegates were able to secretly slip away from the ICD venue and meet with us in private.

We hosted a steady stream of partisans from all sides. From early in the morning until late at night, delegates sought our advice and shared inside information. They usually tried to attract us to support their position. In every case, we made clear our absolute neutrality, but we always gave advice that would help them find a way toward resolution. Some came with astounding hatred for their adversaries, and the task seemed hopeless at times. Alliances among rebel groups and factions within the government would be formed and boldly announced one day only to be shattered and realigned the next.

During a brief break in our meeting schedule, we went to the official ICD site for coffee and to see some of our colleagues. While there, I noticed a familiar looking frame of a man with his back to us. I told the others it looked like Haile Menkerios, and I told them the story of his heroic efforts to help end the Ethiopia and Eritrea war and his courageous stand for freedom and democracy in his country. As I was speaking the man turned our way and shouted out, "Chic, what are you doing here?" It was Haile. I don't think I have ever been more thrilled to see anyone. We embraced in a long, firm hug and smiled like I have never smiled.

I told him what we were doing, and he told us his story. Indeed, he had been charged with treason in Eritrea for speaking out publicly for freedom and democracy. He would be imprisoned and possibly executed if he were to return home. However, UN Secretary-General Kofi Annan knew of his plight, and respected his remarkable talent. Annan hired him as a special envoy to represent the UN in many of the most difficult spots in the world. He had even been dispatched to Afghanistan to try to talk sense with the Taliban rulers—an impossible task, he learned. Now, he was representing the UN at the ICD.

He expressed his extreme pleasure with our engagement in the Congo, and we agreed on the spot to be partners to help move the process towards peace. We made almost daily contact through the rest of the ICD to share information and coordinate strategies.

The ICD had been planned to last for two weeks, but it extended into two months. I was not able to stay for the entire process as I was not being paid, and I had a job to return to. I had used all of my available annual leave for the year to work on the project, and I couldn't afford to take leave without pay. Steve stayed for most of it, however, and we remained in regular telephone and Internet contact.

We asked each of the delegates what instructions or advice they had been given by their families and colleagues before leaving the Congo for Sun City. Without exception, the story was the same—"Don't come home without an agreement. We are tired of war. We want peace."

I am convinced the will of the people to demand peace forced the delegates to reach an accommodation. They dared not return home empty-handed. The people had suffered through unspeakable carnage—death by guns, bombs, landmines, machetes, and rape, pillage, starvation and cannibalism as tools of war. It must end.

Eventually the ICD produced an agreement between the government and most of the belligerents. The Rwanda backed RCD was not satisfied and they were unwilling to sign on at the ICD, but eventually they were enticed to agree and join the coalition government. Our friend Azarias Ruberwa, the leader of the RCD, became Vice President in a government he had fought bitterly to overthrow. Olivier Kamitatu, the second in command of the Uganda backed MLC, became president of the parliament in a government he had tried to destroy.

The agreement to form a coalition government led to elections in 2006. The UN sent Haile Menkerios to oversee the election process, and Steve Smith was also employed by the UN to help plan and monitor the elections.

While the agreement ended the massive civil war, tragic fighting has continued in the Eastern part of the country with the rape and murder of women and exploitation of child soldiers as the most prominent features. I remain in regular contact with Haile and others in the region as we continue to try to find a way to put an end to the tragedy of the Congo. No nation in history has suffered from the brutality of corrupt leaders and warlords as much as the Congo. Starting with Belgium's King Leopold who caused the murder of ten million innocent Congolese, through their war for liberation, the U.S. sanctioned assassination of their first elected leader Patrice Lumumba, and the massive corruption under the U.S.-supported dictator Mobutu Sese Seko, and then this war, the Congo has suffered the curse of its extraordinary mineral wealth. There is too much to be gained through corruption by whoever controls this desperately poor country. So the fighting has persisted.

The Congo has been exploited for its rich mineral deposits and ruined by outsiders and by its own people for over a century. At long last, there is reason to believe the tragedy can and will end. We hope to have played a small part in making it happen. On several occasions, Azarias Ruberwa and others involved at the highest levels have assured me that the progress toward peace "began with your team on that day in Virginia."

FOR THE NEXT GENERATION

I thoroughly enjoyed my colleagues at BoardSource, and consulting with a wide range of nonprofits was stimulating, but I feared our financial model was flawed, and I did not see the consulting team surviving. We should have been a profit center for BoardSource, but we were a drain instead. So, I was open to a move.

I had known and worked with Bill Reese during much of his twelve years as President of Partners of the Americas, and we had stayed in contact after he went to be the Chief of Operations at the International Youth Foundation in Baltimore. A leadership change was in process at IYF, and everyone expected Bill to move into the CEO spot. During this process, Bill invited me to meet for breakfast, and he asked if I would consider becoming Vice President for Development, the top fundraising position. Instead of Bill, David Hornbeck actually became CEO, and Bill served as the Chief Operating Officer, and the offer to me remained firm. I was ready for a move; I liked both David and Bill, and I believed in the mission of IYF. Furthermore, the commute would be much shorter, so I accepted the invitation.

Our department was small, but I inherited Charlotte Kea as an associate from my predecessor Aaron Williams. Aaron is a returned Peace Corps Volunteer and one of the fine people in international development. He had done a terrific job for IYF, but I think the best thing he did was to hire and nurture Charlotte. (Several years later, Aaron was selected by President Obama as the new Peace Corps Director.) I had rarely felt comfortable delegating important tasks to subordinates, but in this case, I gave the toughest challenges to Charlotte and took charge of lesser tasks myself. I had complete confidence in her, and she never disappointed me. Together, Charlotte and I hired Magdalena Koniutis-Nanni, a delightful and dedicated Polish immigrant as our administrative assistant, and we made a very good team.

While Charlotte managed relationships with virtually all of our ongoing donors and sponsors, I helped the IYF staff develop a new program in India and Mexico and cultivated the General Electric Foundation as the donor. GE required extraordinary detail and rigor in the plan, but we prevailed and secured a grant of $1.4 million. That grant, keeping Charlotte happy, and bringing Magdalena on board were my only consequential contributions to IYF.

Before joining the IYF staff, I had been helping Peter Yarrow develop a new program to help combat bullying in schools. John Garamendi was on Peter's board, and he had suggested to Peter that I might be helpful since I had managed several successful nonprofit organizations, and I was considered a bit of an expert on building effective governing boards. Peter asked me to send my recommendations for the development of the organization and building the board, so I drafted a set of comments. I never expected a response, but Peter called after reading my paper, and he urged me to join his effort. We agreed it would be best for me to serve as an unpaid advisor rather than as a board member. That would enable me to remain an outside and objective observer and consultant.

The organization's concept emanated from a powerful song, "Don't Laugh at Me," written by Steve Seskin and Allen Shamblin.

I'm a little boy with glasses
The one they call the geek
A little girl who never smiles
'Cause I've got braces on my teeth

And I know how it feels
To cry myself to sleep
I'm that kid on every playground
Who's always chosen last
A single teenage mother
Tryin' to overcome my past
You don't have to be my friend
But is it too much to ask
Don't laugh at me
Don't call me names
Don't get your pleasure from my pain
In God's eyes we're all the same
Someday we'll all have perfect wings
Don't laugh at me

Peter's daughter Bethany had introduced him to the song at the Kerrville Folk Festival in Texas, and both of them had been moved to tears. Peter introduced it to Noel (Paul) and Mary, and they incorporated it into the Peter, Paul and Mary repertoire. They performed the song at a national conference of elementary school principals, and the response was so enthusiastic Peter promised to create a program to use music, exercises, and lessons to help schools deal with the scourge of bullying.

Peter is a brilliant, passionate, and determined man who had devoted his life to important social and political causes of civil rights, peace, the environment, opposition to nuclear weapons, and support for women's rights. This would be his next and possibly final cause, and he wanted it to be his most significant achievement. He identified with children who are the victims of ridicule and harassment, and he was determined to help alleviate it. School officials were increasingly troubled with bullying incidents and the adverse impact on the learning environment, so they welcomed his intervention.

My modest role was to observe and provide advice as I saw fit. I developed a bond with the founding executive director Flora Lazar, and we consulted each other regularly as the organization was formed and began to grow. Charlotte Frank, a Vice President with McGraw-Hill, the powerful textbook publisher, embraced the concept, and she persuaded the company to provide office space as well as in-kind production and distribution of the materials. Charlotte also became the board chair.

The organization's original name was Don't Laugh at Me (DLAM), based on the title of the song, but many of us urged a more affirming and marketable name. We came up with Operation Respect (OR), and it resonated well with schools and donors, so that became the official name of the organization, but we kept the DLAM title for the school program. The mission was (and still is) to assure each child and youth a respectful, safe and compassionate climate of learning where their academic, social and emotional development can take place free of bullying, ridicule and violence.

Unfortunately, Flora and Peter could not agree on organization structure and direction, and she left. Peter and the board brought Mark Weiss in as the new executive director. Mark was a well known and highly respected New York Schools administrator with a big heart and personal charm. He had retired from the school system after creating and guiding a special school for troubled kids that achieved remarkable results. He was once featured in a cover story in the *New York Times* magazine for his achievements.

Mark strengthened the education quality of the organization, but he was not a skilled fundraiser, and the organization needed more resources to grow and fulfill its promise. Mark agreed and graciously volunteered to change his role and accept a pay cut to make room for a new chief executive. Mark became the Director of Education, a position perfectly suited to his talents and disposition.

Kathleen Kennedy Townsend had been Lieutenant Governor of

Maryland, but she lost a race for Governor in 2004. Since children and education were her priorities, she seemed to be a natural choice to take over the Operation Respect CEO role. On paper and on the surface it was a perfect fit. A team of Peter Yarrow and Kathleen Kennedy Townsend would bring substantial clout, public exposure and access to funds. Those of us who knew both of them, however, were skeptical. Their objectives were similar but not directly aligned, and both were accustomed to being in full control. If they could have modified their respective agendas, it could have worked, but that was not possible.

Peter and Kathleen differed on both style and substance. Since I knew and admired them both, and since I was not aligned with either agenda, the board asked me to try to mediate and find a way for them to work together. When negotiation failed, we agreed to try a different strategy. Whenever either one was upset with the other, they were to call me and let me try to handle it instead of confronting each other directly. If I had nothing more to do, this solution might have worked, but I was busy with IYF responsibilities, and the burden grew from a few hours each week to stressful encounters virtually every day. Furthermore most of the conflicts were far too serious and complex for me to resolve on my own.

Eventually, Peter, Kathleen, and I met at our home on a Saturday afternoon to seek a final solution. It was intense and emotional, and it lasted well into the night. Kay provided food and drink to sustain us, as we explored the issues and struggled to find answers. Finally, Kathleen looked at me and said, "Chic, you have the skills to do this job, and you are committed. If you will take over as President of OR, I will step aside."

≈

I had been with IYF less than a year, and I was just getting settled. The transition would be difficult, and I did not want to break my commitment to Bill Reese. At the same time, Reese and Hornbeck had noticed the amount of time I was diverting from IYF responsibilities, and they knew I had mixed loyalties. I gave the proposition considerable thought, and I discussed it with key OR board members. I was not sure I could work with Peter in an executive capacity either. As the founder and primary funder Peter had a legitimate proprietary interest, but as a seasoned nonprofit executive, I also knew I would have to be in charge of operations. No one else had been able to achieve the right balance, and it was rather naïve to presume I could do any better.

While I was considering my options, Peter called and invited the whole family to be his guest at a special concert at Carnegie Hall for the benefit of the Woody Guthrie Foundation. Peter, Paul and Mary were on the program, of course, but others included Arlo Guthrie, Pete Seeger and the living members of the original Weavers, as well as Theodore Bikel, and Leon Bibb. These had been my musical and activist idols since college. Peter, Paul and Mary's "If I Had a Hammer" (written by Seeger and Lee Hays, both of the Weavers) had inspired me during my cowboy summer of 1962 and again at the civil rights march in 1963. I owned every album Pete Seeger ever made. I had admired Theo Bikel as an intellectual as well as a musical and theatrical star, in spite of our confrontation over national arts policy many years before. The Weavers were the inspiration for all of them, and I had sung Arlo Guthrie's anti-war anthem *Alice's Restaurant* on my way to my draft physical. This would be a special night.

Guthrie opened with some traditional songs as well as a few new tunes. Then a tall, frail gentleman of elegance and distinction walked onto the stage with his banjo. Pete Seeger was 84 years old; his voice was thin, and he lost a few of the words, but it was a magical moment. Our seats were in about the fifth row right in the center, and we absorbed every ounce of the energy and spirit Seeger emitted with his songs, including my favorite "Guantanamera." When he finished, I was the first in the entire hall to rise in applause. The rest of the entranced Carnegie Hall audience followed almost instantly. A few years later, Seeger's life was documented for posterity in the film *The Power of Song.*

That concert is in the film, and my cameo appearance, rising to my feet, can't be missed. For half of a second, I was a movie star in a supporting role for my hero Pete Seeger.

Following the concert, most of the performers gathered at Peter's Manhattan apartment to celebrate the event. Peter had invited us to spend the night in his guest room, so we were there for the entire party. My children were too young to know these historic figures, but I have tried to teach them how significant these people are in America's cultural and political history.

Peter need not have given us such a special night to persuade me to leave IYF and take over Operation Respect leadership, but it didn't hurt. I knew Peter could be difficult to work with, but I admired him, and I believed in the mission. I made the move with pleasure, and with the blessing of Reese and Hornbeck at IYF.

The OR office is in the Penn Plaza Building at Penn Station in New York. I was not prepared to move the family to New York, so we arranged for me to work three to four days out of the New York office and the rest from my home in Maryland. I took an early Amtrak train to Penn Station usually arriving at the office before the local staff. Peter made his guest room available, so I had free lodging in one of the best locations in the city. On Thursdays or Fridays, I caught an evening train back home, usually arriving after 11. It was a tiring routine, but it gave me an opportunity to live and work in New York—an experience I would highly recommend to anyone.

The staff included Mark Weiss as Education Director, Elizabeth Kolodny as Program Coordinator and Caroline King handling administrative duties, finances and development. My task was to assure effective and efficient operations, marketing, strategic planning, and fundraising. My main responsibility, however, was to support Peter and help present the OR concept to education leaders and policy makers throughout the country and worldwide.

Elizabeth is totally devoted to Peter and to Operation Respect.

Her sister had been a victim of cruel bullying, and Elizabeth committed every ounce of her heart and soul to the cause. She worked endless hours and did everything any human could to make a difference. Mark brought his deep knowledge of education theory and his connections to the organization. Thanks to him, we became embedded in the New York City School System to provide training for the principals, staff and teachers for every elementary and middle school in the entire system. It's a monumental task, but we know it has helped spare thousands of children from the trauma of bullying, and it has helped improve school performance.

Peter and I traveled the country and the world together to advance our cause. His star power opened doors and enabled us to reach audiences who otherwise would have ignored our best intentions. All too often, Peter arrived late and spoke too long, but he got away with it because of his engaging personality, genuine commitment, and the wonder of his music.

We made presentations at virtually every national education association in the country plus many others that had little to do with education. We went to dozens of state associations as well. We encouraged the schools within their realms to integrate some form of character education—preferably the Operation Respect/Don't Laugh at Me (OR/DLAM) program—into their systems. As a result, thousands of schools and hundreds of thousands of students have improved the climates of their schools and reduced bullying, ridicule and violence. It was, and it still is a remarkable achievement, due almost entirely to the sheer will, talent and persistence of Peter Yarrow.

At the same time, Peter is a perfectionist, and he could be condescending at times. I confronted him about it, and he seemed surprised. To his credit he promised to improve, and he has. Peter could also be exasperatingly late. Every fundraiser knows never, ever to be late for an appointment with a foundation executive, but Peter never read the memo. He was almost always late. Once, we were staying in a hotel in

San Francisco, and we had an appointment with Paul Brest, President of the Hewlett Foundation in Menlo Park, about 90 minutes away. I called Peter well in advance of our planned departure time to be sure he was awake so he would be ready on time. I called again, just to be sure. When the time came to go to the car, I called yet again and found him asleep. (As a seasoned concert performer, Peter lives and works best late at night—not the daylight hours the rest of us consider normal.) He dressed as quickly as possible, but we hit bad traffic and arrived about an hour after the appointment. Only Peter could get away with it. He just got out his guitar, invited the entire Foundation staff to gather, and we sang "Puff the Magic Dragon," "Blowing in the Wind," and "Don't Laugh at Me." And, we got the grant.

A year or so later, we had a meeting scheduled with Vartan Gregorian, the powerful President of the Carnegie Corporation in New York. Gregorian is a giant of a man in every way, and I doubt if anyone anywhere has ever kept him waiting. I arrived in plenty of time, and Peter was due in from the airport. I tried to maintain conversation with Gregorian while frantically calling Peter on his cell phone. He arrived 45 minutes late. Again, he opened his guitar case, the sophisticated Carnegie staff assembled in Gregorian's office, and we all sang together and enjoyed the experience. This time, however, we never got the grant, but it wasn't Peter's fault. They just didn't fund programs like ours.

Traveling with Peter was a joy. He loves to shop for gifts for friends, and he usually picked up something for Kay. He also appreciates fine food, especially Asian, so we ate well. Furthermore, he always closed his presentations by inviting members of the audience to the stage to sing with him, and he made sure I was one of the first to join the singing. I have sung "Puff," "Don't Laugh at Me," "If I Had a Hammer," "This Land is Your Land," and other great songs with Peter on stages many, many times—though I sing without a mike to protect the experience for everyone else.

We went to Nice, France to speak at a global conference of international school administrators, and we took full advantage of the fabulous setting. We blew the presentation and had to apologize to the organizers for misunderstanding their expectations, but we had a delightful time. We ate the best seafood Nice had to offer, and we toured the amazing antique shops for hours. Peter purchased countless gifts for his friends and family, including a classic silver wine decanter for our home.

Our house is filled with gifts from Peter. Every Christmas something wonderful arrives in a large box shipped from the Monkey and the Rat import store in Portland, Oregon that is owned by Peter's son Christopher. At random times throughout the year other gifts arrive as well. Most, but not all, of them are works of art or craft from Thailand. We treasure all of them, but four are extra special. Peter sent Kai a magnificent Mandala prayer circle that hangs in a classic frame on our living room wall. He sent us an enormous and imposing portrait of an ancient Chinese feudal lord. It is prominently displayed in the foyer of our home, as the centerpiece of our modest art collection. It is worth a visit just to see it. Peter was trained as an artist, and he produced a wonderful painting based on his song *Day is Done*, the song he had dedicated to Kai at Wolf Trap in 2001. And, he sent Grant a large framed black and white photo taken in 1964 at the Hilton Hotel in London with Ed Sullivan, the Beatles and Peter, Paul and Mary. It is an historic photo as the occasion was Sullivan's meeting with the Beatles to sign them for their famous performance on his show. It had been hanging on the wall in Peter's apartment, but spontaneously he took it down and decided to give it to Grant. Peter had his colleagues, Paul (Noel to his friends) and Mary autograph it just for Grant.

Noel is on the Operation Respect board, and he is a tremendous source of wisdom and support. His personality is the polar opposite of Peter—calm, relaxed and easy going—but like Peter he cares deeply about social and political issues. Knowing my commitment to building peace, he sent a delightful "peace" lapel pin as a Christmas gift recently. I met and saw Mary Travers on several occasions, but I never had a chance to get to know her well because she was not directly involved with the Operation Respect program. I spent many long hours with her husband Ethan, however. He and I were both staying at Peter's place in 2005 while Mary underwent extensive treatments for leukemia. We would talk about life's challenges and triumphs over fine wine whenever he returned from the Sloan-Kettering Hospital late at night. Her recent passing hit me hard on both a personal level and as another indication that our era is slipping away.

I can't count the number of special moments with Peter. We went to the Metropolitan Opera together, we had late night dinners, and enjoyed endless conversations about every topic imaginable. I introduced Peter to Haile Menkerios, who was rising higher and higher within the UN system, and we met for dinner frequently for in-depth analysis of politics and efforts to combat corruption, hunger, and war. Peter's apartment was the gathering place for the famous and powerful, and for hopeless cause activists of all kinds. It was always alive, vibrant, and stimulating.

But special moments were offset with confrontations over policies and strategies for OR. If I was going to be the President and CEO, I needed to set the direction of the organization—so long as it was consistent with the overall mission and goals as determined by the governing board—the whole board, not just the founder. That is fundamental doctrine for nonprofit organization management and governance. I was trying to build an organization that would meet the needs of schools and children, that would be a tribute to Peter, and that would be able to survive and thrive beyond his direct involvement.

Peter, on the other hand, wanted to remain in charge of the direction, and he wanted to be the face of the organization. I had noticed that many of the younger teachers and most of the students did not know who Peter was, and they did not identify with his musical style. They liked us and wanted to work with us, but the heart and soul connection didn't always happen. I loved Peter and his music, but I felt Operation

Respect needed to add diversity to its identity and style.

≈

At about the time I began searching for new approaches, I met Jeff Gomez (founder of Starlight Runner Entertainment) an exceptionally creative and talented young man who had lived the traumatic experiences we sought to address. He describes himself as the son of a teenage mother and gang-bang father in the housing projects in Manhattan's Lower East Side. He was born with a prominent facial deformity, and he had been the subject of severe bullying and ridicule in school. Jeff had persevered and overcome the obstacles, and he had created the remarkable "Never Surrender" program for school assemblies. He motivates students with similar challenges to resist the temptation of drugs and street crime, and muster the courage and will to overcome adversity.

I feared Operation Respect's Don't Laugh at Me program was a bit too soft and cuddly for the real hardcore inner-city world. While our program had the power of music and a professionally developed and tested curriculum, Jeff had real life cred and street grit. Jeff's personal story and Hispanic heritage would add currency and vitality to our message. Merging Jeff and Never Surrender with Peter and DLAM could produce a powerful mix.

Jeff introduced us to Jonathan "Baby Jay" Gutierrez, a teenage rapper from Houston who was determined to give hip hop a new message of peace and respect. We concocted the idea of Baby Jay creating a hip hop rendition of "Don't Laugh at Me." It seemed to be an ideal merger.

At first Peter was resistant, and several board members recoiled at the notion of any identity other than Peter and any musical sound other than folk. I argued vigorously that the music that stirs the hearts and souls of late middle-aged prosperous white people does not necessarily resonate the same way with inner-city kids from multiple ethnic backgrounds. The kids were our target population, not the board. We needed to speak their musical language.

My own son Kai was in his early teens at the time, so he was in the target age group, and I knew folk music just didn't connect for him. Peter loves Kai, and Kai admires Peter in return. Kai beamed with pride when he got to introduce Puff the Magic Dragon's creator to his classmates at a middle school assembly, but the music itself was never his style. Peter understood, and with some reluctance he and the board agreed to let us proceed.

Convincing Steve Seskin and Alan Shamblin that their beloved song "Don't Laugh at Me" could be translated into hip-hop proved even more challenging. It was their song, and they had to approve any modification. At first, they rejected the revised lyrics and sound, but we persisted and reached a reasonable accommodation. The final music and DVD has been an enormous hit with students throughout the country. Peter enjoys a small cameo role portraying a street musician in the hip-hop video.

Peter and I also clashed over the 2003 Operation Respect Annual Report that was designed by the famous poster and album cover designer Milton Glaser. Glaser had designed the iconic and ubiquitous "I Love NY" logo and many of the memorable album covers for Peter, Paul and Mary, Bob Dylan, and others. Glaser is a design master, and I love his work. He had donated the designs used in the DLAM curriculum, so it was natural for him to do the annual report. However, when the draft report arrived, I was shocked. It drew all of the attention to the designs, and the designs overwhelmed everything substantive in our work. It was a showcase for Glaser designs, not for OR and the kids. The entire staff agreed when we first saw it.

Peter, however, had already told Glaser he loved the design before I had a chance to express my concerns. After a long and difficult discussion, Peter agreed to talk with Glaser about our objections. Glaser's reaction was clear and absolute. He knew what he was doing, and we did not. He was right, and we were wrong. I stood my ground as best I could. I showed the design to several others, and the reaction was always the same. Unless modified, this document should never see the light of day. After a painful negotiation, Glaser reluctantly agreed to reduce the size and overwhelming presence of the design elements, and the final product was acceptable. Sadly, however, it strained my relationship with Peter.

≈

All of this was happening while I was very sick, and didn't know it. In the spring of 2004, a red spot appeared and grew to several inches in diameter on my left side, directly on the incision line from the nephrectomy. I felt strange, tired, weak, and sometimes confused. I also developed hand tremors. Since there had been a mild infection following the surgery 12 years before, I assumed the infection had been dormant and then regenerated. My medical team reached the same conclusion, and I took normal antibiotics. I felt somewhat better, the red spot faded away, and I assumed all was well.

Nevertheless, the symptoms continued to emerge from time to time, and my brain function diminished. I became confused over anything complex, and I often found myself behind the wheel of the car completely befuddled about where I was and where I was going. It was frightening, as it seemed I might be losing my mind. I told no one, and I hid it as best I could. I didn't want to alarm my family, and I didn't want to risk losing my job. As long as I could function well enough that others didn't notice, I would carry on with hopes it would improve.

That summer, we splurged on a family vacation in Europe. I had been there many times, and Kay had been to Ireland, but neither she nor the kids had been to the continental countries. I designed the trip very carefully, and it went precisely as planned, except for a break into our car by thieves in Milan. Otherwise it was perfect. We started in Frankfurt, visited Heidelberg, then to Strasbourg and nearby Dambach la Ville (an idyllic historic wine producing village), followed by a drive through the Black Forest. We drove south through Switzerland, and then on to Italy and Milan. From there we went west along the Mediterranean Coast to Mougins, France for a few days with friends and then turned north going through Leon on the way to Paris for several glorious days. Paris was the fulfillment of Kay's lifetime dream, and the smile never left her face the entire time we were there. After enjoying the sights, sounds, smells, and tastes of Paris and the opulence of Versailles, we went on to Liege in southern Belgium on our way to Cologne and one last grand cathedral to see. From there we followed the Rhine River enjoying the castles around every bend before catching our flight home from Frankfurt.

My ulterior motive for the family trip to Europe was to teach my children an object lesson in cultures, geopolitics, economics, and power. A century ago, many of the European countries we had visited conquered and dominated various parts of the world. They were global economic, political, and military powers. Now, Europe as a whole has only moderate global influence, and its power has been eclipsed by the U.S. I wanted my children to see just how miserable the people are now that their colonial rule in Africa and Asia has been stripped away, and no one fears their military prowess. I tried to point out all of the sad and depressed people, but we couldn't find them. Everyone seemed quite content. In fact, the people we saw were happy, relaxed, and secure as they enjoyed fine coffee and baguette at outdoor cafés.

Point made. The good life does not depend on national strength and power. Rather, the quality and value of life has no national or cultural identity, and wealth and power are relatively irrelevant. The day will come—possibly within my lifetime and certainly within my children's lifetimes—when the U.S. will not dominate the globe economically, politically or militarily. And, it's okay. People in the U.S. and all over the world will do just fine, possibly even better, in a multi-polar world.

I felt reasonably healthy throughout the trip, but troubling symptoms continued to rise and fall over the next few months. Finally, on Labor Day weekend, I awoke in excruciating pain throughout my body. The headache was intense; all muscles were frozen rock solid, and my joints screamed at any movement. The family took me to the emergency room at Annapolis Hospital, and after a long wait, the medical team ran their usual battery of tests. They found nothing. A group of four physicians gathered with Kay, Alex and me to discuss their conclusion—they had no clue what was causing the pain.

I plaintively pleaded, "Please help me. I am in serious pain."

One of the doctors suggested, "Let's test for Lyme."

The others were skeptical, but he persisted. "Would you mind if we do a spinal tap?" he asked. "Yes, I mind," I replied, "But if that is what it takes, let's do it."

They checked me in, numbed my back, inserted a large needle between the vertebrae, sucked out some fluid, tested it, and announced, "We're checking you in for a long stay. It looks like you have Lyme disease." The spinal fluid test indicated some form of meningitis, but blood tests would eventually confirm that it was actually Lyme. On one hand, it was grim news. Lyme is very serious. On the other hand, we knew what I had, and it could be treated. At least if I was losing my mind, I knew why.

I spent a week in the hospital and six weeks at home with an IV injecting major antibiotics into my system. The treatment worked, and I was able to return to work, but there was permanent damage. I live with serious tinnitus (a loud ringing sound in my head that never subsides); Bell's palsy; hand tremors; weakness and fatigue; some memory loss, and occasional cognitive confusion. Furthermore, every few months, the full force of the symptoms return, and I am incapacitated for a day or for several days at a time. Consequently, I am functional most of the time, but totally incapacitated at other times.

≈

The combination of my medical condition; the stress of the job, and wear from the weekly commute to New York indicated that my tenure with Operation Respect would be limited, but I was determined to make as much progress as possible before moving on.

In order to convince schools that they should incorporate our program or something similar, we had to demonstrate efficacy. Several studies and reports verified the value, but we wanted to make a larger and stronger statement. Therefore, we created a national symposium on the theme "What Works" to showcase successful programs at all levels of education and in all social and economic environments.

We established a process to accept nominations and select schools based on their results so we could honor them and learn how they became successful. We invited the schools that could best demonstrate significant reductions in disciplinary actions and improvement in academic performance. We produced the entire event within a few months, from creation of the concept to full implementation, and it was a tremendous success. The participating schools were thrilled to be honored and studied, and the students as well as faculty and administrators who represented them were inspiring and richly informative. The event attracted leading figures in education as well as foundation leaders, and we encouraged them to increase their investments in character education based upon this proof of its value. The report and video were circulated to schools nationwide, and we helped expand support for Operation Respect and for character education programs of all kinds.

The gala dinner at the beginning of the symposium featured a performance by Peter, Paul and Judy. Mary Travers was undergoing treatment for leukemia, so Judy Collins agreed to substitute. With all due respect to Peter and Noel (Paul) who gave wonderful performances, Judy stole the show. I have heard her many times, but for some reason she was absolutely celestial that night. When she began to sing, I could see that people at my table and around the ballroom were fixated and transformed. None of us had ever heard music so pure, lyrical, and lovely. It was the talk of every table and group at the end of the evening and into the next day. Years later, I still meet people who were there, and they say it was the most magical evening of their lives.

The "What Works" conference marked the conclusion of my role with Operation Respect. We had stabilized the organization after the stressful confrontation between Peter and Kathleen, we had incorporated a vital new dimension with Jeff Gomez and Baby Jay, we had a contract to introduce the program in all New York City elementary and middle schools, we had built stronger connections and greater credibility among school officials nationwide and overseas, and we had produced a significant event.

It was time for me to move on, to return to my home territory of Washington, D.C., and my passion for building peace. The Alliance for International Conflict Prevention and Resolution needed a new CEO; they offered me the job, and I accepted. While my relationship with Peter had been strained over several issues, we retained deep mutual respect and admiration. Our friendship is as strong, if not stronger than ever. Peter hosted a farewell party at his apartment with the OR board and staff as well as dozens of friends and colleagues. Peter's delightful daughter Bethany came, and she and Peter sang their hearts out in a moving tribute.

Operation Respect is still doing wonderful work. It has expanded into China, and started to reach students in Vietnam and in Israel and Palestine. The Peace Corps program in the Ukraine is using it as well. Mark Weiss is busy with the New York City Schools, and travels the world with Peter. Elizabeth has twins, but continues to manage the program as well as the daily operations of the organization, and thousands more children enjoy a bully-free childhood, thanks to this marvelous team.

At last, Peter is fully in charge. Normally, I would strongly recommend against that arrangement. More often than not, visionary founders whose talents are in business, sports, or the arts fail when they try to run their own philanthropic organizations. But Peter is unique, and he is doing it quite well. I admire him, I applaud him, and I love him. The world is a much better place because of Peter Yarrow, and my life is richer because he is my friend.

BUILDING PEACE, PART 1

I began to question the war mentality when I learned that the premise for the war in Vietnam was fabricated. That revelation turned me into an anti-war activist focused on that particular conflict. Further study and analysis, however, led me to reject the concept of war altogether. Therefore, I would welcome any opportunity to devote my career to helping build a more peaceful world.

The Alliance for International Conflict Prevention and Resolution was in trouble when I interviewed for the CEO job in 2005. The previous chief executive had left on less than pleasant terms; the primary funder had cut off all support, and the only other major donor was about to abandon the organization. The mission statement was confusing, the web site dismal, and many friends and colleagues advised against even trying to salvage it. But I saw enormous potential, and I described my vision to the selection committee. The Alliance could be much more than a meeting place for conflict resolution experts to share information and ideas. It could, and should be a vigorous leadership organization expressing a message of peace and mobilizing collaborative action to more effectively help prevent and mitigate violence. I believed the mission should be to help reduce the frequency and severity of warfare. "If that is what you want to do," I told the committee, "I hope you will give me a chance to provide leadership and make it happen." I added, however, "If it is not, please do not hire me as we will be frustrated with each other, and it will never work out."

They hired me, and we went to work. We changed the name, mission and goals. New name: Alliance for Peacebuilding (AfP). New mission: To build sustainable peace and security worldwide. New goals:

1. Initiate, develop and support collaborative action;

2. Build understanding of and support for peacebuilding policies and programs,

3. Increase the effectiveness of the peacebuilding field.

We use the term peacebuilding because peace must be built. It takes hard work by dedicated professionals who roll up their sleeves and take on the most difficult and intractable challenges on the planet. Wishful thinking, praying and preaching about peace and anti-war demonstrations produce little or no progress, but the active construction of systems and mechanisms to resolve conflicts can make an enormous difference. Peacebuilders design and build the frameworks for conflict resolution and reconciliation. Peace is built on a foundation of trust and respect for the rights of others. It requires negotiation and application of laws rather than arms to adjudicate disputes. Sustainable peace requires systems and mechanisms for everyone—regardless of wealth or status—to redress legitimate grievances, and citizens everywhere must have safe and secure environments to raise their families. Peacebuilders address the root causes of conflict including human rights violations, water shortages, poverty and lack of health care. We also help hostile tribes, sects, ideologies and societies embrace peaceful coexistence rather than eternal perpetuation of vengeance and retribution cycles.

From the beginning, my top priority with AfP was to help elevate public knowledge of and support for the concept of peacebuilding, and to build respect for the difference we can make to reduce the frequency and severity of violent conflicts. To achieve that objective, we needed the right language, and I was convinced the word peacebuilding had to become the universally recognized term of reference for all of our work. Other terms in use at the time were inadequate and cumbersome. Conflict resolution wasn't quite right, violence prevention didn't always fit, nor did mitigation, reconciliation or stabilization. Peacebuilding captures it all. The term had been used sparingly and with various meanings, but I was able to convince our board and members to define it and apply it to identify our network. We define peacebuilding as "a wide range of efforts by diverse actors in government and civil society to address the root causes of violence and protect civilians before, during and after violent conflict."

Peacebuilding is distinct from peace activism, though I appreciate the activists. It incorporates but is not limited to peacemaking—bringing adversaries to the table and to a resolution of their differences. Peacekeeping (blue helmeted troops who keep hostile forces physically apart) can also be part of a peacebuilding framework, but our work goes far beyond. Peacebuilders identify the drivers of a given conflict environment, mobilize resources and apply proven strategies to reduce and eliminate the causes of hostility and achieve sustainable stability and security. Peacebuilding is complex, it is time consuming, and it is hard work, but it saves lives and property and it enables diverse societies to coexist and thrive. The typical cost of war, even in less developed countries, is in the tens of billions of dollars. The price of building peace is but a tiny fraction of the cost of war, and no one gets killed.

Since we embraced the term peacebuilding it has been appropriated by writers, policy makers, and agencies throughout the U.S., and it is increasingly applied worldwide. U.S. Institute of Peace Vice President Trish Thompson pulled me aside a few years ago and asked if I would mind if they used the term to describe their work. Of course I gave an enthusiastic endorsement. USIP, the only U.S. government agency focused entirely on peace issues, now defines its mission as peacebuilding, and their magnificent new building next to the Mall in Washington will be known as the Peacebuilding Center.

Every cause and concept needs a name. Ours is peacebuilding.

To the best of my knowledge, the first peacebuilder was Lysistrata, a private female citizen in male-dominated ancient Greece. As Aristophanes told the wonderful story 2,500 years ago, this bold woman mobilized all of the women of Sparta and Athens to deny sex to their husbands until a peace treaty was signed to end the Peloponnesian War. These brave women locked their knees together and denied entry to their warrior men, and it worked. The land disputes that had driven the men to war were resolved through negotiation; peace was restored, and everyone returned to living happily in every way. Unfortunately, since then we have not had very many men or women bold enough to confront the war mentality and make it stop. I often suggest to my colleagues with female-based peacebuilding organizations that they could create peace on earth overnight. They simply need to organize a global and universal Lysistrata Brigade to deny all men everywhere any sex until they put down their weapons and pledge to live in peace. While there are no modern day Lysistrata Brigades, peacebuilders are emerging everywhere, and we are making progress.

≈

With a rather high profile position in the peacebuilding world, I felt compelled to examine and define my own beliefs and philosophy regarding issues of war and peace. I am not a pacifist, but I reject the concept of pro-active war—starting a war. I would bear and use arms in self-defense, and I would go to war for my country and our allies if we were actually attacked by a hostile adversary. I would also take up arms to protect innocents in far off lands from genocide. Those who use violent force must be stopped, and sometimes they must be met and conquered with force. But that is a rare, very rare situation. Yet, the United States has gone to war nine times since World War II. Few of them were necessary, and some of them proved to be disasters.

The neo-con policy wonk Robert Kaplan described the U.S. as a *Dangerous Nation* in his remarkable book by that title. Kaplan documents America's consistent penchant to deploy troops and employ violent force to achieve our national objectives. Kaplan thinks our aggression has been and continues to be a good thing. He is willing to sacrifice a given portion of our young people on battlefields to advance U.S. political and economic interests. Furthermore, if tens of thousands, hundreds of thousands, even millions of Dominicans, Vietnamese, Iraqis, or others need to die to satisfy America's thirst for power, security and prosperity, so be it. Kaplan sees no problem. I do.

It is one thing to *defend* national interests with force when attacked with force. It is quite another matter for the U.S. (or anyone else) to use violent force to *advance* our interests. I am all for active, even aggressive, global engagement to promote democracy, human rights, and economic progress. But I am adamantly against imposing those qualities and values with guns and bombs. I also believe we need to approach relations with other nations and cultures as a two-way street by listening and learning as well as promoting and teaching our ways. Why should anyone else listen to us if we aren't willing to listen to them? We have a lot to learn from others. Respect and humility towards others begets respect and humility in return.

With few exceptions, I have been a vocal critic of U.S. invasions of other countries, but voices like mine are usually drowned out by the overwhelming national impulse to rally around the flag and "support the troops". I support the troops. I just don't support the policies that force the troops to kill and be killed for nefarious reasons.

War, or any application of violent force, does nothing to determine who is right or wrong in any dispute. It only determines who can inflict more pain and suffering on the other side. The only guaranteed outcome is death and destruction. As Bertrand Russell said, "War does not determine who is right—only who is left." In almost every violent confrontation, the same outcome could be achieved through negotiation or mediation without the destruction of life, limb, and property. The world community has created systems and mechanisms based on international law and reason to resolve conflicts through the UN and regional institutions. Therefore, war is not a reasonable, rational, or acceptable way for anyone anywhere to resolve their differences. Ninety percent of

violent conflicts are now settled through negotiation rather than conquest. Why not bypass the death and destruction and go straight to the
negotiation and reach a settlement?

I continue to hear the absurd argument that war is good for the
economy. It is not. Period. The only way war stimulates any economy is
through massive government spending of taxpayer money. But it is the
ultimate in government waste because the money is spent to kill and
destroy. Government spending on the same scale for bridges, roads,
schools and hospitals would be an economic stimulus and constructive, but government spending on war is destructive. Fighting for self
defense may be a necessary expense on rare occasions, but it is not an
economic plus. Furthermore, if war was good for the economy, the U.S.
would have enjoyed extraordinary prosperity during the Bush administration when we were fighting two large wars at once. Instead of growth,
the economy collapsed.

The Institute for Economics and Peace commissioned several pre-
eminent economists to analyze the impact of war and preparation for
war on the global economy, and they found the net negative impact to
exceed $7 trillion per year. If the whole world could be at peace, the net
global economic productivity would be over $7 trillion dollars (about
13%) higher. It's time to put the ludicrous notion that war is good for
the economy to rest for good.

The advent and proliferation of weapons of mass destruction makes
the use of force even less reasonable or tolerable. More and more countries have the capacity to destroy everything everywhere. Keeping these
weapons away from rogue nations and irrational non-state extremists
will not be possible forever. We must rein these weapons in before they
reach more dangerous hands.

My complaint about a war mentality however, does not only concern the U.S. In fact, I believe we are on the right side of most global
issues. I object to any country embracing a war mentality and active use
of force to achieve social, economic or political ends. Two great chal-

lenges for America and all mankind in this generation are to change attitudes about the viability and efficacy of war, and to establish and apply more credible and effective mechanisms to resolve conflicts through negotiation, mediation, and international law. That is the full-time focus of my life in this, the latest and possibly final chapter of my career.

≈

Changing nation states and social structures to embrace peacebuilding principles takes time, patience and persistence, but it can be done, and it is happening. Just within the past two decades, thousands of new nongovernment as well as government organizations and institutions have been created to provide alternatives to weapons and battlefields. Now, more than ever before, adversaries can turn to informal negotiation opportunities as well as the United Nations, regional institutions and sympathetic but neutral nations for constructive facilitated dialogue and expert negotiation.

For example, large-scale civil war seemed inevitable following a corrupt 2007 presidential election in Kenya—but it never happened. Within days after the votes were counted (or miscounted) and results announced, over 1,000 citizens were killed, and longstanding hostilities were enflamed. But the United Nations responded immediately, and former Secretary-General Kofi Annan was there with Haile Menkerios and a strong leadership team to negotiate a reasonable resolution. At the same time the Kenyan civil society leaders built a coalition of Concerned Citizens for Peace (CCP) to promote dialogue and persuade citizens at the grassroots throughout the country to stop the violence. The combination of official diplomacy led by the UN and citizen-based action led by CCP calmed the tensions and stopped the violence before it could escalate out of control. Kenyan Ambassador Bethuel Kaplagat wrote, "The core group of concerned citizens had no force, no organization and no money, but they discovered that they had other resources in abundance than these—they had commitment, hope and conviction that the problem the country was facing was their problem and therefore had an obligation to make their humble contribution to save the nation." Civil society organizations continue to address the core issues that drive the conflict in order to achieve justice and stability and to prevent a return to violence. The violence was contained, civil war never happened, and the country is working out its troubles with wisdom and reason rather than brute force.

The last century marked the most violent in history, but the new one is off to a remarkably good start. The wars in Iraq and Afghanistan as well as high profile terrorist attacks and a few brutal conflicts in Africa dominate the news, but overall there are 40 percent fewer wars and casualties have declined by 80 percent since the mid-1980s. Andrew Mack and analysts at the University of British Columbia have documented these amazing developments in the *Human Security Report 2005*. They attribute the progress to the end of the Cold War, the effectiveness of the United Nations, and "the World Bank, donor states, a number of regional organizations, and thousands of NGOs..." Working together, these institutions constitute a powerful new workforce dedicated to the hard labor of building peace.

The trends are in the right direction, and peacebuilding concepts, principles and practices are making it possible. At the same time, ominous signs indicate the potential for reversal and a precipitous decline into unspeakable violence. The development and proliferation of biological, chemical and nuclear weapons makes the potential for disaster exponentially greater than ever before. These weapons in the hands of non-state actors who are not constrained by traditional standards adds to the threat. Population growth, declining access to water, and the impact of climate change all build greater pressure on societies and political systems worldwide. The global community must embrace this new concept of building peace before the dreadful alternative overwhelms us all. That's what we are all about. *Carpe diem*. May we seize the day.

I believe we are on the cusp of an historic transformation with enormous potential. Scholars used to study war to determine how to win the next one. For the first time in history, hundreds, even thousands of scholars worldwide are studying war to determine how to *prevent* the next one. They are learning how to build peace. For the first time in history, hundreds of academic institutions worldwide have created peace studies curricula. Virtually none of these programs existed only a few decades ago. Thousands of bright young students have just emerged from the most respected colleges and universities with graduate degrees in conflict resolution. New civil society organizations have been created specifically to promote peace and apply conflict resolution skills locally and globally to reduce the frequency and severity of warfare. Established international relief and development agencies like CARE, Mercy Corps, Catholic Relief Services and Oxfam have incorporated conflict resolution into their missions and programs. The United Nations has created a new commission and a special fund focused on building peace, and governments everywhere are studying and embracing new policies and programs designed to prevent and mitigate violent conflicts. Even militaries in the U.S. and worldwide are exploring ways to use their power and influence to prevent wars so they won't have to fight them. All of this is new. Virtually none of it existed three decades ago. Something remarkable is happening.

The Alliance for Peacebuilding and our members as well as the Global Partnership for the Prevention of Armed Conflict (GPPAC) and other coalitions and networks are gaining strength and influence here in the U.S. and worldwide. Building peace is not yet a priority for the U.S. government, and the peacebuilding concept is not well known or understood by the global power elite, but we are gaining exposure and respect. If we succeed, this will become the most peaceful century in history.

≈

The AfP platform has enabled me to connect with some of the world's most remarkable people. Some are on the staff, some are on the board, some are colleagues, donors and advisors, and all are integrated into our mission in one way or another. For example, Milt Lauenstein made a modest fortune with Telequip, the company that makes automatic change machines—the apparatus used in grocery stores and fast food restaurants with a slide and cup for coins. After a life devoted to business success, Milt was determined to invest in the alleviation of human suffering. He conducted a thorough analysis, and he determined that violent conflict was the primary cause of needless death and destruction. Furthermore, he found that few others were doing anything about it. Since wars are manmade, mankind should be able to prevent them. Milt embraced, with passion, the concept of preventing wars before they begin. Once a war has started it's too late. There will be unspeakable death and destruction, and the belligerents will become entrenched. If violence can be prevented, the damage will be averted, and a resolution can be achieved and sustained.

Milt formed a working group of experts to develop a basic concept of violence prevention and to conduct an extensive analysis of the places where that framework could be applied. He was determined to invest in actual violence prevention where it was needed and could be effective. After studying volatile and vulnerable countries throughout the globe, the small West African nation Guinea-Bissau was selected for a pilot project. Milt enlisted Michael Lund, a Returned Peace Corps Volunteer and one of the world's premier experts on violence prevention, to help develop the conceptual framework. Ben Hoffman, former director of the conflict resolution program at the Carter Center and founder of the Canadian International Institute of Applied Negotiation, was retained to lead implementation of the project. Since local ownership and leadership is a fundamental principle for effective peacebuilding, the Citizens' Goodwill Task Force and Macaria Barai, a remarkable local business woman and civic leader, became the primary local partner. The project had started well before I arrived, but I have been deeply involved with it from my first days in the office.

No one can make an absolute claim to have prevented war from breaking out, but Milt and this project come as close as anyone. Virtually all analysts had anticipated civil war in Guinea-Bissau, but it never happened. Even when the head of the military and the elected president of the country were assassinated, no wide-spread violence ensued. Something had changed in Guinea-Bissau that made it possible to resolve their conflicts without violence. Macaria's local leadership, Ben's tactics, Michael's strategies, and Milt's support have to be a major factor.

Our objective now is to sustain the progress in Guinea-Bissau and apply the model and lessons learned to more places. We have formed a partnership with Swisspeace, based in Bern, and we have given the program a new name, the BEFORE Project. Heinz Krummenacher of Swisspeace is now the program's CEO, and I brought Melanie Kawano on board in our office as program manager with primary fundraising responsibilities. Heinz is an experienced and wise conflict resolution expert and an able executive to lead the program. Melanie adds vital insight and attention to every detail to keep it on track. Prior to the partnership with Swisspeace and Melanie's arrival, management of the project rested on my inadequate shoulders. Between Heinz and Melanie we have an extremely competent team, and I am able to pay more attention to big picture and strategic issues.

The Guinea-Bissau project has demonstrated that a modest investment of $300,000 to $500,000 per year to build peace in vulnerable countries can reduce the probability of the outbreak of war. The cost of war would be hundreds of times that amount. Yet, philanthropists, other than Milt, have been reluctant to make the investment. It's a new concept, so it will take time to catch on, but the case should be obvious, and the potential is enormous.

Working with AfP put me back in direct and regular contact with Haile Menkerios, Eritrea's former ambassador to the UN who had been a key part of our work on the Ethiopia–Eritrea border war and the Congo civil war. The new UN Secretary-General Ban Ki Moon had named Haile Assistant Secretary-General, and he brings remarkable wisdom and perspective to the toughest challenges. The world would be a far more dangerous place for millions of innocent people were it not for Haile's skill and the intervention of the UN. He has been dispatched to virtually every other trouble spot to cool the rising temperatures and restore order and civility. He was a key player in the quick resolution of rapidly escalating violence following a flawed election in Kenya, and he has helped steer Zimbabwe away from violence as the dictator Robert Mugabe's disastrous rule wanes.

We invited Haile to be our keynote speaker for an AfP conference at the marvelous Shawnee Inn on the Delaware River in Pennsylvania, and I was honored to be able to introduce him as a courageous hero for democracy, one of the world's most effective men of peace, and my dear friend. Haile affirmed as clearly as possible the absolute imperative of civil society, citizen-based organizations like ours, in the peace making and peacebuilding process. There are roles that only governments and official bodies like the UN can play, but civil society is the only player in the process with peace as its primary objective. Governments act in their own national interest, and the UN is a creature of governments. As Menkerios assured us, "You represent the ability to seek peace for its own sake… Civil society's partnership in peace making and peace consolidation is central." Haile continues to be a special friend, trusted advisor, and an integral part of our work in Africa.

I made sure we brought John Garamendi onto our advisory board. John had returned to California where he was elected Lieutenant Governor—a Democrat working with Republican Governor Arnold Schwarzenegger. During his campaign, I suggested we take a break to go fishing. John has a cabin in the High Sierras in Calaveras County, and the headwaters of the Stanislaus River are within a short drive and then a long hike from the cabin. We spent the night in the cabin and drove to the trail early the next morning. The hike made waders impractical—too hot to wear and too bulky to carry—so we would wet wade. John knew the trail conditions, and I didn't. He wore Levi's, and I wore shorts. John's legs were untouched, and mine were scratched and cut to bleeding on the sharp thorns and brush, but it was worth every bit of the pain.

The setting was picture perfect. John hooked a few nice rainbows on a generic Royal Wulff dry fly pattern. I tried to be fancy and match the hatch with caddis and midge patterns with no luck. When I switched to basic hare's ear nymphs, however, I began to attract big hits, and I landed several sizable trout. Out of habit, I gently returned mine to the stream, but John brought his home for dinner. We also spent a little time discussing his campaign strategy and our peacebuilding projects and fundraising needs, but this was a real and relaxing break all the way.

≈

The spring before that trip to California, I had received an invitation to a reunion of our Oklahoma State football team. The team was famous in Stillwater for defeating the Oklahoma Sooners twice in a row, and most of the former players live within driving distance, so the gathering of aging Cutchin Cowboys draws a nice crowd. I was far away in mind as well as miles, however, so I didn't make the trip.

Shortly after the reunion I received an email from Jim Click with pictures from the event. I sent Jim this flippant note: "Thanks for the pictures, but you sent the wrong ones. These are a bunch of fat old guys playing golf. Where are the fit athletes?" I just wanted to say thanks and poke a little fun, but a few minutes after hitting the send key my phone rang. A unique and unforgettable voice with a distinctive Oklahoma accent on the other end barked out, "Hey, Dambach. It's Click. I just saw your note and I see the name of your organization. We've got to talk." (My email messages include my name, organization and contact information.) Jim had just returned from a trip to Kigali, Rwanda with the famous mega-church pastor Rick Warren. Jim provided his private jet for the trip. Warren has adopted Rwanda for a missionary program that focuses on health care and building peace. Unlike many initiatives created by other evangelical pastors, Warren's actually provides quality health care without requiring conversion to Christianity. I knew of it, and I admired it.

I was quite surprised but very pleased to know Jim was supporting Warren's project and that he had developed an interest in this amazing African country—a country I had come to know and admire. I was also gratified to know he would reach out to me. I knew Jim was one of the country's leading automobile dealers, and that he had become very wealthy. I also knew he was a prominent Republican. Therefore I assumed we would have little in common. I was wrong.

Jim and I had a lengthy and enthusiastic conversation catching up on each other and discussing Rwanda's President Paul Kagami. I had never met Kagami, but I had visited the country in 1996; I knew some of Kagami's advisors, and I had followed Rwanda's progress closely. Jim had been quite taken with Kagami, and he wanted to do all he could to help Rwanda cope with its problems and become a success story. I told Jim of my direct involvement a decade earlier in the immediate aftermath of the genocide, so we had a new bond—far more important than sharing over-the-hill football teammate status.

When we hung up, Jim called Dr. Zac Nsenga, Rwanda's ambassador to the U.S., and Nsenga called me immediately. The embassy was only a few blocks from my office, and he came straightaway to see me. Obviously, Jim had made a strong impression on President Kagami and Ambassador Nsenga. Zac and I became acquainted, and we worked together on several issues until he was reassigned to a major position back home in Kigali. We even feature him in some of our AfP materials. A few months after Jim and I reconnected and talked about our mutual interest in Rwanda, President Kagami visited the U.S., and he included a special trip to Tucson just to have dinner with my old teammate Jim Click.

Since I was going to be in California to meet and fish with John Garamendi, I decided to swing through Tucson and see Jim as part of the trip. All of the arrangements had been made, but two weeks before leaving, Jim called. "I really want to see you," he said, "but (Vice President) Cheney's office called and he's going to be in Phoenix that day. If you don't mind, we could go together and have lunch with him." Jim was one of the largest donors in the country to the Republican Party and the Bush campaign. He and the Bush family were very close friends, and he was a frequent visitor to the White House during the George H. W. Bush Presidency and George W's as well. He knew everyone in leadership positions in the Party, including the Vice President.

I am no friend of Dick Cheney, but I would never pass up an opportunity to have lunch with the Vice President, no matter who he is. I stayed at a cheap airport motel the first night in Tucson with plans to meet Jim the next morning, go see Cheney, and then have dinner and spend the second night at Jim's house.

Jim picked me up early—in his new Continental Town Car, of course. We hadn't seen each other for forty years, but nothing had changed. Jim was the same trim, high energy, enthusiastic, and talkative guy I knew and admired on the playing field and in the dorm. He took me to a breakfast rally for Steve Huffman, a Republican candidate for Congress. Jim was backing the moderate Huffman in the Republican primary against Randy Graf, a far-right anti-immigrant firebrand. That was a good sign.

We could drive 140 miles to Phoenix in a bit over two hours, but it only takes twenty minutes in Jim's private jet. So, we flew. On board the plane, we had a few minutes to talk, so we covered the customary family and life stories fairly quickly and then got right into politics. Since I was his guest, I didn't want to be combative, but I feared we would be polar opposites on just about everything. We weren't. We actually agreed or found ourselves close to agreement on most issues, even foreign policy. We're both libertarian at heart, but we are also pragmatists with a different tilt—his to the right and mine to the left. He's in a very different income bracket, and we weren't exactly aligned on tax policies, but the main point of departure was unions. Jim hates unions and I don't. I don't love them either, but I don't hate them. They have a very important place in our society and economy, from my point of view. Unions have made the large American middle class possible. Without them, we would be like a third-world country with a few extremely wealthy families at the top, a very small middle class, and an enormous hard working but impoverished underclass population.

The meeting with Cheney was interesting and informative, if a bit awkward. There were eight or ten dedicated Republicans in the room, including Senator Jon Kyle. Jim's friend Chic was the odd one. He knew all of them well, and before the Vice President arrived, Jim introduced me to everyone as his old friend, and a Democrat! He appeared to delight in the shock value. They were reasonably gracious, but not sure they liked the idea of sharing time and space with a guy from the other side. At the same time, they were curious about the friendship between their loyal Republican colleague and this Democrat. If nothing else, I hope we conveyed a message to them (and to my Democratic friends as well) that friendship can and should cross party lines and that we can conduct civil and mutually respectful dialogue.

Cheney was obviously pleased to see Jim as he greeted him warmly. I found Cheney to be as troubling in person as I had anticipated. He was obsessed with the terrorist threat. Obviously the trauma of September 11, 2001, had shaken him deeply, and he could talk of little else. There was one and only one theme—"There are evil people out there who are out to destroy us, and we have to get them before they get us."

I object to Al Qaeda and dangerous extremists as much as anyone, and I am absolutely committed to do all I can to help build a world that is safe and secure from anyone anywhere who would inflict pain and suffering on others. I just put it all in a different perspective, and believe in a very different strategy. First of all, Muslims are not the problem, and Muslim extremists aren't the only threat. The overwhelming majority of Muslims are normal, moderate and peace-loving people. Extremists of any ilk are the problem. White-middleclass-conservative-Christian extremist Timothy McVey was responsible for the second worst terror-ist attack in the U.S. Perhaps we should also profile people like him for extra searches at airports. Should we have tortured him when he was in prison before his execution to obtain more information? The atrocities carried out by Serbian Christians like Slobodan Milosevic and Rado-van Karadzic against Muslims make Osama bin Laden seem moderate. Their ethnic cleansing was responsible for the murder of some 200,000 innocent Muslims. I think the world community needs to unite and overcome sectarian, ethnic, and political violence in *all* of its dreadful forms. So, I couldn't share Cheney's obsession with Muslim-based ter-rorism.

Second, we know from experience that military conquest alone will not suppress terrorists. It may, in fact, feed sectarian hatred and fuel recruitment of more extremists. Most of our massive and techno-logically advanced weapons systems are almost useless in this battle. At $350 million each (nearly the entire Peace Corps budget), not one of the 184 F-22s in the Air Force arsenal has seen action in Iraq, Afghani-stan, or Pakistan. It is a colossal waste. The drone unmanned planes fir-ing missiles at targets in Pakistan and Afghanistan have fomented deep hatred toward the U.S. in the places where we need to build support. They may have some military utility, but this is a political and moral struggle, and they counter our moral strength.

Muslim extremists don't hate America because we are free. They hate us because—from their perspective—we have humiliated them, occupied their land, and exploited their resources. Now U.S. planes without pilots fire explosives into their homes with impunity. U.S. mili-tary bases in Arab countries are insulting. We would react much the same way if Arab military bases were to be built in Kansas and Georgia. How, then, can enlarging our military presence and dropping bombs on Muslim populations overcome extremists? A few more anti-terrorism strategists need to read *Three Cups of Tea* if we ever hope to turn the tide.

This is a struggle between extremist elements and moderates—regardless of theology, geography, or ethnicity. When we resort to the tactics of the extremists, we are no better, and we will lose. I fear we have come close. This crisis calls for a new and different strategy, one based on building up vulnerable societies and winning allies rather than killing perceived potential adversaries and destroying their homes and their societies. Fortunately top U.S. policy makers seem to be learning these lessons, and we are behaving better, but much of the damage has been done. With support from philanthropist Paul Stevers, the Alliance for Peacebuilding is developing a new "Peace through Moderation" project to support citizen-based initiatives to help overcome extremist movements that lead to violence. I am convinced we can do more to reduce extremism and the threat of terrorism with a few million dollars than our military can with tens of billions.

For Cheney, fear of Islamic terrorists had become the *sine qua non* and any strategy or tactic that might conquer and destroy the enemy was justified to protect American lives. This is the only possible explanation for violating the U.S. Constitution and international law, attacking Iraq and the torture of prisoners. Cheney himself told an American Enterprise Institute audience, "I'll freely admit that watching a coordinated, devastating attack on our country from an underground bunker at the White House can affect how you view your responsibilities." Sadly, his view and the policies he promulgated have proven counterproductive and they have cost America dearly in treasure, respect and support. It could take decades to recover. Nevertheless, I am very proud of the picture on my wall with Jim and the Vice President—one a great friend, and one not.

Jim invited Carl Hodges to join us for dinner that night. Hodges had been among the visionary creators of the famous Biosphere project in Arizona, but Jim asked him to join us because of our mutual interest in Eritrea. When our Peace Corps team was in Asmara in 1999, we were told about the Seawater Farms project on the Red Sea coast, and had our schedule allowed, we would have traveled to Massawa to see it. This creative and entrepreneurial venture used seawater to flow through an inland river to farm shrimp and fish. The effluent from the sea animals served as fertilizer as it flowed into fields of salicornia and mangrove before running back out to sea as naturally filtered clean water. (Salicornia is a unique edible plant that grows in saltwater and extreme heat, and it has multiple commercial uses.) Eritrea's government officials were extremely proud of the project as a model of its industrious culture and its commitment to become a contributor to rather than a drain on global resources.

Seawater Farms was the work of a genius, and the genius was Carl Hodges. I knew him by reputation, but we had never met. He knew me by reputation as well. Like so many others concerned about the Horn of Africa, he knew all about our successful engagement in the Ethiopia—Eritrea peace process. Who could possibly have imagined we would meet through my old friend and teammate Jim Click?

In addition to our mutual interest in the same people in a remote land, Carl and I also shared dismay over President Isaias Afwerki's turn from enlightened leadership to dictatorial rule. My friend and colleague Haile Menkerios had been charged with treason for expressing his concern. Fortunately, Haile was in New York at the time representing Eritrea at the United Nations, so he was not arrested and incarcerated. He lost his job, but not his freedom. Carl's friend and colleague Petros Solomon, Minister of Maritime Resources, however, was living in Asmara, and he was sent to prison where he remains nearly a decade later. The imprisonment of Solomon cast a pall over Seawater Farms, and it has fallen into ruin. Carl desperately wants to return to Eritrea and rebuild the project, but he cannot and will not until his friend is exonerated and free. So Carl and I share a commitment to do all we can to free the Eritrean patriots who have sacrificed their own liberty for the freedom of their people and the future of their country.

After dinner and again over breakfast, Jim and I continued to share stories, philosophies, and plans. While we have fundamental political differences, we also respect each other's points of view. Both of us want to see a more just, peaceful, and prosperous world. We can agree on those objectives, and then debate the best ways to get there. If Jim could be the leading Republican in Congress and I the Democrat, we would find bi-partisan solutions to nearly every issue. Even more important than national policy, however, we are in total agreement on the fundamental virtue and value of fly fishing. One day soon, we will meet on a river and wrestle some magnificent steelhead into a net, take some pictures, and let them go.

≈

Before leaving, I met with Jack Hood Vaughn who has settled in Tucson for his semi-retirement. Vaughn had been Peace Corps Director when I signed up, and he had intervened during the strike with our training group. He had become ambassador to Colombia while I was serving there, and then he was briefly the presidential campaign manager for Senator Fred Harris. We had connected at each of these intersections, but I wasn't sure he would remember. Not only did he remember, he seemed genuinely thrilled to meet up again.

We engaged in a very warm and enthusiastic discussion of the Peace Corps and Colombia, Harris, the current political climate, and the book he is writing. I told him about my meeting with Vice President Cheney, and he confirmed my assessment. He had known Cheney well over the years, and he always respected him. Vaughn, by the way, had been appointed to major positions by presidents of both parties. Like many others, Vaughn felt that the shock of September 11 had shaken the Vice President so deeply that he had lost the ability to be reasonable and rational.

Vaughn appreciated and approved of my career and the work I was doing to try to reduce the frequency and severity of violent conflict. But he has always been a hard-nosed realist—a gentleman of love and compassion, but also a tough former Marine with both feet firmly on the ground. (In 1988, the *New York Times* ran a story about Vaughn, then sixty-seven years old, physically subduing a street mugger, leaving the young thug in pain on the ground.) Vaughn agreed that most leaders can be led to the negotiating table and that the use of violent force is, at least in theory, not a reasonable, rational or acceptable way to resolve conflicts. But, he asked, "What about those who are not reasonable or rational? What do you do about them?" He cited Hitler, Mao, Stalin, Pol Pot, Idi Amin Dada, and, of course, Osama bin Laden.

I had to admit the path of reasonable dialogue, negotiation, and mediation will not always be possible or effective. Until a better system to protect innocent lives can be found, some of these despots will have to be taken out by force. But, I argued, more often than not, they can be isolated and denied the support base they need to operate and inflict harm. Attitudes and paradigms can change, and they are changing all over the world. Fewer and fewer nations and societies tolerate violence as a legitimate instrument for the state or for insurgents. Open societies and legitimate democratic institutions provide a framework for extremists as well as moderates to express themselves and be heard. The moderates almost always prevail in the marketplace of ideas, and the opportunity to speak out can often diffuse the extremist's rage.

Nevertheless, when reason fails to deter rogue extremists or aggressive nation states, the civilized world still needs the capacity to thwart them with force. I would prefer to see that capacity in the hands of a legitimate international body with the authority to make decisions and mobilize an effective response. That will take time, but it can happen, and eventually it will happen. I hope my government will become a leader toward that goal instead of continuing to be the primary obstacle.

As I shared these concepts and visions, Vaughn smiled and seemed pleased that his protégé, this aging returned Peace Corps Volunteer, maintained the idealism and commitment that had brought us together decades earlier.

≈

In 2007, I returned to the OSU campus for a reunion of the FA-TAGS—our loosely connected student activist group that had published *The Drummer* underground newspaper, protested for civil rights, for free speech, for the environment, and against the war in Vietnam. We gathered on the campus that had scorned us to celebrate the 40th anniversary of our trials, tribulations, and triumphs. Aside from Keith McGlamery, Ron Stevens, Bob Swaffar, Connie Kantzer, and Gene Reid, I had not seen anyone from the group in four decades.

The university seemed to have forgiven our transgressions as they welcomed us and gave us open access to the archives in the library to revisit the stories in the *Daily O'Collegian* and yellowing copies of *The Drummer*. Even after trying to shut down *The Drummer*, the university preserved every edition. We weren't sure if we should be pleased or insulted! About thirty old friends who would never recognize each other without name tags gathered in the library and whooped with delight upon discovering a photo or story of our exploits. We had created quite a buzz back in 1967 and over the next several years. I seriously doubt that any other period in OSU history compares. It was unique, it was challenging, and it was historic. It was also fun. We really liked each other as students, and we enjoyed being together again.

Sherry Caves found the original letter to the editor of the *O'Colley* that Bill Dawson and I wrote blasting Arts and Sciences Dean Scales that led to my friendship with him, and she gave me a copy to keep. I was very excited to share the experience with Kay and Kai. Unfortunately, Grant was about to start at the University of Maryland, so he couldn't make the trip.

At the same time, knowing teenager Kai might be bored with a bunch of grown up meetings and Dad reminiscing about the "good old days", I made an effort to do something special for him. He is obsessed with sports, so I arranged for us to see one of the football team practices. I called the athletic department in advance, told them I had played, and asked if we could get in. They welcomed us and even assigned a coach to give us an inside orientation and take us to a special place to watch the practice.

Shortly before going to the practice session, we discovered an OSU football jersey for sale in a local store with my number 51. I bought it for Kai, and I could tell it was very special to him. He went on the Internet and found out who on the current team had the same number—Jared Glover, a highly recruited linebacker from Bixby, Oklahoma. Kai took the jersey to the practice with a waterproof felt-tip pen hoping to find Glover and get his autograph. Unfortunately, the team was focused on their practice, and we could never move in close enough to attract his attention.

We had to leave for the reunion dinner before practice ended, so Kai came away disappointed. After we had been at dinner for a while, Kai asked to be excused. I certainly couldn't force him to stay and listen to our tiresome stories of war protest and free speech movements, so I let him go—assuming we would find him watching TV when we finished reminiscing and socializing.

When we finally reached the room, Kai was there beaming with pride. He had retrieved the jersey with #51 from the room; found his way across campus to Bennett Hall (the place I had called home and still the athletic dorm); found Jared Glover; told him the story about his dad, and got his autograph on the jersey. Then, my son looked up at his dad and said, "I want you to sign it, too." I could barely contain tears. After all we had been through with his health, having given him a kidney, having endured sleepless nights in emergency rooms, and seeing him mature and gain strength, and then for him to ask for my autograph on an Oklahoma State football jersey with my old number was about as good as life gets. I've signed a lot of important documents, and even a few autographs, but no signature ever meant more to me. Kai wore that jersey to school on the first day back, and I wish I could know what stories he told his friends about the trip to Stillwater and what that jersey means to him. I can tell him it means life and joy to me.

BUILDING PEACE, PART 2

To turn the Alliance for Peacebuilding into a viable and more meaningful organization, we built a stronger board, created an advisory board with national and international leaders, and we found new sources of funds. I went to old friends for financial support, and many came through. Susan Hackley, Managing Director of the famous Program on Negotiation at Harvard Law School, became the board chair and she added credibility along with wise leadership. We assembled a new staff supported by a team of talented interns. The new mission demanded a growing network of peacebuilders to enhance our effectiveness. Organization membership has nearly doubled. We have added individual and student membership categories, and we are now able to link hundreds of peacebuilders worldwide. Eventually it could reach into the thousands. The economic crisis almost crippled us, but extraordinary support from Chip Hauss and his wife Gretchen Sandles as well as Milt Lauenstein, Steve Killelea, Julilly Kohler and others kept us alive.

We also began, for the first time, to address major policy issues. During our annual conference in the fall of 2007, we gathered the membership for an open discussion of any issues or concerns on anyone's mind. When the topic of Iran was mentioned, there was a collective gasp. The Bush administration had been escalating its bellicose rhetoric and building fear of an existential threat from Iran to Israel and even the U.S. The signs were ominous, and a U.S. attack on Iran appeared inevitable.

Virtually everyone in the room agreed the prospect of a violent confrontation with Iran was the world's greatest threat to peace. An attack would be catastrophic for everyone everywhere. After some discussion, the group also agreed that the peacebuilding community had a moral obligation to speak out and offer alternatives to military action to diffuse the tension and help resolve the issues. Fortunately, a new National Intelligence Estimate in early 2008 indicated the perceived threat from Iran had been exaggerated, and the pressure eased. Nevertheless the prospect of a U.S. or Israeli attack remained on the table as the presidential campaigns in both parties tested the degree of testosterone among the candidates.

Once again, Iran, a country I have yet to see in person, became a priority. We formed an Iran Working Group to share information and ideas and to develop strategies to express our position. I also helped my friend Sanam Anderlini, an Iranian born and internationally prominent scholar, writer and peacebuilder, to plan and facilitate a gathering of the nation's leading experts on Iran. Ambassador Tom Pickering (former US Ambassador to the UN), Ambassador Jim Dobbins (former Presidential envoy to Afghanistan), Trita Parsi (President of the National Iranian-American Council) and other diplomats, scholars and policy analysts met and produced the *Joint Expert's Statement on Iran*. The *Statement* debunks several persistent myths that prevail on both sides and exacerbate hostilities. The *Statement* also indicates key steps the U.S. could and should take for an effective diplomatic strategy. The document generated substantial national attention, and we know it has been read and embraced by President Obama's foreign policy team. Even though street demonstrations and chaos in Tehran in the aftermath of the suspect 2009 elections make the entire situation more volatile, diplomacy is still the only reasonable path to a positive resolution.

War sabers no longer rattle, and vigorous diplomacy is underway. Iran's President Mahmoud Ahmadinejad may be an odious tyrant, but the Supreme Leader Ali Khamenei and the Council of Guardians are known to be pragmatists rather than fanatics, and they wield much more power than the President. It will never be easy, but Iran will negotiate to protect its interests, just like any other nation. I don't believe it will blow the earth, or even Israel, to bits.

≈

I had a unique opportunity to gain special insight into U.S. negotiating behavior in the summer of 2007 when the U.S. Institute of Peace (USIP) sponsored a workshop at the pastoral Airlie House in Virginia to examine what it is like to be on the other side of the table negotiating with the United States. Participants included top level diplomats from Russia, France, the UK, Turkey, and several other key nations. Israel's great negotiator Itamar Rabinovich and Sa'eb Erekat, the Palestinian chief negotiator, were part of the group, and I was most impressed with the warm and mutually respectful relationship that had obviously developed between them. USIP President Dick Soloman presided, and seasoned U.S. diplomats like Chester Crocker, Casimir Yost, and Charles Freeman were active observers. I was invited as well because we provided administrative and logistical support for the event.

The purpose of the workshop was for U.S. diplomats to learn what others had to say about us. Diplomats from other countries would speak, and we would listen. The results were to be published in the book *American Negotiating Behavior* written by Soloman and Nigel Quiney.

Ambassador Chan Heng Chee of Singapore spoke first, and she set the tone and theme for the earlier workshop. Ambassador Chan had represented Singapore in the U.S. for more than a decade, and over the years she had been a senior negotiator on several economic issues. Her small stature and innocent charm belie her brilliance, tenacity and courage. She dared to open the meeting by saying, "Americans don't really negotiate and don't know how to negotiate very well." As she explained in *American Negotiating Behavior*, "Americans often present their views at a forum and negotiating table using a very direct approach and expect the other party or parties to accept them and adjust to them. In short, they will try to talk to the other party until it accepts their proposal." All of the other participants in the workshop nodded in enthusiastic agreement with Ambassador Chan. Americans don't listen to or try to understand the needs and aspirations of others, the diplomats intoned throughout the retreat, and our attitude is resented worldwide.

Many said this was the first time they had ever participated in an event where U.S. diplomats came to listen, and they appreciated it. I came away with a much better understanding of why we are perceived as arrogant and obstinate in international circles. As long as we persist in demanding our way or no way on Iran, Israel/Palestine and China, reaching mutually acceptable resolutions to intractable issues will be nearly impossible.

The subtitle of *American Negotiating Behavior* is *Wheeler-Dealers, Legal Eagles, Bullies, and Preachers.* The most senior U.S. diplomats at the USIP sponsored book launch event acknowledged the accuracy of that description. Perhaps this workshop exercise and the new book will have some positive influence on future U.S. negotiating behavior.

≈

Working for peace and security worldwide is a lofty mission, and it brings me into contact with wonderful people who share my vision. None is finer than Harriet Mayor Fulbright. I had met Harriet a few times while working in the arts, but we didn't know each other. Sherry Mueller, my friend and faux ex-wife on our trip to Saudi Arabia, lives on the same block in Arlington, Virginia, with Harriet, and she invited us to get better acquainted over dinner. We were kindred spirits from the first few sentences.

Harriet, widow of the late Senator J. William Fulbright, is a highly respected, accomplished, and influential figure in Washington. Whenever I mention her name, doors open. She ran the Fulbright Association for many years, and President Clinton appointed her Director of the President's Council on the Arts and Humanities.

Since few young people know the significance of Senator Fulbright, I often make the video *Fulbright, The Man, the Mission, and the Message* required viewing for interns in my office. The Fulbright story is too powerful and important to be forgotten and ignored by future generations. Fulbright had been a heroic figure for me back in college, and I believe the book he wrote in 1966, *The Arrogance of Power* should be required reading for anyone with any influence over U.S. foreign policy. Had President Bush and his advisors read and understood it, the U.S. would not have gone to war in Iraq.

During the time I was getting to know and build a partnership with Harriet, I encountered Steve Killelea, a highly successful technology entrepreneur and philanthropist from Australia. Steve is unique among the many amazing people I have encountered and embraced as friends and colleagues. He was a high school drop-out in Sydney who would rather surf the waves and meditate than study. However, he enjoyed playing on computers; he took courses, and he figured out how they work. Within short order, he had designed programs that help run securities exchanges worldwide, including Wall Street, as well as the global ATM network. Consequently, he has become a wealthy man.

Steve had come to Washington to find an organization to serve as his North American base for the Global Peace Index, his creative new initiative. He had invested tens of millions of dollars in development projects in Africa and Asia, and he devoted an extraordinary amount of time to personal visits to the sites of his projects. He had observed first-hand the damage to development—let alone the tragedy of death and destruction—caused by violence. As a creative entrepreneur, however, he brought a different perspective to the issue. While everyone else looks at violence in search of a cure, Killelea decided to study peace in search of models of success. He asked the experts which are the world's most peaceful nations, and what do we know from their experiences. No one had an answer. There had never been an effort to determine the world's most peaceful nations, and as a result, there had not been a credible study of the factors and drivers of peace.

Hundreds of books and research papers were available on war and the drivers that cause violence, but there was little or nothing on peaceful nations. Academic peace studies programs have emerged by the dozens, but they usually study war in search of cures rather than peace and models of peaceful behavior. The Global Peace Index would rank the nations of the world based on their peacefulness. The ranking would enable experts to study the history of peaceful countries to understand the qualities and characteristics that enable some nations to live in peace when so many others are consumed with violence.

Steve and I met over lunch, and within a few minutes I recognized the enormous potential of his concept. For me, the Global Peace Index would help us dispel the pervasive myth that war is natural and inevitable. If world leaders and policy makers can get past that mental barrier, they can create systems and mechanisms to build a more peaceful world. The Index would validate the concept of peace as a natural and achievable state. If the nations identified in the Index could be peaceful, so could others—all others. Furthermore, I was confident that the most peaceful nations would, for the most part, be among the most successful in other ways as well. More often than not, nations and societies achieve safety, security, and prosperity through peaceful means rather than military conquest and authoritarian rule.

Many on my board of directors were skeptical of the value and efficacy of the Global Peace Index project, but I was able to persuade them to give it a chance. Virtually all of the critics have since acknowledged that our affiliation with Steve and the GPI is one of the best things we have done as an organization. Some of our member organizations were also skeptical, but Ambassador John McDonald, President of the Institute for Multi-Track Diplomacy, understood the value from the beginning. McDonald is one of the pioneers and giants in the peacebuilding world. If he was on my side, I knew I was on solid ground.

Steve assembled a panel of highly respected experts to develop the criteria for ranking countries for peacefulness, and he commissioned the Economist Intelligence Unit (EIU) in London to produce the data and analysis. The EIU is the world's premier research and analysis firm for the study of the social, political, and economic characteristics of nations, and its credibility is unmatched. The Index project examined internal factors such as homicide and incarceration rates as well as external indicators including arms sales, overseas troop deployments, and engagement in armed conflicts. Participation in UN peacekeeping operations counts as a plus for the country.

I joined Steve in London to meet with the EIU team working on the project as well as executives of the Edelman Group and Fenton Communications to plan the launch. While there, we set the date for late May and carefully analyzed the questions and objections that might be raised. Though the study was not complete, we anticipated a low rank for the United States. Americans don't take kindly to criticism of any kind, so we feared this would not sit well with some commentators. At the same time, we knew we were on solid ground with the quality of the data and the objectivity of the criteria and analysis. We prepared for the critics, and were ready.

Steve asked me who would be the best person in the U.S. to introduce the Index at the launch event we planned for the National Press Club in Washington. We considered several foreign policy celebrities, but none seemed quite appropriate. Some would draw attention to themselves rather than the Index, and others lacked media appeal. Harriet Fulbright, however, would be perfect. The Fulbright Program is respected throughout the country and worldwide, Senator Fulbright had been a proud and prominent advocate for peace, and Harriet is dignified, elegant and articulate. She was the perfect choice.

Steve handled the launch event in London, and his colleague Clyde McConaghy joined Harriet and Leo Abruzzese of the EIU on the platform in Washington. Clyde had been the head of the EIU in London before returning to Sydney, and he had connected Steve with the Economist team in the first place. He had become President of the Global

Peace Index to provide management for the project.

By the time of the launch, the GPI had endorsements from half a dozen Nobel Peace Prize winners as well as leading academics, political and religious figures, and famous corporate executives. The event attracted a full house including several well known dignitaries and many respected academics. It was broadcast nationwide over C-SPAN television, and news cameras from many other countries, including Russia, recorded the event. Harriet was eloquent, Clyde was rock solid, and Leo filled in all of the details. As we anticipated, some in the audience objected to the low rank of their favorite countries. A gentleman from South Africa was particularly indignant, but neither he nor anyone else could assail the credibility of the study. Media coverage worldwide was remarkable with print and broadcast stories in over 100 countries. *Financial Times*, *Newsweek* and the *Economist* all reported on the ranking and its significance. We were on our way.

After the release of the Index, we participated in several public forums, and it gained attention and respect with each new audience. I had the honor of filling in for Steve when he could not be in the U.S. for forums and lectures. The next year, we decided to announce the results at the Center for Strategic and International Studies, one of the premier foreign policy think tanks in Washington. Rick Barton, my old friend from our project in Rwanda, was a senior policy analysis at CSIS, and he recognized the value of the Index. He made the arrangements, and he gave the welcoming remarks. The same team, Harriet, Clyde, and Leo presented the results, and press attention was even greater than before. CSIS served as host for the GPI launch again in 2009, and Rick arranged for Linda Jamison, Dean of the Abshire-Inamori Leadership Academy at CSIS, to provide the welcome comments. Linda had joined the international panel of experts that shapes the criteria and helps guide the analysis of the GPI. Her opening remarks caught my attention as particularly pertinent. The emphasis is hers, just as she sent the text to me:

As someone who has spent time scrutinizing political leadership and training rising leaders, what the GPI provoked in me was this question: *If we demand competent and creative leadership in times of war, shouldn't we also demand the same character of leadership to achieve peacefulness?* We know a lot about war, especially in this country. We know far too little about peace—how to organically promote it, how to incite it in others, mine it within ourselves, and manage it in our own cities and neighbohoods.

The United States ranked 96th out of 121 countries in the 2007 Global Peace Index. By the time the fourth edition of the Index was published in 2010, the U.S. position had improved to 83rd out of 149—still quite low. Some proud Americans object to the ranking, but no one can deny that America is a relatively violent country—both internally and globally. The U.S. is fighting two major wars; our military budget equals that of the rest of the world combined, we have one of the worst murder rates, and our per capita prison population is the highest in the world. How could anyone expect the U.S. to rank well on a Global Peace Index? When we review the data, most critics nod in silent, reluctant agreement. The United States is not a peaceful country. That can change, and this stark revelation of just how low we rank in the peace index should stimulate new thinking, and it should embarrass us into action.

We have convinced ourselves that America is best in the world at everything. I am as proud as anyone to be an American, and I've waved our flag at events all over the world, but I also know we have many flaws. Excessive violence is just one of them. In reality, the U.S. ranks well but not at the top on most global comparisons, including the Economist Intelligence Unit's highly respected Worldwide Quality of Life Index. Our own CIA places us 49th in life expectancy, for example. The GPI is just the latest study to give the U.S. a less than stellar review. We're still a great country. We may be the greatest nation in history. But that is for others to proclaim and for history to verify.

For now, I wish we would spend less time trying to convince ourselves and others of our greatness, and just do a better job of meeting the needs of our people, while contributing more constructively toward a more peaceful and prosperous world. A little humility and global collegiality would serve us well.

≈

Steve Killelea provided us with a grant to hire staff to focus, at least in part, on the Index. Shortly before Steve offered the funds, I had interviewed Zoë Cooprider at the insistence of Chip Hauss, our special head of government liaison, board member, and benefactor. We had no openings when I met Zoë, but I was determined to find funding and get her on board if at all possible. Organizations like ours succeed or fail based on the quality of the people on the team. I saw Zoë as a rising superstar, and wanted her on my team. Steve's support made it possible, and she has met, if not exceeded, all expectations.

Shortly after the launch of the first GPI in 2007, Harriet Fulbright and I met for lunch at Aria, our favorite restaurant in the Reagan Building complex on Pennsylvania Avenue. I had been contemplating ways to increase the value and impact of the Index, and a new idea came to me on the way to that lunch. We should convene and honor the most peaceful nations and study them. We give medals and heap praise on people and teams for running and swimming fast. Why not honor nations for being peaceful? We could publish the results to demonstrate to the world that peace is possible, and we could provide a road map to get there, based on countries that had successfully traveled that positive path. I shared the idea with Harriet, and I suggested we work together to make it happen. Harriet agreed and we began to develop the concept and implement it.

The Alliance for Peacebuilding and the Fulbright Center created and produced the Global Symposium of Peaceful Nations to celebrate the most peaceful countries on earth, to learn whatever we can from their experience and to encourage them to become leaders to build a more peaceful world. Nothing like this had ever been done anywhere in the world. For the first time in history, nations would be honored for being peaceful, and the peaceful nations would be studied to provide lessons and possibly indicate policies, programs and strategies that might help guide others to peace.

Most of the top ten peaceful countries are Scandinavian plus comfortable places like Canada, New Zealand and Japan. We knew the rest of the world would find a study of those countries to be irrelevant to their concerns, so we carved the map into nine regions and agreed to honor and study the two most peaceful nations in each region.

Producing an event of this magnitude, however, required a substantial budget—and both of our organizations were underfunded and understaffed. Neither of us had enough support to sustain basic operations let alone produce a world class event. The challenge was enormous, but the result could be monumental. We needed an angel to make it happen.

In the spring of 2008, the U.S. Institute of Peace held a ground breaking ceremony for a new building overlooking the Potomac River and next to the Mall. Rob Ricigliano, the conflict resolution expert we had commissioned to help our team on the Congo was there as was my board chair, Susan Hackley. Following the ceremony (where President Bush gave the single worst speech I have ever heard) Rob, Susan and I discussed the persistent precarious financial condition of the Alliance for Peacebuilding. Rob has always been a great source of inspiration and ideas, and he suggested a potential donor for new funds. His friend Julilly Kohler had been sending us $5,000 per year based on his recommendation, but I had never met her, and we had no direct connection. Rob suggested that if I were to make a trip to Milwaukee and meet with Julilly, she might take greater interest and offer more support. The Kohler name is synonymous with high quality plumbing fixtures, and

Julilly is a beneficiary of that corporate wealth. This had promise.

Rob invited me to speak to one of his classes at the University of Wisconsin—Milwaukee, and he arranged for me to meet Julilly. She and I connected immediately based in no small measure to our mutual history of social and political activism. It was clear from the beginning we were kindred spirits destined to share the same vision and values. I outlined the full range of AfP initiatives with her, including the BEFORE violence prevention work in West Africa, our Collaboration Connections program, our emerging advocacy initiatives, and the Global Symposium of Peaceful Nations. When I mentioned the Symposium, she lit up like a halogen bulb. She wanted to know more. I went into detail about the concept and its potential impact. She asked what the budget was, and I told her half a million dollars. "We'll do half of it," she said on the spot. She explained she would have to secure approval from her foundation board, but she was confident they would share her enthusiasm, and they did.

As soon as the 2009 GPI was announced, we knew which countries would be honored, and we started meeting with their ambassadors. The embassies responded enthusiastically to the concept. On November 1, 2009, the first Global Symposium of Peaceful Nations began with a gala at the Mayflower Hotel in Washington, where 220 guests gathered to celebrate peace. Harriet and I shared the podium to explain the concept and introduce delegates from the most peaceful nations. Helen Clark, former Prime Minister of New Zealand and current Administrator of the United Nations Development Program, gave a remarkable keynote address. Tom Pickering, former U.S. Ambassador to the UN, Rick Barton and several other top diplomats and political leaders attended, and the response was both inspiring and moving. House Speaker Nancy Pelosi's Chief of Staff John Lawrence sat at our table, and his thirteen-year-old son Elijah moved everyone singing "What a Wonderful World."

One-by-one, we presented awards to delegates from each nation. New Zealand topped the list, but places as diverse as Botswana, Canada, Chile, the Czech Republic, Japan, Norway, Oman, and Singapore all qualified. The last one, in alphabetical order, was Vietnam, and I was overwhelmed with emotion as Harriet and I presented the Peaceful Nation Award to Hong Quang Nguyen, Chief of the North American Division in the Ministry of Foreign Affairs and Van Chuong Pham, Vice President of the Vietnam Peace and Development Foundation. They had flown in from Hanoi to receive the award and participate in our analysis of peaceful countries. I had lengthy discussions with Mr. Pham over the next few days, and found him to be wise, kind, considerate, respectful, and a genuine man of peace. The dreadful chapter in U.S.–Vietnamese history seemed to vanish, at least for the two of us.

While the American press showed no interest in the event, we generated substantial media attention worldwide. Saudi Arabia's KSA TV 2 presented a lengthy story broadcast throughout the Middle East. Several newspapers in Botswana, Canada, Costa Rica, Denmark, Singapore, and Vietnam published articles about the award and the story behind it. A few bloggers picked it up as well with enthusiastic commentary.

Over the next two days, delegates described their own countries and listened to each other to better understand how they became more peaceful than their neighbors. While nothing shocking or profound emerged from the sessions, the messages are very significant. Peaceful nations are more prosperous, as well as being safe and secure. Countries that treat their own people and others with respect tend to be peaceful. Countries that trust their own leaders and others are peaceful. Following a civil war in 1948, Costa Rica abolished its military and it lives in peace, trusting others to refrain from attacking them. Costa Ricans enjoy a safe, secure and relatively prosperous way of life. By the way, they also rank number one on the Happy Planet Index.

Equity and inclusivity are common characteristics of the most peaceful nations, and they tend to be pragmatic and generous rather than ideological and aggressive in their foreign policies. Perhaps most significantly, societies that focus on the present and future rather than striving to avenge historic grievances tend to live in peace and prosper. While none of these characteristics are surprising, the Symposium helps affirm these fundamental values for peace, stability, security and happiness to prevail. They can be applied everywhere, including the intractable conflicts in the Middle East.

The results will be published and distributed to world leaders in a book and video documentary. If they are willing to listen and learn, other nations might soon be able to compete successfully for the highest achievement I can imagine—peace, safety, security, prosperity and happiness for their own people and their neighbors. Several delegates promised to work with us to follow up and possibly produce regional conferences to advance the message and help each of the regions become less prone to violence. The potential long term impact of this initiative is enormous.

≈

The Israeli—Palestinian confrontation, of course, remains the epicenter of intractable political, ethnic and sectarian conflict. It is a malignancy that infects virtually every other major clash to one degree or another. For decades, the best minds and most compassionate souls on the planet have done their best to find solutions, but to no avail thus far. Irrational fears and fanatical doctrines on both sides continue to prevail.

I have precious little to contribute to the mix, but that hasn't kept me from trying. A decade ago, Ambassador Dane Smith, my successor as President of the National Peace Corps Association, and I went to Israel and Palestine at the invitation of Returned Peace Corps Volunteers living in the area. Elana Rozenman (sister of Gordon Radley of LucasFilm and Larry Radley, the first Peace Corps Volunteer killed in service) had served in the Peace Corps in Colombia. Elana lives in Jerusalem, and works with the Peace X Peace initiative to bring Jewish, Christian and Muslim women together to build mutual understanding, respect and trust. Her son was badly wounded in a bus bombing, but she has responded by seeking resolution rather than retribution.

Tom Neu, another RPCV, headed the American Near East Refugee Aid office in Jerusalem. ANERA is one of the few NGOs sympathetic to the Palestinian cause that enjoys financial support from the U.S. Tom and Elana, representing Palestinian and Israeli affiliations respectively, hoped Dane and I would be able to bring the dozens of RPCVs living in the area together to develop projects on both sides of the divide and help build bridges.

Our trip coincided with the start of the Second Intifada, and the climate was tense. Israel had imposed a strict quarantine on much of the West Bank, and residents in sensitive sites like Bethlehem were confined to their homes and shot if they wandered out at any time of the day or night. Nevertheless, we met with officials in the Israeli government and the Palestinian Liberation Organization as well as civil society leaders, and we toured special sites in Israel and Gaza in hopes of finding some opening for a small breakthrough.

However, even within the Peace Corps community, those who identified with one side feared and distrusted those affiliated with the other side. Dane and I were able to bring them together for a reception and brief program where they made awkward connections, but the divide was deep, and the prospects of developing a successful project seemed dim. Upon returning home, we tried to find support to continue, but it proved to be an impossible task.

Tensions remain high today, but many Alliance for Peacebuilding member organizations persist with active engagement in the long and hard search for peace. I have the honor of working directly with Sulaiman Khatib and Gadi Kenny, two courageous young men who helped create Combatants for Peace, a remarkable and uniquely effective movement started jointly "by Palestinians and Israelis, who have taken an active part in the cycle of violence; Israelis as soldiers in the Israeli army (IDF) and Palestinians as part of the violent struggle for Palestinian freedom. After brandishing weapons for so many years, and having seen one another only through weapon sights, we have decided to put down our guns, and to fight for peace."

Since Souli and Gadi are based in Ramallah and Tel Aviv respectively, we help manage their People's Peace Fund in the U.S. to support grassroots initiatives that bring Palestinians and Israelis together on joint peacebuilding projects. It is our small contribution to an enormous task. In addition, Peter Yarrow has taken the Operation Respect program to Jerusalem and the West Bank, in yet another of the many citizen-based projects that may yet bring peace to the Holy Land.

Even though both sides of the conflict remain belligerent, and sporadic violence erupts, solutions are available and on the table. There are wonderful people in both camps who strive every day for a peace that will enable Israelis and Palestinians to move beyond their mutually destructive past and embrace a safe and secure present and hopeful future. We won't give in to those who perpetuate hatred and violence, and one day peace will prevail.

≈

I have traveled the world and embraced people and diverse cultures, and I never anticipated or feared discomfort or alienation—until my first visit to the U.S. Military Academy at West Point. Peace activists and military officers are as far apart as east and west, north and south. There is no way we could relate to each other and find common ground—or so I thought.

Shortly after starting to work with the Alliance for Peacebuilding, I received an invitation to lecture at the Academy. Some AfP leaders had worked with the West Point Social Sciences department to develop curricula for the cadets on conflict resolution, and several of our members had been invited to provide guest lectures. Now, it was my turn. I grappled with my phobias and biases about the military, but I knew it was a remarkable opportunity, and I looked forward to the trip. I never resented or opposed people in the military. I simply thought we had fundamental cultural and political differences, and I rarely if ever socialized with career soldiers. I was afraid if I ever tried to engage a career military person in a serious conversation, a fight might break out and ruin my reputation for peaceful behavior. Paul Barnette, my friend from childhood, was the only career military guy I knew well, and we rarely touched on this touchy subject.

I took Amtrak to Penn Station in New York where a friendly driver in uniform met me with a smile and took me up the scenic drive to the picturesque campus. I passed through security, and Col. Cindy Jebb gave me a warm greeting in her office. We had lunch with members of the faculty and administration, and the West Point people welcomed me as though I was family. I was the odd one in the family, perhaps, but I was family nonetheless. I felt a bit disoriented as I had anticipated at least some aversion to my values. After all, they knew my background and my singular focus on preventing and stopping warfare. If I succeed in my mission, their careers will become irrelevant—not that there is any likelihood of that in my lifetime or theirs. Yet, they assured me they shared my opposition to war, and they stated emphatically that they detest violence even more than those of us who express our views from the safety of the soap box.

Military people don't like shooting at people, and they certainly don't want anyone shooting at them. They have seen the horror of battle, and they have lost friends in mortal combat. General and President Dwight D. Eisenhower had said, "I hate war as only a soldier who has lived it can, only as one who has seen its brutality, its futility, its stupidity...." I thought that was the musing of an old, retired General, but I found it to be the tune of the current and serving military brass as well.

This is not meant to understate our differences. Military officials are prepared to go to war, and they tend to view the world through red, white and blue glasses—a purely American perspective. They should. They follow orders, and their job is to protect the interests of the United States. They volunteered to be trained to kill, and they are ready and willing to do so. I respect and appreciate their role and perspective, but it is not mine. I am not prepared to accept a call to arms just because the

Commander in Chief orders it, and I have a global perspective on the value of peace and the consequences of war.

As an American citizen, I want our interests to be protected, and I want my family to be kept safe from adversaries who would do us harm. But few of the wars we have fought in my lifetime bear any connection with the safety and security of my family or of the United States. Furthermore, I value the lives of Africans, Afghans, Persians, Asians and Latinos as much as Americans. Human life is human life regardless of geography, culture, ethnicity, language, or creed.

The cadets I lectured were smart, well informed, respectful, attentive, and inquisitive. We engaged in lively dialogue, and after class several lingered to talk further. I have been back several times, and I find the same experience every time. I am very encouraged about the future of U.S. military leadership. There may be a few young Curtis LeMay devotees lurking in search of some odious enemy to nuke, but they are few and far between, and I doubt they will ever again rise to senior leadership positions.

The next year, I was invited to spend two weeks with the officers studying at the U.S. Army War College in Carlisle, PA. This would be a unique opportunity to connect with the brightest colonels rising to general rank, and perhaps I might have some impact on their attitudes and perspectives. They, of course, would also seek to influence me, and I had to be open to them if I wanted them to be open to me.

As with West Point, the students and faculty at the War College shattered all stereotypes about a military eager to hunt and kill enemies wherever they could be found. Col. Roger Machut, a rock solid Marine who had just returned from Iraq, was assigned to be my host, and we thoroughly enjoyed our extended dialogue. We don't share basic political philosophies, but we found substantial common ground and deep mutual respect. I want him to succeed in his mission to keep Americans safe, and he wants me to succeed in making it unnecessary for him or anyone else to fight, kill, and be killed in battle. We stay in touch and encourage each other.

In the spring of 2009, I was invited by Col. Mike Meese back to West Point to help plan and then participate in the *Senior Conference*. This annual event brings top military leaders together to address a major issue of the day, and this year the theme was "Bridging the Cultural Divide: US Military/NGO Relations in Complex Environments." About thirty key military leaders and some fifteen NGO representatives exchanged perspectives and concepts on our respective roles in assuring national security and building a more peaceful world. For the military, national security is the top priority. A more safe, secure and peaceful world is ours. At West Point, we explored our inextricable link and the ways we could build on it—to build peace. When I became a war protester and Peace Corps Volunteer many decades ago, I never would have dreamed I would find myself, in effect, singing *Kumbaya* at West Point with a bunch of friends wearing uniforms with stars on their shoulders. But that is where we were, and I am a better man for it.

≈

We at AfP are building collaboration among peacebuilders and helping bring the military and peace communities together—with full respect for our fundamental differences as well as opportunities for convergence. We have launched exciting new initiatives, and we are putting the whole concept of active engagement by civil society as well as government agencies on the map. The next, and possibly most important challenge however, stares us in the face. Our own government is lagging, and it is time for the U.S. to join the world's leading peacebuilders. Lisa Schirch and I are determined to make it happen. The timing is right. Peacebuilding has matured as a professionally developed framework for social and political interaction with thousands of highly trained and skilled experts available to implement the policies.

The world community has come to recognize the futility and potentially cataclysmic consequences of war. Governments the world over are embracing peacebuilding frameworks, and the United Nations has created a Peace Building Commission and a special Peace Building Fund. Hundreds, even thousands, of civil society organizations are poised to add their unique perspective and talents. It is time to make a firm commitment and invest in building peace, and it's time for the U.S. government to step up and help lead the way. The Congress wants to revise the Foreign Assistance Act, and it is an ideal vehicle to incorporate peacebuilding into the law of the land with a robust peacebuilding component written into the new Act. We are working closely with the House Committee on Foreign Affairs and the Senate Foreign Relations Committee to develop the framework for peacebuilding policies, structures and programs. The process is just getting started, but our initiative could make an enormous difference. A robust peacebuilding policy emerging from the government of the United States of America could change the world.

≈

In the spring of 2008, I received an invitation to give the graduation address for the Institute for Conflict Analysis and Resolution at George Mason University. ICAR is among the oldest and largest peace studies and conflict resolution schools in the world. I was overwhelmed with the honor of addressing such distinguished faculty and graduates, and several peacebuilding heroes like Susan Allen Nan, Marc Gopin, Kevin Avruch and Andrea Bartoli were in the audience. I laid out my perspective on the growth, the significance and the potential of the peacebuilding community for the new and very impressive generation of peacebuilders. I assured them we are on the leading edge of a growing movement to significantly reduce the frequency and severity of violent conflicts.

Imagine the implications of this movement. Throughout history, ethnic groups, religious sects, tribes and nation states have wantonly resorted to violence—open warfare—to assert and impose their will. When my children study world history, they study the story of war, and few people anywhere believe it will ever change. But that's what we are doing. We're changing it. It's too early to prove we can bend the course of history, but that is our aspiration, and there is reason to believe we are on the right path.

Just as medical science is still perfecting the tools and skills to overcome disease, we are still developing our peacebuilding tools and skills. The good news is that it is happening, and private citizens are leading the way. The U.S. government, the UN and many other national governments are also essential to the cause. Together, we can design and build a pathway to peace. It's up to the new and rising generation of peacebuilders to complete the task, and I believe they will.

AFTERWORD

As I age, memories fade but reminders of the early years come into view and spark them back to life. Some are powerful and poignant, while others are sublime. A recent story in the *Washington Post* juxtaposed the beauty and emerging wealth in Cartagena, the beautiful historic Caribbean coastal city of my Peace Corps years, alongside the wretched poverty in the barrios. A large color photo of a barefoot child walking through the mud amid shanties with pigs in the background could have been taken in Albornos forty years ago where I worked and lived among friends. Nothing had changed.

The story described glittering prosperity in the old center city and the peninsula Boca Grande where classy tourist hotels are flourishing, but it focused on conditions on the barrio Villa Hermosa where living standards are as bad if not worse than ever. I'm sure my efforts and those of my Peace Corps colleagues helped some individuals and families live better, but we were not able to help narrow the giant chasm between the wealthy and the extremely poor. That will require a much larger commitment of resources and systemic change than anyone seems willing to make.

I don't care how wealthy the rich become. May they thrive and enjoy their prosperity. But I do care about how dreadfully poor those at the bottom remain, and I care when the rich and powerful exploit the poor, powerless, and uneducated. I care about peace and justice. I will go to my grave feeling inadequate in the face of this overwhelming humanitarian tragedy and human failure. At the same time, I have done the best I could, and I am encouraged by the progress we are making.

The world today is far better than the one I entered over six decades ago. The nations devastated by World War II have recovered, and they are thriving. Colonial rule that oppressed the people in much of Africa and Asia is gone, and democracy is emerging as the predominant form of governance on every continent. While hunger and poverty persist, massive famine is rare, and food production and distribution has improved dramatically. Thanks to miraculous medical advances we live longer. After a long and bitter struggle, the apartheid nation I was born into is now integrated. And the frequency and severity of violent conflict has declined. This represents enormous progress within just one lifetime.

President Barack Obama's election and inauguration represented the symbolic fulfillment of the promise of the movements that started more than five decades ago. Back then, we were for the rights and opportunities for every American, regardless of race, creed, or color; we were against war; and we were concerned about freedom of speech and the environment. The Obama campaign embodied all of those causes in his person and in his message. Whether or not Obama proves to be a successful president, his election alone is great for America and the world. Entrenched and powerful interests will fight and resist the changes he seeks, but I am confident he will move the nation forward, if only in small increments.

The Presidential Inauguration was intoxicating. Washington has never been so happy. Millions of people came from near and far to celebrate the end of a dreadful era and the dawn of a hopeful new one. I spent Saturday before the inauguration in the office catching up on work, but then joined John Garamendi for dinner at the Palm restaurant just a block away. The Palm is well known to Washington insiders as the gathering place of prominent Democrats, and they were out in force and smiles that night. John was planning to run for office again, and this was an opportunity for him to connect with major donors to advance his campaign. Ambassador Kathryn Hall and her husband Craig arrived in elegant ball gown and black tie as they were between high powered events. Craig is part owner of the Dallas Cowboys and together they own two prominent Napa Valley vineyards. Katherine had been appointed ambassador to Austria by President Clinton. New York public affairs consultant Joan Dean was with us, as was Karen Teal of the Patton Boggs law firm, along with John's wife Patti and their youngest daughter Ashley.

There was ample discussion of John's campaign, but he also made sure everyone at the table knew about our peacebuilding mission and achievements—and our financial needs. Dean and Teal both offered their help with contacts, and the Halls expressed great interest and suggested the possibility of financial support. This was supposed to be an event for John, but his generous spirit prevailed once again, and he helped me, his friend, instead.

I returned to the office on Sunday and I was finally making progress on memos and a boring financial analysis when Peter Yarrow called. He was about to perform for a children's inaugural program at the Historical Society, and he wanted me there, so I happily turned off the computer and drove over to the event. Peter was particularly pleased to be performing with seventh grader Elijah Lawrence, the son of our mutual friend John. A very proud father John and I watched the performance together and Elijah was superb as always. Peter was his usual manic and wonderful self, engaging the kids with dynamic interaction and group sing. He went beyond the allotted time, but everyone loved it. Nothing has changed!

Peter and I slipped out to a Starbucks across the street and pondered the historic significance of the Obama victory. We agreed that Peter's wonderful song "Sweet Survivor" is his best ever, and this national transformation is an affirmation of the impact and value of the persistence of the social and political movements. I am particularly honored

that Peter has dedicated this song to me on many occasions in front of
audiences large and small. It is the ultimate tribute to those of us who
have kept alive the dream of peace, justice, respect for our fragile planet,
and an end to race-based bias.

SWEET SURVIVOR

You have asked me why the days fly by so quickly
And why each one feels no different from the last
And you say that you are fearful for the future
And you have grown suspicious of the past
And you wonder if the dreams we shared together
Have abandoned us or we abandoned them
And you cast about and try to find new meaning
So that you can feel that closeness once again.
Carry on my sweet survivor, carry on my lonely friend
Don't give up on the dream, and don't you let it end.
Carry on my sweet survivor,
Though you know that something's gone
For everything that matters carry on.
You remember when you felt each person mattered
When we all had to care or all was lost
But now you see believers turn to cynics
And you wonder was the struggle worth the cost
Then you see someone too young to know the difference
And a veil of isolation in their eyes
And inside you know you've got to leave them something
Or the hope for something better slowly dies.
Carry on my sweet survivor, carry on my lonely friend
Don't give up on the dream, and don't you let it end.
Carry on my sweet survivor, you've carried it so long
So it may come again, carry on
Carry on, carry on.

Peter Yarrow -Barry Mann -Cynthia Weil- Silver Dawn

I watched the inauguration of President Barak Obama on TV at home. I wanted to be on the Mall and march in the parade with my Peace Corps colleagues, but I was recovering from a seriously pinched sciatic nerve, and I couldn't stand or walk the distance without severe pain. It would have been extraordinary to share this amazing moment with two million proud, enthusiastic, and hopeful flag waving people. Decades of struggle among courageous colleagues who have been vilified as un-American by faux patriots of the right wing had culminated in this triumph. Even my rational Republican friend Jim Click agreed it was a great day for America.

The inaugural address hit all of the right themes—personal accountability and shared responsibility, humanitarian values, and a global embrace. We will not know for many years if this president will be able to lead the nation and the world out of the economic and moral abyss left by his predecessor, but he has the right instincts, and the right message. I am inspired once again as I was forty-eight years ago when another exciting young president challenged us to a higher mission. I don't have the strength, the stamina or the energy of youth, but I hope I still have something to offer to do my part.

My 65th birthday came the day after the Inauguration, and of course many of the greetings from friends made reference to the celebration of the new president as well as my special day. Rachel Jackson, of Peter Yarrow Productions, sent the best line of all: "We all got together and got you a new president for your birthday. Enjoy!"

≈

The next day, I participated in a conference hosted by Swanee Hunt, daughter of the famous H. L. Hunt, the oil billionaire from Texas. Hunt has become a major leader in the women's rights and peacebuilding communities. Walking (painfully) back to my office with Julilly Kohler and my Board Chair Susan Hackley we ran into Rick Warren who was about to leave for the airport.

Warren had been invited by President Obama to give the invocation, but his participation was controversial due to his outspoken support of a California referendum that would ban gay marriage. Many liberals, including many of my good friends, expressed outrage at Obama for inviting him. At the same time, many conservative Christian groups were furious at Warren for accepting and associating himself with Obama. I was with Obama. Inviting Warren sent a signal to America that we can reach out to those with whom we disagree. After Obama invited Warren to participate in the event, Warren removed the incendiary references to homosexuality from his website, and he backed away from the issue in national television interviews. I still disagree with Warren on many issues, but the constructive engagement between Obama and Warren has softened the rhetoric. That is important progress.

I walked toward him and announced, "You look like Rick Warren. I appreciate your work, and I am a friend of Jim Click." (Jim is one of Warren's major backers and he had flown him to Rwanda in his private jet a few years before to help Warren develop his remarkably effective health, peace, and development programs there. That was the work I appreciated.) Warren smiled broadly and gave me a huge hug. We had a brief conversation about Rwanda and about my peacebuilding work. I introduced him to Susan and Julilly, both of whom had been seriously disappointed when he was selected for the inaugural prayer. They weren't shy about expressing their political positions. "I'm a liberal, in fact I'm a radical liberal!" Julilly proclaimed. Warren went right to her, gave her a bear-hug and then did the same with Susan. "Don't believe everything you read about me," he said.

With that gesture of personal embrace, Warren disarmed all of us, and he demonstrated why demonization of the other is wrong. I am also a proud liberal, but I don't think all conservatives are racist and cruel-hearted monsters. Even if they are, we should give them a bear-hug and engage each other in respectful dialogue. We can disarm others just as Warren did us, and then we can make peace through dialogue. That is what I am all about—finding and celebrating the humanity in all of us.

≈

I don't know if it is serendipity, synchronicity or fate, but sometimes things just work out in amazing ways. For obvious reasons, our family has been passionate about health care reform, and the Obama election renewed our hope. With a serious preexisting condition, Kai had no hope of obtaining health insurance on his own.

After a long and bitter struggle the House of Representatives finally scheduled the final vote on their reform package for Saturday, November 7, 2009. I was supposed to tape a program for Saudi Arabia's KSA TV 2 that afternoon, but it was postponed at the last minute. Coincidentally, Kai happened to be in D.C. for a class tour of the Newseum, Washington's wonderful news museum. Since I was already in town and had unexpected free time, I called Kai to see if he wanted to get together.

John Garamendi had won a special election to Congress the Tuesday before, and he had been sworn in on Thursday. (John invited me to sit with his family for the ceremony, and we celebrated in his office after the event.) Since the health care debate was underway, I suggested to Kai we go watch it. We stopped at Congressman Sam Farr's office and had a delightful chat with him and his staff. Then we went to John's office to say hello and introduce him to Kai. John told us he was scheduled to give a one minute speech on the House floor about how bad the health insurance companies are. As we described Kai's remarkable story, John exclaimed, "That's it! That's my speech!" We filled him in on some details and then left him alone to prepare. We returned at the designated time; met up with John; rode on the Member's subway from the Rayburn Office Building to the Capitol; John escorted us to the special Member's guests section of the gallery, and we watched the debate.

When John's turn came to address the Congress and a national audience on C-SPAN he said, "Today we are faced with a choice… do we vote to provide every American with a comprehensive, affordable, and available health care policy? One example of why we must vote yes on HR 3962 and end the healthcare crisis that millions of Americans face each year is Chic Dambach and his son Kai. Some of you may know Chic as the former President of the Returned Peace Corps Association. Chic and his family had a comprehensive family health insurance policy. At the age of two, Kai's kidneys failed. Their insurance refused coverage for kidney transplants. Chic and his wife Kay were faced with a choice, enormous personal debt, or their son's life. They chose life. A decade of battles with their insurance company ensued—together with a crushing burden of debt. When Kai becomes 23 he will be uninsurable. Like millions of other Americans, he has a preexisting condition. HR 3962 is America's opportunity to end this despicable situation..." This statement is now in the Congressional Record as part of the procedures leading to the historic vote for health care reform.

Several of my friends who are Members of Congress looked up at the gallery, saw us and came up to say hello and meet Kai. A few hours later the Affordable Health Care for America Act passed 220 to 215, and the prospects for affordable health care for Kai and everyone like him improved significantly. It was an unexpected special day for Kai, and his dad. Now that universal health care is finally the law of the land, Kai and millions like him can look forward to a relatively normal life instead of the constant threat of financial ruin and premature death. It is that important.

≈

I've almost exhausted the limits of my possibilities, and health issues make the remaining boundaries more restrictive. My head rings constantly with tinnitus, and the entire left side of by body is permanently numb from four different causes. Nerve damage from Lyme disease has deadened half of my face; my left shoulder and arm have been asleep for 45 years from sports injuries; my left torso is numb from the nephrectomy, and a pinched sciatic nerve makes my hip and leg weak and tingling. None of it is debilitating, but it is limiting. My neurologist has determined that I have Persistent Lyme Syndrome, emanating from that deer tick many years ago. It leaves me with hand tremors, forgetful and tired, and with no cure. Slowly, my body parts are wearing out. I still put in a full and productive work week, but at the end there is little left—the limits are nearly exhausted.

Fortunately, as my generation—the 1960s civil rights, anti-war and pro-environment generation—fades, new leaders are emerging. The Student Peace Alliance invited Harriet Fulbright and me to speak as "elders" in the peacebuilding world at their 2010 national conference held at Southwestern College in Texas. It was an honor for us to be there. The college students and recent graduates who produced and participated in the event already surpass most of us "elders" in their intelligence, knowledge and commitment.

Many, if not most, of my contemporaries have retired or will soon. I can't afford to, but I probably wouldn't stop even if I could. There are still rocks to push and mountains to climb. There is so much more to do. Fortunately, however, I will soon begin to ease off and leave the heavy lifting to younger and smarter colleagues like Rob Ricigliano, Lisa Schirch and Sandra Melone. The current crop of students and recent graduates like Aaron Voldman and Julia Simon-Mishel, leaders of the Student Peace Alliance, are just awesome. Recent Hamilton College graduate Riada Asimovic, a brilliant and multi-talented young woman from Sarajevo, and many like her could well lead a new generation of global citizens to build a better world. The future is in good hands.

I can look back with satisfaction at the rocks pushed and the mountains climbed. I've never reached the summit, and I never will. No one ever does. But I found my place and my joy. Building peace is a heavy rock to push, but I have been privileged to be among those who move it ever higher. And now, as Peter Yarrow urges all of us in song, "For everything that matters carry on."

BUILDING A PATHWAY TO PEACE

Charles F. (Chic) Dambach
President, Alliance for Peacebuilding

Institute for Conflict Analysis and Resolution

George Mason University
Graduation Ceremony Address
May 17, 2008

Thank you, Sara Cobb for all you do for this remarkable institution and for giving me this opportunity. Several of the people on your faculty and staff are very special to me. I wouldn't even be here if it weren't for Susan Alan Nan who was vice chair of the Alliance for Peacebuilding board when I was hired. Kevin Avruch currently serves on our board, and he provides wise advice whenever I need it. I also want to recognize Michael Shank who is raising the public consciousness about peacebuilding with his essays that appear regularly in major media outlets. Dennis Sandole also deserves an award for his frequently published letters and op eds. *Financial Times* should pay him, as he gets more ink than their staff journalists!

I am here today because I admire you, the graduating students. I hope your families are proud of you. They should be. You have chosen a vital path; you have studied hard, learned a lot, and passed your exams. I know many on your faculty, and they are among the very best. You have met their high standards, and you are well-equipped to launch your careers. You have taken that famous first step on your thousand mile journey. May the rest be enjoyable and fruitful.

Every older generation criticizes the next younger generation. It's a prerogative we earn by living so long. But I can't do that today. Yes, I worry about self-indulgence, eyes glued to computer screens, and muscle-bound thumbs from excessive exercise on the X-box controls. But that's not what I see. I've met hundreds of students and young professionals, and I am overwhelmed with your knowledge, your values, your skills, and your commitment. You inspire me, and I know the world is in good hands. I'm not the older generation criticizing the younger generation. I look to you as the generation that will correct the dreadful mistakes my generation has made and put squarely in your laps.

We have done a miserable job on the environment and the federal debt. We've allowed our national leaders to entice us into ill-advised and poorly executed wars. We've created political chaos. I don't even want to mention the whole student loan issue! All I can say is, I'm sorry.

Yes, we've made a mess. But at the same time, we have started something quite remarkable. It's called peacebuilding—a concept that barely existed when I was born. Now, I'm happy to say that it is gaining traction and momentum. As graduates today, you have an unprecedented opportunity to take the driver's seat and make peacebuilding a central feature in everyone's policy book.

You get to start your careers in conflict resolution at a remarkable time in human history. We are on the leading edge of a growing movement to significantly reduce the frequency and severity of violent conflicts. Can you imagine the implications of this movement?

Throughout history, ethnic groups, religious sects, tribes and nation states have wantonly resorted to violence—open warfare—to assert and impose their will. When my children study world history, they study the story of war, and few people anywhere believe it will ever change. But that's what we are doing. We're changing it. It's too early to prove we can change the course of history, but that is our aspiration, and there is reason to believe that we are on the right path.

Until the advent of medical science, humanity accepted suffering and early death from disease. Few believed it would ever change. But research into the causes of illnesses, the development of effective treatments, and the training of professionals to apply them has transformed the quality of life and extended life expectancy.

Likewise, humanity has always accepted war between tribes, cultures and nations as inevitable—until now. Just as medical science emerged a century ago and changed our lives, the concept of peacebuilding and the conflict resolution profession has the potential to transform the way societies resolve intractable differences. In the absence of treatments, diseases took their inevitable toll. In the absence of systems, mechanisms and skilled practitioners to resolve conflicts, war will continue to take its toll.

That is changing. We are in the midst of a remarkable convergence of new, distinct, and synergistic phenomena that could transform the way nations and societies manage conflicts. We are designing and building a pathway to peace, and you are a central part of it. Let me give you some examples.

Look at the change in research. We used to glorify war and study the history of war largely to learn how to win the next one. Now, we are studying the history of war to learn how to *prevent* the next one. Furthermore, just as medical research studies wellness to understand and model healthy behavior, we are beginning to study peace—the stories of peaceful nations—so we can learn how everyone can live peacefully. We are developing systems and mechanisms within governments, through the United Nations and in civil society to provide national leaders and belligerents with alternatives to machetes, guns and bombs. And, we are training a whole generation of conflict resolution experts to teach the lessons we have learned and apply the skills needed to prevent and mitigate violence.

The remarkable emergence of private citizen engagement is the most exciting and promising dimension of the growing capacity to build peace. Women, in particular, are providing leadership. War and peace have always been the province of national leaders along with their armies and diplomats. Private citizens were merely passengers on the ships of state with little or no impact on the decisions and actions of those in power. Today, private citizens and citizen-based organizations play a role—a vital role.

The concept of citizen diplomacy emerged in the United States following World War II with tremendously important exchange programs like Sister Cities, AFS, the Experiment in International Living, and of course the marvelous Fulbright Scholars program. Rotary International and other civic organizations add a vital dimension to mix. My favorite, the Peace Corps, was created in the Cold War climate to build friendships and mutual understanding in remote parts of the world. All of this helps tear down walls and build bridges as a foundation for a more peaceful world.

But peacebuilding, as applied by conflict resolution experts, goes another step. We become directly engaged, at all levels, with groups and nation states that are at war or about to go to war. We seek to address the drivers or causes of conflicts and help opposing sides find a path to resolution without resorting to violence.

Saint Egidio, and its remarkable work in Mozambique, was among the first success stories, and our colleague Andrea Bartoli was part of it. New books are appearing every year with more and more examples of civil societies building peace where there would otherwise be war.

Track two diplomacy, or multi-track diplomacy is now recognized everywhere. Some of the people you have encountered here at ICAR created track two diplomacy and gave it credibility. Ambassador John McDonald, for example, left the Foreign Service and became a private-sector peacebuilder decades ago. His Institute for Multi-Track Diplomacy is a model for all of us. Ambassador McDonald, Joe Montville, and Chris Mitchell are among the great pioneers upon whose shoulders we stand today. You have studied among the giants in this field.

During the years you graduating students were born, degrees and careers in conflict resolution barely existed. Yes, there were careers in diplomacy, but that is different. Official diplomats serve the interests of their countries, and that can mean support for and defense of war just as much as it can be work for peace. Peacebuilding places a priority on non-violence—finding ways to resolve differences without war.

When you were born, there were but a handful of citizen-based organizations trying to penetrate the realm of violence prevention and conflict resolution. Today, there are dozens of degree granting programs, and there are hundreds of NGOs as well as government agencies and the UN working every day to help reduce the frequency and severity of violent conflicts.

Just within the past few years, the Global Partnership for the Prevention of Armed Conflict (GPPAC) was formed to link peacebuilding organizations in each of 15 regions. Their networks of conflict resolution professionals and organizations provide local leadership. In Kenya, for example, Florence Mpaayei of the Nairobi Peace Initiative helped tame the violence that erupted in the aftermath of a corrupt election. That tragic situation could easily have deteriorated into large scale civil war. But it didn't. It didn't because the UN stepped in, and it didn't because Florence and her team went to work. Government officials, UN officials, and civil society worked together to build peace.

In 2005, GPPAC sponsored a conference at the United Nations that attracted over 1,000 peacebuilders. Nothing like it had ever happened, and it stimulated the creation of the UN Peacebuilding Commission. The UN has also established a new "Peace Building Community of Practice" to facilitate interaction among all of its departments. This is new.

The U.S. Agency for International Development has an Office of Transition Initiatives and a Conflict Management and Mitigation department. The State Department has a new bureau called the Coordinator for Reconstruction and Stabilization. Even the Department of Defense has recognized peacebuilding with a liaison to our community based in the Joint Forces Command. West Point and the U.S. Army War College now offer courses on peacebuilding. All of this is new.

An international panel of "eminent persons" is being formed to build the political will among nations to turn warnings of possible violence into action to prevent it. This, too, is new. Nothing like this has ever been tried. Think about it .... the potential impact of a team of former heads of state, foreign ministers, Nobel Laureates, scientists, artists, and philosophers all speaking with one voice of reason to press the world community to prevent wars wherever and whenever they seem most likely.

CARE, Catholic Relief Services, World Vision, Mercy Corps and many other relief and development agencies have incorporated conflict resolution into the services because their social and economic development initiatives depend on it. This is new.

Several NGOs and government agencies now monitor volatile states and provide vital information and policy recommendations to help avert disasters. In addition, the Global Peace Index ranks the countries of the world based on their peacefulness—highlighting the countries that have actually achieved a relatively high degree of peace. What a fabulous idea. Let's learn who has succeeded, honor them, and learn from them. The second edition of the Index will be released this Tuesday.

The Alliance for Peacebuilding is a new participant in this rapidly growing community. We were incorporated just five years ago, and most of our members are less than two decades old. We facilitate collaborative action among dedicated and talented organizations and professionals, and we are developing (in cooperation with Swisspeace) a Global Crisis Prevention Mechanism. We are also becoming a united voice in support of conflict resolution policies and programs in the halls of Congress and in the national media.

All of this is new.

- Dozens of graduate programs in conflict resolution,
- Hundreds of private peacebuilding organizations,
- A UN focus on peacebuilding,
- An international panel of eminent persons speaking with one voice of reason,
- New agencies within the U.S. government and other governments worldwide,
- Conflict resolution capacities within the relief and development community,
- Monitoring volatile states and creating responses to prevent violence before war breaks out,
- Studying peaceful nations as role models, and
- An alliance of peacebuilders to improve effectiveness through collaboration and outreach.

If only two or three of these initiatives emerged at once it would be significant, but probably inadequate. The fact that it is all happening simultaneously means that something big is underway. It will still take time; sufficient resources have yet to be committed to the task, and there is no guarantee peace will prevail.

But, this is the best opportunity the world has ever seen for a change of course. This is your opportunity.

You have the potential to embrace these new opportunities and transform the course of history—and not a day too soon. Alienated and disenfranchised groups, called terrorists, are creating fear and inflicting enormous suffering. The proliferation of weapons of mass destruction makes the potential damage from any conflict too fearsome to contemplate.

Furthermore, growing pressure from expanding and migrating populations, as well as dramatic changes in climates and shrinking access to water, could trigger a new wave of violence on a global scale. We must find ways to resolve these conflicts at the negotiating table. If not, the battlefields will expand, and death and destruction will become catastrophic. No one will be immune. Peacebuilding is arriving on the world stage in the nick of time. You are arriving in the nick of time.

I am convinced that the use of violent force is not a reasonable, rational or acceptable way to resolve differences. Conflicts can be resolved through reason, negotiation and mediation. It takes time, patience and persistence, but it is almost always preferable to violence.

The only assured outcome of violence is death and destruction. There is absolutely no assurance that fairness, rightness or justice will prevail in any conflict that is settled on the battlefield. All warfare determines is who can inflict more pain and suffering on the other, and which side is willing to endure more loss of life and property in order to claim victory. That's a lousy way to settle anything.

My wife Kay and I are raising two boys, one 18 and the other 16. They argue like any healthy siblings. Our 18 year old is much bigger, and he can beat up his little brother any time he wants. Do we let him do it, and have his way? Of course not. But, that's what we've allowed among nations, isn't it? If one can destroy the other, they can prevail and reap the spoils. What nonsense.

Furthermore, in a world of asymmetrical warfare and offset strategies, size and power don't guarantee a winner. The battle between Israel and Hezbollah last summer was an example. Israel expected a quick and decisive conquest, but it didn't happen. The U.S. experiences in Vietnam and Iraq clearly demonstrate the failure of overwhelming force to assure victory. Every side feels bold and confident at the outset of war, but the reality is quite different. More often than not, no one wins.

Please don't get me wrong. I don't embrace absolute pacifism. There are situations where military force is necessary to prevent even greater violence and loss of life. Hitler had to be stopped, and it took military force to do it. Mao Zedong and Joseph Stalin should have been indicted and hauled before an international tribunal for their crimes against humanity—even if it took an armed force and an invasion to do it. I believe the international community finally did the right thing to topple Slobodan Milosevic and put him on trial. The genocide in Rwanda could have been stopped, but the international community failed to commit the forces available to end the killing. The failure to use force when it was needed resulted in preventable and unspeakable violence.

Unfortunately, universal world peace is still a distant dream, and megalomaniacs still seize power. We still need people in uniforms and carrying guns to prevent extremists, brutal dictators, and aggressors from inflicting more damage. But that will become less and less necessary if we are willing to invest in and develop our peacebuilding capacity.

Most wars, however, are led by rational people who feel compelled to resort to force to redress their grievances or achieve their goals because they see no other way. Most ethnic groups, tribes and cultures, even those with deep-seeded and centuries old hostilities would rather co-exist than fight. Sometimes, however, they feel trapped or trampled upon, and in desperation they resort to violence to escape or restore their dignity. Our job is to provide another way and help them find it and embrace it.

News reports often create the impression that one side is right, the other wrong and that conquest of good over evil is the only answer. Yet, the real world is rarely that clear cut. I have come to know rebel leaders who have been portrayed as evil incarnate. I have listened to them and learned that they, too, have a story to tell and a compelling case for their position. I may not agree with it or approve of their behavior, but I have found that when I am willing to listen, they are willing to listen to me. When I am willing to show them respect, they return it in kind. When I trust them, they trust me. These are the three keys words in building peace: *listen, respect,* and *trust.* Each builds on the other in that sequence.

I had a unique opportunity to apply this concept successfully just a few years ago. In the spring of 1999, John Garamendi and I formed a small team of former Peace Corps volunteers and staff to facilitate communication between the leaders of Ethiopia and Eritrea to help them end their border war. (John had been a Peace Corps Volunteer in Ethiopia, and now he is Lieutenant Governor of California.) We met regularly with both ambassadors, both foreign ministers, and both heads of state over a two year period. We were willing to listen, and listen, and listen to both sides over and over again as they explained why they were right, and why the other side was wrong. As a result, they trusted us.

We didn't come in with the answers. We came in with our ears, listening. By hearing them out, we demonstrated respect for them, and they reciprocated with respect for us. Eventually, we were able to find a path to peace—together.

There were ups and downs and periods of frustration and exasperation, but they consistently came to our small unofficial group for guidance and to convey messages to the other side. In September, 2000, Eritrea's President Isaias Afwerki informed us in a phone conversation that he would accept the final condition for settling the conflict. I jumped into a cab, and went straight to the Ethiopian embassy to convey the message.

A few weeks later, we were invited to meet with Ethiopia's Prime Minister Meles Zenawi. Over breakfast, the Prime Minister said, "I am here to tell you the war is over, and I want to thank you for helping make it happen."

Obviously, we were thrilled beyond words with the news, and moved beyond description with his expression of appreciation. Shortly thereafter, we were contacted by President Isaias who invited us to the agreement signing ceremony in Algiers. It was the best trip of my life.

A few years later, we played a similar role with the leaders of the major rebel groups and President Joseph Kabila in the Congo. In that case, we helped them agree to form a coalition government leading to elections and an end to the most deadly conflict since World War II. We were successful because we built their trust by listening to them and respecting all of them.

Permanent peace is far from assured in either of these cases, and we continue to meet with key leaders to urge further progress, but at least the military war between Ethiopia and Eritrea is over, and the major fighting in the Congo has stopped. Only lower grade battles with renegade militias continue.

I share these stories to convey two very important messages. First, it is possible for individuals and citizen-based organizations to build peace. We can help belligerents, even when they are heads of state, find a path to peace. The U.S. and other governments play geopolitical chess trying to manipulate the outcome to serve foreign policy interests. We, as private citizen peacebuilders, serve one and only one purpose, and that is peace.

We know how to listen, to learn why people and nations feel compelled to go to war. We can build a special trust relationship. On that basis, we can explore—with them—the paths that will lead to peace.

I believe these are the keys to conflict resolution success:

Always be on the side of peace

Listen, really listen to learn and understand

Demonstrate respect

Build trust

Be patient, and

Be persistent

That set of skills and qualities apply to virtually any conflict resolution environment, be it within a family, at work, in a community, or at the national and international level. Violence is not acceptable. Conquest is rarely possible or sustainable. Virtually every conflict has a mutually acceptable and peaceful resolution. Our task is to help opposing sides find it and embrace it.

At long last, we are studying war to prevent it rather than just to win it. We are developing systems and mechanisms to help prevent and mitigate violence, and young people like you are developing the skills to make it happen. The impossible task of reducing the frequency and severity of violent conflict is no longer impossible. It can be done, and you will do it.

Some of you will find jobs as conflict resolution professionals right away. Others will find related work, in which you can apply these skills. Others may have to create your own opportunities. The world does not yet offer peacebuilding jobs the way it does for mechanical engineering graduates. But you are creative people on the cutting edge of an exciting new field. You will make it happen.

Just as medical science is still perfecting the tools and skills to overcome disease, we are still developing our tools and skills. The good news is that it is happening, and if we persist, we can change the course of history.

Private citizens are leading the way, but the UN and many national governments are also part of the cause. Together, we are designing and building a pathway to peace. I wish it could be a superhighway, but a walking path will do for now. It's up to you to complete the task. It can happen in your lifetime. You will make it happen.

Congratulations and best wishes.

ACKNOWLEDGEMENTS

Several of my family and friends volunteered to read this text as it emerged, and their comments and suggestions helped correct mistakes and improve the flow. My sister Charlou Howald read the first very rough draft, and her enthusiastic response encouraged me to continue writing. Mark Weiss read a very preliminary draft and he guided me—page by page—through badly needed changes and corrections. Elizabeth Kolodny made sure the narrative was accurate and respectful. Award-winning novelist Dan Fesperman read the entire book and taught me how to rearrange it and make it more readable.

Gregg Wilhelm gave me encouragement, and he guided me through the publishing process. Melissa Henderson provided expert editing while Amy Scioscia and Kathleen Boehl produced the design. These delightful Loyola University in Maryland students, as well as the faculty at Apprentice House, made the publishing experience a joy. Special thanks to Uta Allers for her extraordinary editorial advice, and to Emily Mallozzi and Mary Leopold for a final proofreading. My dear friend Carissa Champlin sent vital corrections all the way from Berlin at the very end of the process. Brooke Hall added a special creative concept and design for the cover and developed the marketing plan. She has been a terrific partner in this project.

Earl Jones was the early inspiration for my values and for this book. I could have done nothing without a special friendship with and support from Congressman John Garamendi and his amazing wife Patti.

Congressman Sam Farr was an early mentor, and he remains a consistent and reliable friend and ally. Peter Yarrow's music and values aroused my own ideals and our enduring friendship lifts my spirits in the face of every new challenge.

Dozens of friends and colleagues waded through the evolving drafts, advised me, and kept me motivated to polish it, and get it published. Special thanks to: Adrianna Amari, Sarah Armstrong, Ron Beales, Jon Benner, Bob Berg, Harry Blaney, Emily Campion, Ersel Coates, Zoë Cooprider, Geri Critchley, Jared Dunn, Maryo Ewell, Cathy Finney, Outi Flynn, Sharon Gafford Furstenwerth, Melissa Long Goers, Larry Goetz, Jeff Gomez, Gul Mescioglu Gur, Susan Hackley, Tex Harris, Wardell Hollis, Melanie Kawano, Charlotte Kea, Ginny Kirkwood, Sandy Kleinman, Milt Lauenstein, Laurence Myre Leroux, Michael and Brenda Lilly, Jim Luce, David Mason, Keith McGlamery, Faye McNeil, Sherry Mueller, Maria Nazareth, Gail Perry, Jeanne Reed, Gene Reid, Rob Ricigliano, Christopher Czaja Sager, Paul Stevers, Arnd Wächter, Steve Werner, Karen Williams, Yeshu Habitegioris Woldemicael, John and Nancy Wyant, and, of course, my love and best critic Kay.

The future of publishing...today!

Apprentice House is the country's only campus-based, student-staffed book publishing company. Directed by professors and industry professionals, it is a nonprofit activity of the Communication Department at Loyola University in Maryland.

Using state-of-the-art technology and an experiential learning model of education, Apprentice House publishes books in untraditional ways. This dual responsibility as publishers and educators creates an unprecedented collaborative environment among faculty and students, while teaching tomorrow's editors, designers, and marketers.

Outside of class, progress on book projects is carried forth by the AH Book Publishing Club, a co-curricular campus organization supported by Loyola University's Office of Student Activities.

Student Project Team for *Exhaust the Limits:*
    Amy M. Scioscia, '12
    Kathleen M. Boehl, '11
    Melissa Henderson, '10

Eclectic and provocative, Apprentice House titles intend to entertain as well as spark dialogue on a variety of topics. Financial contributions to sustain the press's work are welcomed. Contributions are tax deductible to the fullest extent allowed by the IRS.

To learn more about Apprentice House books or to obtain submission guidelines, please visit www.ApprenticeHouse.com.

Apprentice House
Communication Department
Loyola University in Maryland
4501 N. Charles Street
Baltimore, MD 21210
Ph: 410-617-5265 • Fax: 410-617-2198
info@apprenticehouse.com

CPSIA information can be obtained at www.ICGtesting.com
263191BV00004B/5/P